Con Brio

OTHER BOOKS BY NAT BRANDT

Nonfiction

The Man Who Tried to Burn New York

The Town That Started the Civil War

The Congressman Who Got Away with Murder

How Free Are We? What the Constitution Says We Can and Cannot Do (with John Sexton)

Mystery

Land Kills (with Yanna Brandt)

Con Brio

Four Russians
Called the Budapest
String Quartet

NAT BRANDT

New York   Oxford
OXFORD UNIVERSITY PRESS
1993

Oxford University Press

Oxford   New York   Toronto
Delhi   Bombay   Calcutta   Madras   Karachi
Kuala Lumpur   Singapore   Hong Kong   Tokyo
Nairobi   Dar es Salaam   Cape Town
Melbourne   Auckland   Madrid
and associated companies in
Berlin   Ibadan

Copyright © 1993 by Nat Brandt

Published by Oxford University Press, Inc.,
200 Madison Avenue, New York, New York 10016

Library of Congress Cataloging-in-Publication Data
Brandt, Nat.
Con brio :
four Russians called the Budapest String Quartet /
Nat Brandt.
p.   cm.   Includes bibliographical references and index.
ISBN 0–19–508107–2
1. Budapest String Quartet.
I. Title.
ML398.B76   1993   785′,7194′0922—dc20   92–31447

Extracts from Joseph Wechsberg's article on the Budapest String Quartet, which appeared in
the Nov. 14, 1959, issue of *The New Yorker*, are reprinted by permission of The New Yorker
Magazine, Inc. Copyright © 1959, 1987 by The New Yorker Magazine, Inc.

2 4 6 8 9 7 5 3 1

Printed in the United States of America
on acid-free paper

In memoriam, to Papaci

Preface

The Budapest String Quartet. One of its recordings is playing as I begin writing this book—the stormy, atonal *Grosse Fuge* (the *Great Fugue*) by Beethoven—"the first of the modern masters," according to Boris Kroyt, who was my father-in-law.[1] The music sounds so contemporary, so jagged, so full of conflict and rage. Listening to it brings to mind the first time I heard the piece.

I was in Washington to attend one of the Budapest's performances at the Library of Congress, where it was the quartet-in-residence. The members performed on the Library's Stradivarius instruments. I can picture entering the auditorium and hearing the sounds of their warming up coming from behind the center door back of the stage. The auditorium—an intimate hall, sharply raked so the sight lines are excellent—is full. Those who cannot get in are taking folding chairs in the pavilion nearby, where the music will be piped in. Their concerts are so popular that music lovers line up in droves at dawn to get tickets, and the same program is performed two nights in a row. Seated in the very first row, several seats in from the aisle, is the woman whose money has built the auditorium and after whom it is named—Elizabeth Sprague Coolidge, America's preeminent music patron, now in her late seventies. Her archrival—they do not speak to each other—a woman just a few years younger who always wears a funny little hat, is present in the second row from the back, in a seat on the aisle especially fitted with an electronic hearing device that she can plug into—Gertrude Clarke Whittall. It is she who donated to the Library the Strads the musicians are using.

Suddenly the muted sounds of tuning up end, the lights dim, and an expectant hush falls over the audience. Everyone's head turns when Mrs. Whittall calls out loudly in her squeaky voice, "There are my boys!"[2] as the center door opens and the players enter. Applause rings out as the musicians take positions beside their chairs, bow slightly in acknowledgment, and sit down. Their parts are already on the music stands in front of them. They adjust their seats, turn a page or two of the music to make sure they will be able to flip them with ease, and then wait as the second violinist fusses with a handkerchief he is adjusting over his chin rest. The first violinist scans his part, the tip of his bow resting on the stand. The violist sits patiently, impassively looking over the audience, his instrument propped on his thigh. The cellist wraps a loose hair from his bow around his wrist, pulls it away, and lets it drop to the floor. Finally, the second violinist nods his head that he is ready. The two violinists and violist take up their instruments; the cellist brings his toward his shoulder. Their bows are poised. Almost imperceptibly, the first violinist leans slightly forward and they begin playing. Music suddenly floods the hall—deep mournful chords from the cello and viola that the first violin rides high above with a melodic passage that the second violin picks up and repeats.

The Budapest String Quartet. Joseph Roisman sits almost ramrod erect, unemotional, every so often cocking his head to the side, listening to himself as he plays a phrase; when he leans to the side, his tongue pushes out his cheek. Next to him, a hunched-over Sasha Schneider sits on the edge of his chair, thrust forward so intensely that he seems about to burst from it; though not a big man, he surrounds his Strad in such a way that it seems like a child's instrument. Next to him, to the listener's right, is Sasha's brother Mischa, looking down through his horn-rim glasses and pursing his lips as he bows, looking so much like the paterfamilias that he is; his fingers flick up and down the strings on the neck of the cello as he pouts. The ordinarily genial Boris Kroyt appears unnaturally somber playing the viola, perhaps because pressing his jowl against the chin rest forces him to look grim; when he has a solo passage to play, he gracefully turns toward the audience so that the notes fill the hall.

Joe. Sasha. Mischa. Boris. A writer has likened them to the four movements of one of the most popular pieces they play, Beethoven's

Opus 59, No. 1. Joe is *Allegro*, Sasha is *Allegretto vivace e sempre scherzando*, Mischa is *Thème russe: allegro*, and Boris *Adagio molto e mesto*.[3] Four men with personalities as varied as their ways of playing. Yet they have stayed together longer than any other contemporary quartet, and that despite six major crises—among them, a serious accident, a suicide, and a heart attack. The myth is that they do not like one another and do not speak to each other outside the concert hall; but the truth is that almost constant touring, rehearsing, and performing over the years has taught them the value of having moments to themselves. All four are Russian Jews, products of a rich middle-European cultural environment that had once dominated the world of Western music. They fled from Nazi Germany and, like so many other talented musicians—Jew and Gentile alike—carried that heritage to the United States, to help make it the musical center of the world. Though they all trained in Germany and afterwards pursued their careers there, they refused after leaving to return and play there. The Schneider brothers lost their mother and sister in the Holocaust, and Roisman's wife blames the Nazis for the fact that the couple is childless.

They are world famous, have played on every continent, traveling by car, bus, train, ship, and, since the end of World War II, plane. They have performed more than three thousand times—to audiences as small as three persons and as large as thirty-five hundred—before men preparing to go off to war against Japan and before the Empress of Japan in Tokyo—in private homes, churches, synagogues, public-school assembly halls, and the largest opera house in the world. They have introduced chamber music in communities as diverse as Macon, Georgia; Tulsa, Oklahoma; Cedar Rapids, Iowa; and Charleston, West Virginia. Their standard repertoire comprises more than sixty quartets, but they have performed over the years more than 265 different works and played with more than 130 guest artists and four symphony orchestras. They are known as classicists, yet they have premiered thirteen contemporary pieces—three of which were dedicated to them—and although they abjure Berg and Webern, they commissioned Hindemith to write a quartet for them, and quartets by Barber and Piston are in their repertoire as well. They are lionized for their interpretation of Beethoven, Mozart, Schubert, and Brahms, but they have also played works by such relatively obscure contemporary composers as Easley Blackwell, William Denny, Benjamin Lees, and Nikolay Medtner.

The Budapest String Quartet. Four gifted musicians with a passion for playing the finest works any composer has written. Their name has become synonymous with chamber music. Indeed, they can claim credit for radically changing the way people regard and appreciate what once was considered the most esoteric of musical forms—for making chamber music an intrinsic, influential, and enriching part of America's musical world. And it all happened in an incredibly brief time.

New York City   N. B.
October 1992

Acknowledgments

I initially began this book with taped interviews of Boris Kroyt and Mischa Schneider in the mid-1960s. However, I had to postpone the project because of the unavailability of Joseph Roisman and Sasha Schneider. Roisman was at that time committed to working with two other writers, Tibor Bartok and Alan M. Kriegsman, and Schneider had started a memoir. So, I put the idea for the book aside—except for a brief flirtation with renewing my endeavors in the early 1980s, when I interviewed Mischa Schneider again.

Bartok and Kriegsman never did write their book. However, their notes survive. I am indebted to Kriegsman, who made them accessible to me, and to Bartok's widow, Sidonie S. Bartok, who holds the copyright on her husband's contribution, for use of the material.

I am also indebted to June Schneider, who made available to me the papers of her husband, Mischa, including the manuscript of his unfinished autobiography.

I am indebted as well to Sasha Schneider, who gave me permission to quote at will from his autobiography, which he published privately in 1988. Although he answered a number of written questions, he said that he had divulged all he wished to disclose about the Budapest String Quartet in the chapter devoted to the Quartet in his book.

A number of individuals have also been very cooperative. I wish to thank all those whom I had the opportunity to interview—each of whom knew or performed with members of the Budapest String Quartet—for giving me their time and offering their frank appraisals. I am tempted to single out several for special mention but am reluctant to do so because everyone deserves my gratitude. They are, in alphabetical order, Mrs. Isidor (Rose) Alpher, Mrs. Cameron (Jane) Baird, Artur Balsam, Howard R. Brubeck, Lee Fairley, Natasha Schneider Furst, Felix Galimir, Frances Gewehr, Mrs. Jac ("Honey") Gorodetzky, Virginia Harpham, Paul Hume, Anna Lou Kapell-Dehavenon, Milton Katims, Paul Katz, Mrs. Ernst Křenek, Alan M. Kriegsman, Jaime Laredo, Ruth Laredo, Caroline Levine, Julius Levine, William Lichtenwanger, Margaret McClure, Joseph Machlis, Madeleine Milhaud, Irving Moskovitz, R. Peter Munves, David Oppenheim, Edgar Ortenberg, Leslie Parnas, Gail Rector, Samuel Rhodes, Mary Rogers, Sol Schoenbach, Harold Schonberg, Howard Scott, Thomas Z. Shepard, David Soyer, Arnold Steinhardt, Walter Trampler, Michael Tree, and Mrs. Edward N. (Lilly) Waters.

Among those who have been especially helpful in the research for this book, I would like to mention Ann McLean of the Music Division of the Library of Congress. The book could not have been written without her assistance and support.

Others deserving my thanks are Steven W. Siegel, Library Director and Archivist, 92nd Street Young Men's & Women's Hebrew Association, New York City; Michelle Errante of Product Marketing and Josephine Mangiaracini of Photo Archives, Sony Classical, New York City; Lillian Knapp of the onetime Annie Friedberg Management; Dean Stein of Chamber Music America; Clementina Fleshler of the Buffalo Chamber Music Society; Nancy Bren Nuzzo, Reference Librarian, Music Library, and Christopher Densmore, Associate Archivist, University Archives, State University of New York at Buffalo; Hans Hirschmann, former chairman of the Cleveland Chamber Music Society's Program Committee; Carol S. Jacobs, Archivist, Musical Arts Association of Cleveland; Mariann Carlin, Concert Manager, Department of Music, Cornell University, Ithaca, New York; Gail Rector, former Director, University Musical Society, University of Michigan, Ann Arbor; Olive McDuffee, Executive Director, Coleman Music Society, Pasadena, California; Jean Gelrich, Media Coordinator and Archivist, Ravinia Festival, Highland Park, Illinois; Martin Antonetti, Reference Librarian, Rare Books and Archives, Mills College, Oakland, California, and Hilde Limondjian, Program Manager, Concerts and Lectures, Metroplitan Museum of Art, New York City.

I am also grateful to the following persons for translating articles, letters, and other written materials: Maria Saffioti (Italian); Elliot Junger (German); Remi Saunder (Russian); Loes Schiller (Dutch), and my wife, Yanna Kroyt Brandt (French and Spanish). Yanna was also invaluable as a guide to understanding the members of the Quartet and in helping me to prepare my manuscript for publication.

Joseph Machlis graciously gave of his time to read my manuscript from the standpoint of a musicologist. Any errors or misinterpretations that still exist are, however, solely mine.

Contents

Con Brio

One Russian is an anarchist; two Russians are a chess game; three Russians are a revolution; four Russians are the Budapest String Quartet.

(attributed to Jascha Heifetz)

1

A Close Call

It is late afternoon of a Friday in March 1938. The four musicians of the Budapest Quartet are standing in line, inside the ballroom of the liner *Manhattan,* waiting to be questioned by immigration authorities. The ship rests in the Narrows of New York Harbor, steam still up, ready to make her way to her berth up the Hudson River once the formalities are finished. The musicians' American agent, Annie Friedberg, is waiting at the dock on West 18th Street to greet them. They are scheduled to play a concert on Sunday in Town Hall in Manhattan and then to perform fifteen other recitals over the next several weeks during this, their sixth tour of the United States. It is a tour that they are not particularly looking forward to. There are not enough concerts—in fact, considerably less than on their prior tour, and they are concerned that with all their traveling expenses, they may end up making almost no money.

The line moves. Mischa steps up to the table where one of the inspectors sits. He hands him his passport and visa.

"Where do you live?" the inspector asks in routine fashion as he looks through the papers.

"I have no residence," answers Mischa. The inspector looks up sharply.[1]

The scene shifts. The four musicians, angry and frustrated, are on the deck of a coal barge, huddled inside their black overcoats, the bitter wind flaring back the brims of their homburgs. To their left is the Statue of Liberty; ahead of them, Ellis Island; at their feet, their luggage and their instruments. They watch helplessly as their ship, the *Manhattan,* proceeds from the quarantine station to her berth without them.

The usually unflappable Roisman stares silently as the coal barge lumbers through the waters of New York Harbor; not so the others. Sasha Schneider is visibly distraught. Several years earlier, he was forced to stay overnight on Ellis Island in a room with five strangers—a sleepless, miserable experience that made him so "mad" that he composed a letter of complaint to President Roosevelt: "how dare he treat artists this way who come to his country to play concerts."[2] Upset at the thought of having to repeat that indignity and fulminating at the stupidity of it all, Schneider is certain that the only reason that he and his colleagues are being detained is because they have arrived a day before their concert contract indicated that they would be coming.

His brother, Mischa, who handles the group's travel papers, knows otherwise and feels guilty. Maybe he looked at the inspector the wrong way. "He didn't like perhaps my looks or something." Thinking about it, he gets furious. "Here I had all the papers. You go to a consul in Europe, you get all the papers, the consul gives you a visa, and then suddenly some guy here decides he doesn't like it and puts you in prison—because that's what it is, a prison. And you pass by the Statue of Liberty—you know, you look at the torch, the beautiful torch, and they take you on a coal sweeper—this horrible, the dirtiest little contraption that you can imagine." He feels, the cellist says, "like the lowest of the lowest."[3]

If the cellist is angry with himself, Kroyt is even angrier—"disgusted," in fact. They are all stateless—traveling on so-called Nansen passports issued by the League of Nations. It is true, Mischa does not have a permanent residence. None of the Quartet members does. They live out of suitcases in hotels, even in Paris, where they now make their base. But Mischa—"a very straight person," Kroyt says disparagingly—answered the question literally.[4] All he had to say was that he lived in Paris. No wonder they are being detained. And, the next day being a Saturday, there will be no examiners on the island until Monday to hear their case.

The four musicians fear being sent back to their homeland; Roisman, for one, escaped across the border from the Soviet Union after the Bolsheviks took over the government. And although all four have lived and concertized extensively in Germany, as Jews they do not dare to return now that Hitler is in power.

Meanwhile, across the bay, Annie Friedberg is waiting at the West 18th Street berth for the *Manhattan* to dock. She scans the disembarking passengers eagerly, looking for the members of the Quartet. It seems like hours before the last passenger walks down the gangway. But where are Joe, Mischa, Sasha, and Boris? Friedberg confronts a ship's officer, who tells her the four Russians have been taken to Ellis Island. Friedberg is beside herself.

On Saturday morning, as the four musicians grouse about their confinement and worry that immigration authorities will force them to return to Europe, a frantic Friedberg finally gets through to Ira Hirschmann. Hirschmann and his wife, Hortense Monath, a pianist, had, in 1937, founded the New Friends of Music, which is sponsoring the Budapest's concert at Town Hall. Hirschmann ordinarily does not engage string quartets that he has not personally heard, but Friedberg sent him several of their records, and he broke his rule and scheduled them for two concerts, the first on that Sunday.

A successful business executive, Hirschmann is also a political associate of Mayor Fiorello La Guardia, and La Guardia, a lover of classical music, is on the board of New Friends. Hirschmann decides to ask for the mayor's help. He reaches La Guardia by phone at his home on Sunday morning.

"Coming to the concert today?" he asks.

"Yes," the mayor replies. "Why?" Hirschmann explains the situation. Reacting to his friend's seemingly flippant attitude, La Guardia merely laughs and hangs up. Hirschmann calls back. La Guardia, enjoying his friend's discomfiture, suggests they take a boat to Ellis Island and "have the concert over there all to ourselves." To Hirschmann's dismay, the mayor hangs up again.[5]

But La Guardia is only kidding Hirschmann, is actually sympathetic, and immediately phones a friend who is in charge of Ellis Island. A federal judge is quickly dispatched to the island to hear the Quartet's case. Soon, Mischa stands before him, angry at both himself and the immigration authorities. "Your honor," he begins, "I would like to know why am I here. What did we do wrong that we are brought here?"

"You didn't do anything wrong," the judge assures him. "It's just that the immigration officer wasn't sure about something. Perhaps the answer that you gave him—or somebody of you four gave him . . . you know, there are a lot of possibilities."[6] The judge smiles. He tells them that they are free to go.

Exhausted—they have not slept—Joe, Mischa, Sasha, and Boris are whisked aboard a launch. It lands them at the tip of Manhattan, where a car is waiting to speed them to Town Hall on West 43rd Street. The concert is scheduled for 5:30 P.M., and it is already past four o'clock. There is no time to do anything but change into their

striped pants and cutaways—wrinkled and creased because they
have not been able to have them pressed—and tune their instruments before going out on stage. They are to play Mozart's Quartet
in C and then, after Efrem Zimbalist plays a violin sonata, the Schubert A Minor Quartet. "Frankly," Sasha declares afterwards, "none
of us remembers how we played that concert."[7] But Boris does. "I
don't think," he says in an understatement unusual for him, "we
played exceptionally well."[8]

No one is more astonished than they are when the next day's
newspapers come out. The critic for the *World-Telegram* calls the
Quartet "one of the foremost ensembles of the kind."[9] The reviewer
for the *Sun* says their "excellent qualities have never before been so
completely revealed here."[10] Their rendition of the Schubert, says
the *Herald-Tribune* reviewer, was "flaw-less."[11] The *New York
Times* critic Noel Straus is ecstatic:

> If there is a finer string foursome in existence than the Budapest Quar-
> tet, it has not made itself known on this side of the Atlantic. . . .
>
> Here is a quartet unrivalled for balance and blending of suave, soul-
> ful and immaculately pure tone, which achieves a unity of effect that
> could hardly be bettered, and brings a poetry and understanding to its
> interpretations unmatched by any other organization of the kind to-
> day. . . . The results were such as one habitually awaits in vain. For
> beauty of sound, richness of imagination and absolutely satisfying expo-
> sition of the content of the works attempted this amazing group could
> unhesitatingly be said to stand in a class by itself.[12]

Straus's review is unprecedented. No other chamber ensemble
has ever won such high praise from a critic in as influential a newspaper as the *Times*.

2

A Fertile Field

America in the 1930s was not exactly a musical wasteland—on the contrary—but the nation was only just beginning to understand and enjoy serious music. It was no longer the same country of a decade earlier, when, Kroyt said, musicians in Europe had "a very low opinion, artistically, about America." Those who came to this country in the 1920s did not come to study; rather, Americans went to Europe to study. As Kroyt put it, "You go to America to make money but not make art."[1]

One reason for the change in the way that musicians regarded America was the influx in the 1930s of composers and top-ranked musicians fleeing Nazi Germany and, as war threatened Europe, a corresponding flood of middle-class refugees familiar with the music they played and accustomed to attending performances. Sol Hurok, who became the leading concert manager of this era, used to say that each time one of the European immigrants died, he lost a customer. Previously, well-known performers had been sought to head American music schools—pianist Josef Hoffman and violinist Efrem Zimbalist by the Curtis Institute in Philadelphia, pianist Ossip Garbiolowitch by the Cincinnati College of Music. Now, in the 1930s, composers are being selected, and faculties burst with creative energy. Stravinsky, Schönberg, Bartók, Hindemith, Milhaud, Křenek, and Martinů all found a home in America. They composed, they conducted, and they taught—Hindemith at Yale and Tanglewood, Schönberg at UCLA, Milhaud at Mills College and Aspen, and Křenek at Vassar and Hamline University. They, and the fleeing musicians who joined them here, were in the process—though unaware of it—of creating a revolution in music. American schools were slowly but inexorably becoming the centers of contemporary music and performance studies. It was no longer necessary for a young American to go to Europe to study either composition or an instrument.

Some of the performing musicians made it to the West Coast, and soon studio orchestras in Hollywood were filled with extraordinary players, many of whom, like Daniel Karpilovsky and Toscha Seidel (who played the violin solos that John Garfield mimicked in *Humoresque*), were of soloist standing. Films were the major cultural medium of the time, and some were made about composers like Chopin and included such pianists as Paderewski, José Iturbi, and Oscar Levant. Singers such as Deanna Durbin, Nelson Eddy, and Jeanette McDonald were stars. Even Walt Disney got into the spirit with *Fantasia,* which included performances of Beethoven's "Pastoral" Symphony and Stravinski's "Rite of Spring" by Leopold Stokowski and the Philadelphia Orchestra. The movies were primarily entertainment vehicles, but they made the public aware of classical music and prepared the ground, so to speak, for touring performers. And then there was radio. Both the National Broadcasting Company and a spin-off network created by the Columbia Broadcasting System had their own symphonic orchestras, which performed on weekly broadcasts; Toscanini, hired to conduct the former, made it one of the outstanding orchestras of its time. "It was incredible what went on and who was here," said violinist Felix Galimir, who reached America from Germany via Palestine in 1938. "Rachmaninoff, Heifetz, Elman—everybody—and Kreisler. I went once to three concerts one Sunday in Carnegie Hall."[2] The climate was ripe for making America, and New York in particular, the musical capital of the world.

This growing audience for music did not yet include devotees of chamber music, which had always been considered elitist, a musician's music. In many ways, it is special. Music created for only three, four, five, or six musicians has none of the vivid color effects and dazzling passages that an orchestra, with its wind, brass, and percussion sections and row upon row of violins, violas, cellos, and double basses, can achieve; no mass of tone that can shake a concert hall's walls. Instead, chamber music calls for close listening—to hear the interplay of musical lines. Chamber music is honest music—that is, there is none of the blurring of phrasing that can occur between orchestra sections; rather, it is clear, with seldom more than three musical lines to follow—like "the interweaving of scarlet with gold and blue and purple threads," as one chamber-music lover put it. Four sensible people conversing—that was the way Goethe described a string quartet. One Columbia recording executive said he did not appreciate Beethoven's symphonies until he listened to the great composer's quartets. He learned to recognize the basic exchange of musical ideas by hearing them expressed by only four instruments.[3]

The trouble was that not many people appreciated the clarity of musical expression composers realized in their chamber music or could afford to indulge in an appreciation of it. Until Beethoven's time, it was generally performed by amateurs, who played with friends gathered for an evening of making music. There had always been nobles and gentry who played instruments themselves or were the patrons of musicians. The Industrial Revolution in the nineteenth century created a middle class that hungered for the cultural status that chamber music seemed to symbolize. It became traditional in Germany, for example, to present a bride with a piano for her new home.

Chamber music was confined to small rooms and private rooms until the man who taught Beethoven how to play both the violin and the viola, Ignaz Schuppanzigh, took a daring step. Schuppanzigh was the leader of a string quartet underwritten by Beethoven's patron, Count Rasumovsky. He started performing in public, much to the dismay of the tightly closed musical circle.

Schuppanzigh unleashed a new era in chamber music—recitals by professional musicians before audiences composed of the very amateurs who liked to play the trios, quartets, quintets, and sextets at home. His ensemble was followed by a number of other quartet groups: the Koella, composed of four brothers of Swiss parentage; the Muller, also four brothers, which toured throughout western Europe and Russia; the Helmesberger, which featured the late quartets of Beethoven; and, the best known of them all, the Joachim. It soon became even more fashionable to listen to chamber music than to play it.

Europe experienced a proliferation of chamber-music groups in the late nineteenth and the early twentieth centuries. America, on the other hand, lagged far behind, with only sporadic interest and a mixed bag of results; there chamber music just was not popular. The first string quartets believed to be heard in the United States were works by Haydn performed in Bethlehem, Pennsylvania, sometime in the eighteenth century. We know that Mozart trios were first heard in that same city in 1785. As often happened in Europe, when chamber music was performed in public, it was on a concert bill with other kinds of music. A quintet by Johann Hummel, for example, was heard in 1842 as part of the debut of the Philharmonic Society of New York.

What interest did exist in this country for chamber music was so minimal that any efforts to foster seasonal performances were short-lived. The Harvard Musical Association started in 1844 an annual series of six chamber-music concerts, but the program lasted only about five years. In 1851 a series of chamber-music concerts was begun in New York, and four years later William Mason and Theodore Thomas started their own series there that lasted for thirteen years. Because of the lack of interest, quartets often folded after two or three years of performing in public, "disheartened" and "in despair," as one observer ruefully noted, "from lack of appreciation and patronage."[4] The first professional ensemble of any duration was the Mendelssohn Quintette Club, made up of five Boston players, which was formed sometime around 1850. Its members, two of whom could also play flute and clarinet, toured North America in 1859 and brought the European repertory of classical and romantic works to the West Coast and Hawaii in the early 1880s.

It was not until 1885, however, that the first American string quartet of real note was established—the Kneisel, organized by the concertmaster of the Boston Symphony and including three other members of that orchestra. It was the first group to perform all the Beethoven quartets in the United States. Kneisel continued performing both with the symphony orchestra and the quartet until 1903, when he devoted himself totally to the quartet, which lasted until 1917. The Flonzaley, formed in 1902 in New York, performed for twenty-six years, disbanding in 1928. By then, a host of groups from Europe had begun making regular tours of America and some of them—the Busch, Kolisch, Lener, Pro Arte, and Roth quartets—eventually settled in the United States. As good as they were, none could make a living from only playing concerts; nor could any of the more than a score of ensembles formed in America that were already performing in the early 1930s—quartets such as the Stradivarius, Adamowksi, Culp, French-American, Hart House, New World, Spargur, Swastika (of Philadelphia), West Sisters, and Zoellner. There were not enough engagements available, and a vicious cycle was started: quartet members had to commit themselves to teaching or performing with other groups, which, in consequence, limited their ability to tour as extensively as they would have liked.

There was another reason as well. "There are a lot of very good musicians who come together and want to play quartet," said Mischa Schneider, "but some of them don't want to lead the life that we led—the gypsy life. You know, you have a family, and you have children. How many times did I leave my wife and my children, and went on a tour for three months? Who does it?" Few quartet musicians did. Only the Budapest, which prohibited its members from outside activities, had the time to travel wherever or whenever a concert date was available. "We were free agents twelve months of the year," Mischa explained. "If we wanted to go to Australia, we went to Australia. If we wanted to go to America, we went there."[5]

It was not just that the members of the Budapest String Quartet were flexible, able to go anywhere, any time. In 1938, when they ran into difficulties with immigration authorities, they had no country they could call their own; they were not staying in any one place for more than a few weeks at a time. By the time she was four years old, Kroyt's daughter Yanna could speak five different languages, the result of having Russian parents and living for a few months virtually every year in France, Italy, England, Germany, and Indonesia. The Quartet members wanted very much to settle down.

Ironically, within a year of their famous Town Hall concert, they were offered a home, a guarantee, stability—a country—but at first they turned it down.

3

Quartet-in-Residence

"Please treat this matter confidentially as it is doubtful if we shall consider the plan with another quartet."[1]

The head of the Library of Congress's Music Division, Dr. Harold Spivacke, and Gertrude Clarke Whittall, who had donated five Stradivarius instruments to the Library, had come up with an unusual idea in February 1939. The Strads needed to be played. If they were not used, they would deteriorate and lose their delicate sound, just as Paganini's Guarnerius del Gesu—a violin dating from 1742, which he had donated to his hometown of Genoa—had lost its tone when kept in a glass case in the Municipal Palace.

Different quartets had been engaged to perform on the Strads at Library concerts in the Coolidge Auditorium, but the players had grumbled about having to get used to unfamiliar instruments within a matter of days. (It ordinarily takes a string player at least six weeks to grow accustomed to a new violin, viola, or cello.) "Suppose," said Spivacke, who held a doctorate in musicology from the University of Berlin, "we had a quartet in residence here, and the players had time to make friends with these beautiful instruments?"[2] What better idea, he wrote Annie Friedberg, than to engage the Budapest Quartet to play the instruments regularly, at twelve concerts every month and "for extended periods of time" rehearsing?[3]

Spivacke's letter to Friedberg did not receive a positive answer. For one thing, the Budapest Quartet members had tried the instruments two months before, at three concerts at the Library in December 1938, and thought they were difficult to play and needed repair. They were "hard in response," said Joe: "You played something like

12

a whisper on your own instrument. When you did the same on another one [one of the Strads] it whistled. You never knew what will come out."[4] Also, in addition to the group's growing popularity in Europe, Friedberg was receiving so many offers for U.S. engagements that the future of the Budapest's performing around the country regularly looked, for the first time, promising. Friedberg was quick to point out that "the Quartet has too many duties and contracted tours to remain in America for a whole year." They already had so many concert dates that they were going to have to confine themselves to America for most of the 1939–40 season and were also committed to return to the Dutch East Indies in March 1940. "I have had so many inquiries for them," she wrote back to Spivacke. "I had another tour for January and February which I had to refuse." She said that "they are a great deal in demand and more so every year" and, misunderstanding Spivacke's offer, said that it was "impossible for them to play twelve concerts in twelve months" without their being able to perform elsewhere.[5]

Spivacke immediately responded. "It occurred to us," he hastened to correct her, "that, with a guarantee as large as this one, they might be willing to establish their semi-permanent residence in Washington instead of New York. We have no idea, of course, of limiting their engagements elsewhere and handicapping them in any way."[6] However, because of the Quartet's tight schedule, Spivacke and Friedberg could only work out five appearances at the Library for the fall of 1939—two in November, three in December.

Understandably, the Quartet was the only group approached by Spivacke to play the Strads on a permanent basis, given the reviews and audience response of their initial three concerts at the Library—on December 8, 10, and 30, 1938. The very first—in which they played quartets by Haydn, Schubert, and Brahms—prompted Alice Eversman of the Washington *Evening Star* to declare: "Such exquisite sound as this combination of instruments has never been heard in this auditorium dedicated to chamber music." Such praise was unusual coming from Eversman, who had been a soprano at the Metropolitan Opera in New York and for many years the leading dramatic soprano for the San Carlo Opera in Italy.

> Yesterday's concert will remain in memory as one where the perfection of string ensemble was vouchsafed to the seekers of beauty in musical tone. . . . The gamut of their tonal color is so even that they merge one into the other without perception and one hears, as it were, a single instrument whose voice is clear and sweet, deep and sonorous, at the

same time. It is so free and unconfined that its origin is undetectable
and its limit never felt.

Eversman continued her review in that vein, ending by saying, "Outbursts of applause greeted the artists at the conclusion of each number, applause which held a very special note of enthusiasm."[7]

At the time of Spivacke's correspondence with Friedberg in February 1939, the Quartet was back in Paris for a thirty-four-recital
tour, concertizing there, in Amsterdam, in Brussels, across Norway,
and throughout England until well into May—again to increasingly
favorable reviews. A critic in an Aberdeen newspaper spoke of them
as "virile musicians" who "had such gifts of phrasing and a way of
getting at the heart of the work they were playing that a critical
attitude faded out in admiration."[8] A London reviewer said that "of
late nothing has proved finer, in both strong and delicate senses" and
that they played with "exquisite sheen."[9] A Romanian critic who
heard the Quartet's Beethoven cycle at the Salle Gaveau in Paris said
that the six concerts

> will remain unforgettable. There is no misuse of *fortissimos*, a tremen-
> dous advantage especially where a quartet is concerned, where the dy-
> namic possibilities are inevitably limited. In exchange, they obtain a
> *pianissimo*, the like of which I have not heard from any other quartet.
> My entire gratitude belongs to these true musicians who can be taken as
> the paradigm of the true performer, the performer who never sacrifices
> musical thought to the instrumental technique.[10]

That summer, instead of remaining in Paris, the Quartet members spent almost three months at Mills College, an all-girls school
in Oakland, California, where they were engaged to play and to
teach. It was an idyllic setting—a campus fringed with tall palms and
perfumed by eucalyptus in southern California, with swimming and
other sports facilities, comfortable quarters, and glorious sunshine
every day—the perfect place to rest up from a hectic concert season
and prepare their repertoire for the next one. Moreover, the atmosphere was cosmopolitan. The school, which had a French-language
department, attracted a number of French writers as well as composers as the political situation in Europe grew ominous—among
them, Henri Troyat, André Maurois, and Darius and Madeleine Milhaud. The Pro Arte Quartet ordinarily spent its summers there, but
its members wanted to return that year to their home country, Belgium. Mischa and Sasha, both bachelors without ties, were against
going to Mills, while Joe and Boris were for it. A tie vote usually
meant no; but this time, for some reason, they decided to pick

matches, and the tie was broken in favor of going to Mills. The Pro Arte was expected back at the school in 1940 but never did return (its first violinist died before then), and in its place the Budapest Quartet became Mills's quartet-in-residence, spending almost every summer there for the next fifteen years. It was "destiny," said Mischa, who later met his third wife at Mills.[11]

News from Europe shattered the warm afterglow of that summer of 1939. A few days after Germany invaded Poland in September, the Quartet, about to begin its American concert season on the West Coast, received a brief, shocking message from its agent in London, Ibbs and Tillett: "As you are doubtless aware, an outbreak of war automatically cancels all existing contracts between Concert promoters and artists in this country."[12] Clearly, not only the concerts that the London agents had already booked in advance were doomed but also recitals scheduled for France, Holland, and Belgium, as well as the Indonesian trip, were in jeopardy.

Suddenly, the Library of Congress offer looked good, indeed. Friedberg quickly got off a note to Spivacke, informing him that, despite earlier plans, the Quartet would now remain "all season" in America "owing to the European conflict" because "they can not return to any other country." Backtracking on her previously negative response to his offer that the Budapest commit itself to the Library, she wrote to him that "in case you need them later on they will be delighted to come again to Washington."[13]

Spivacke played it cool. "I do not see any other opening for the Budapest Quartet during the coming season," he replied, "but if anything unexpected should happen I shall let you know."[14] The Quartet members, however, were not put off by his reply. It was now clear to all of them that their future was in the United States, where they all wanted to settle permanently. Joe and Boris had already applied for immigration visas and been granted first papers leading to citizenship. They had no trouble being accepted as part of the Russian quota—few Soviet citizens were being allowed out of Russia, so there were always vacancies. But the Schneider brothers were not so lucky. Vilna, where they were born, was now part of Poland, and the Polish quota was filled.

With their desire to remain in America in mind, as well as the fact that tours anywhere else might soon be impossible, Mischa wrote on behalf of the Quartet directly to Spivacke, in answer to his original proposition. "We could make our headquarters in Washington," he said, but it had to be understood that "our concert engagements elswhere [sic] shall not suffer from our obligation to live in

Washington." And one thing they wanted to make clear. The Quartet had purposely shunned being tied to a patron. Some wealthy supporters treated the musicians they helped as servants, expecting command performances, even dictating repertoire. "Nobody except Mrs. Whittall shall be allowed to attend our rehearsals," Mischa wrote, "and we shall rehearse works which we need not only for Washington concerts but for elsewhere too." The Quartet would be willing to use Washington as its base for nine months of the year, performing twenty-four concerts at the Library, for a fee of fifteen thousand dollars.[15]

That was more than the foundation could afford, Spivacke wrote back, and a back-and-forth round of letters followed until finally a compromise was reached. On May 10, 1940, Joe, Mischa, Sasha, and Boris put their signatures on a contract for the first of twenty-two annual seasons that the Quartet would perform at the Library. The four Russian Jews—aliens, still learning the language, and novices when it came to American ways—thus became not just the Library's quartet-in-residence but also, by extension, the nation's official quartet-in-residence.

The contract called for twenty-four concerts during the 1940–41 season for ninety-six hundred dollars, or four hundred dollars a performance. In turn, the Quartet members agreed to "acquire a familiarity" with the Stradivari instruments and to perform on them. They also had to agree to reside in Washington during three specified periods of the year and, when concertizing at the Library, to rehearse on the Strads "at least four times weekly, each rehearsal to last at least two hours." If for some reason, they were unable to rehearse, they had to make up the time at a future practice session. Moreover, their programs were to be "planned in consultation with and must be approved by" the head of the Music Division, and the choice of any guest artists that might appear with them "shall rest entirely with the Whittall Foundation."[16]

On the surface, it looked like the Quartet was conceding a great deal by allowing Spivacke—and, by inference, Mrs. Whittall—a say in their programs and the right to choose guest artists. But that was legalese protection for the Library and the foundation. As it worked out, the choice of programs became a matter of mutual agreement, and the Library always bowed to the desires of the Quartet members when it came to engaging other musicians to perform with them piano quartets, cello quintets, and other chamber music. Moreover, moving to Washington was no hardship, though it rankled Sasha Schneider, who always preferred New York. Washington was provincial in his eyes, so he took an apartment on Beekman Place in Manhattan and stayed in Mischa's apartment when he had to be in Washington for rehearsals and concerts. Joe and Boris also rented apartments in the Capital.

Patron or not, Mrs. Whittall and the members of the Budapest Quartet drew close. She liked to invite them to her apartment at the Shoreham Hotel for tea, and they made it a point to treat her courteously and affectionately. She was, however, positively possessive about the four Russians. If someone tried to silence her when they came on stage for a recital, she would snap back, "Don't hush me. Those are my boys."[17] She was seventy-three years old in 1940, a native of Nebraska who was first exposed to chamber music thirty years earlier when the Flonzaley Quartet played a private concert for her family. Her husband, who had made a fortune in rugs and carpets, died in 1934, and she decided to move from Nebraska to Washington.

Mrs. Whittall was a tiny, fussy old lady who, despite her wealth, lived alone without a maid or help of any kind in her Shoreham quarters, which she frequently set on fire while smoking in bed. She dressed very plainly, with a choke of pearls at her throat and a tiny hat perched on her upswept coiffure. She ordinarily rose at seven in the morning, fixed breakfast, fed the pigeons that roosted on the terrace outside her suite, and, if she could, arranged a game of canasta, her other addiction besides cigarettes. "I'm a wild, woolly Westerner and a friend of Buffalo Bill," she liked to say. She wore glasses without lenses; they disguised the hearing aid she had to wear because she was virtually stone deaf. Despite her hearing problem, she likened chamber music to "a rainbow of color." After hearing the Flonzaley all those years ago, she "decided to have a quartette [*sic*] of my own."[18]

Though perhaps she would not admit it, the Strads and the foundation were a direct slap at the Library's other great benefactor, Elizabeth Sprague Coolidge, the country's foremost supporter of chamber music. Mrs. Coolidge was a native of Chicago, a pianist in her own right who had performed with the forerunner of the Chicago Symphony. She was three years older than Mrs. Whittall, though she looked younger. She was taller, too, and bore herself like a patrician. In some ways the two women were similar. Like her rival, Mrs. Coolidge dressed simply and sometimes wore a funny little hat. She was hard of hearing, too, though not nearly as deaf as Mrs. Whittall.

Mrs. Coolidge did everything possible to encourage and promote chamber music. She underwrote such string quartets as the Berkshire and the Coolidge (named after her); commissioned chamber-music works by Benjamin Britten, Paul Hindemith, Darius Milhaud, Maurice Ravel and Igor Stravinsky; founded the Berkshire Chamber Music Festival in Pittsfield, Massachusetts; and in 1924, just before she settled in Washington, offered to build a recital hall on the grounds of the Library of Congress. She wanted to make possible, she wrote the Librarian of Congress, "performance of music in ways which might be considered too unique or too expensive to be ordinarily undertaken."[19] A friend of numerous congressmen as well as of the House Speaker, Mrs. Coolidge had no difficulty in having a joint resolution adopted in January 1925 allocating part of the federally owned property for the hall. The sixty-foot-square Coolidge Auditorium was built in the northwest inner courtyard of the Library, the first building ever donated to the United States government. It had a platform stage thirty feet wide and twenty feet deep, a seating capacity of 511, and rows of seats that were slightly concave and inclined so sharply that each seat had an unobstructed view of the stage. The auditorium took less than a year to construct and attracted a growing audience of supporters to chamber-music concerts and solo recitals.

Mrs. Coolidge could hardly prevent Mrs. Whittall from funding a series of concerts in the auditorium or paying for a pavilion to be built adjoining it to house the Strads and a whole bevy of priceless, original music manuscripts she was collecting. The Strads, though, were the heart of the display—a cello, a viola, and three violins.

Like all of the more than eleven hundred string instruments Antonio Stradivarius made, most of which were violins, each of those in the Whittall collection has unique qualities, though they all enjoy the velvety tones and an ease in bowing that a Guarneri, for example, does not. The cello, called the Castelbarco after a Milanese count who once owned it, is slightly larger than the standard modern cello. It responds quickly to the lightest bowing, more so than even a smaller cello does. Its tone, Mrs. Whittall used to say, "was unforgettable."

The viola—named for Alexander Cassavetti, a member of a noted Greek family who lived in England—"can wring your heart," Mrs. Whittall claimed. Constructed in 1727, the viola has enormous projecting power, though like all the Strads the low C string is a bit weak. The viola tends to sound a bit nasal and blends in more easily with violins than with a cello in a quartet.

One of the violins was also owned by Castelbarco and carries his name. It has what one musician called a "very creamy sound," much like that of another of the violins, the Ward. The latter was owned in the nineteenth century by an English instrument maker and named after him. Mrs. Whittall referred to the Castelbarco violin as "feminine," while the Ward was "sophisticated" because "it lived long in London and knows so many things."

The third violin, the Betts, was "royalty" to Mrs. Whittall.[20] It got its name from a London dealer who supposedly purchased it for one guinea from a stranger who just walked into his shop with it in 1820. Made by Stradivarius during his so-called Golden Period, between 1700 and 1720, the Betts's tone is brighter than the other violins. Because it is considered the best instrument of the five, Roismann was expected to play on the Betts, but he preferred the feel of the Castelbarco. To go with the Strads, Mrs. Whittall also purchased and donated to the Library five bows made by the master bowmaker François Tourte, all finer than the ones Stradivarius made for his own instruments.

The possibility that Washington might be bombed during the war frightened Spivacke, who felt responsible for the safety of the Whittall Collection of instruments and bows. The Budapest members played the Strads on December 18, 1941, for the anniversary of the death of the instrument maker, but then the brief acknowledgment that the Quartet members were playing the Strads donated by Mrs. Whittall printed on the inside of the Budapest programmes disappeared, as did the instruments. For several years they were not even played or brought out for display at any annual concert in mid-December commemorating Stradivarius's death. Nobody had an inkling of where they were.

One day, not long after the Japanese bombed Pearl Harbor, Spivacke's assistant, Edward N. Waters, had left Washington in a truck and had headed west. No one but Spivacke and Mrs. Whittall knew where he was going. It was all very hush-hush. Perhaps it was a matter of being overcautious, or paranoid, but they refused to divulge what had happened to the Strads. The Quartet members, though, were soon informed. In early January 1942, they had a recital coming up in Newark, Ohio. Waters wrote them and asked if they could plan to drop by nearby Granville to check on the instruments' condition—though, careful as ever, he never mentioned them by name. They were to bring a complete new set of strings for each of the instruments, so they could try them out—the Whittall Foundation would reimburse them for the expense.[21] Waters had trucked the Strads to Denison University, where they were put in a special room. Unfortunately, the report back to Waters from the Quartet

after the visit to Denison was not good. The humidity in the area
where the instruments were being kept was not conducive to pre-
serving them, Mischa wrote.

No mention is made of the instruments in concert programmes
until three sets of twin performances in the late fall of 1944. Then
they disappear again until March 7, 1946 (almost a year after the war
ended), when the Quartet resumed playing them on a regular basis as
part of the tenth anniversary of the Whittall Foundation. What had
happened to them between 1944 and 1946 is unclear, though it is
likely they were being overhauled by the Washington luthier the
Library used, Albert F. Moglie.

Each summer before the Quartet returned to Washington for its
fall round of concerts at the Library, Mischa would get off a letter to
Spivacke, requesting that Moglie check out what he jocularly referred to as the "Strad saxophones."[22] There were the usual problems associated with a string instrument—cork on the underside of a
chin rest that needed replacing, a peg or bit of purling that had gotten
loose, a bridge that had to be moved slightly, or the Tourte bows
required rehairing. "The G and C Strings *have to be very thin*,"
Mischa warned once about the cello. "There should be a set when I
come." And, he added, "I might come . . . and play a while on the
instrument as I heard from Joe that you had some troubles with all of
them."[23]

Radio broadcasts of the Quartet's performances were customary
almost from the beginning of its association with the Library. The
second and third of its recitals in 1938, before it became the Library's
quartet-in-residence, were broadcast in part over Station WMAL in
Washington and NBC's Blue Network. The five concerts performed
the following year were aired in part over WMAL and to Latin America. During their first full season as quartet-in-residence, they performed on Saturday afternoons, one hour of which was carried by
WRC in Washington and NBC's Red Network. Beginning the next
year, CBS picked up coverage of the Saturday programs, though a
CBS official had to apologize when an affiliate opted to carry a baseball game one summer Saturday in 1942. "We are all distressed," he
said.[24] CBS also carried the Quartet's first Beethoven cycle at the
Library, a series of eleven recitals in all—which featured other Beethoven works as well—at 11:05 on Sunday mornings and, during the
same hour in the fall of 1942, seven performances that the Quartet
played with guest artists.

The response to the radio programs was overwhelming. The Library received almost thirteen hundred letters for the CBS broad-

casts of the Beethoven cycle alone. They came from every one of the forty-eight states, the District of Columbia, and four provinces in Canada. Requests for copies of the printed programmes came from twelve military camps and hospitals and from both faculty and students in forty-five schools. There were even some complaints—that the hour CBS broadcast the series on Sunday mornings conflicted with local church services or that a CBS affiliate carried only part of the program. Otherwise, the messages were positive: "These concerts are certainly a high point in radio programs for the week" (Washington, D.C.); "the finest program which I have ever heard on the radio" (Houston); "they are the happiest part of my whole week" (Cambridge, Mass.); "by all means let us have more and more chamber music" (Cincinnati); "I have the Beethoven Quartett [sic] scores and play the first part with them. My wife, as the local music club radio chairman, will show your information to her club members" (Jackson, Mich.); "there are many people in this town who arrange their time so they can listen to this" (Bethlehem, Penn.); "a little more than a year ago I listened to my first symphony concert over the air, and now I have an understanding of many types of classical music, but the quartet is one type which I am just learning to understand. Therefore your programs will be of timely assistance to me" (New Brunswick, Canada); "I'm not in the habit of writing 'fan letters,' but I hope, by writing, to encourage you to continue the Sunday morning programs of the Budapest String Quartet" (New York City).[25]

The Budapest concerts were so popular in Washington that to handle the demand for tickets in the fall of 1941 the Library began to schedule repeat recitals, with the Quartet playing the same program two nights in a row. But even then, a local newspaper noted, the demand "has not materially eased."[26] Originally, the two nights chosen were Friday and Saturday, but in the spring of 1943 the twin recitals were held on Thursday and Friday nights. Tickets to the concerts were free—except for a twenty-five-cent handling charge—and distributed from a downtown music store. They were limited to two a customer. The tickets became available Monday mornings when the store opened at 9 A.M., and the queue for them would begin to form as early as six o'clock and soon curl around the block. "Washington is used to lines," the *Sunday Star* reported. "Cigarettes, buses, meat, stage shows, movies, and now nylons. . . . There's one line, though, that has nothing to do with the war. This one forms on G street from Thirteenth to Fourteenth. . . . And it's there as many as 25 mornings a year, during the fall and winter, and regardless of weather."[27] Spivacke's assistant, Ed Waters, accused his wife of marrying him so she would not have to stand in line. Tickets were put aside especially for military personnel, so audiences in the Coolidge Auditorium took on a wartime look with a large group of fresh-faced, uniformed servicemen and servicewomen. The dual Thursday–Friday concerts became a Washington tradition. The Beethoven, Haydn, and Debussy were "a joy," the president's wife, Eleanor Roosevelt, wrote in her syndicated column, "My Day," after attending a concert.[28] Library officials crowed that the Coolidge Auditorium had become the center of chamber music in the United States.

Meanwhile, the Schneider brothers were trying to get quota visas so they could officially immigrate. They hired a lawyer in Toronto to arrange for their entering the United States through Canada and purposely scheduled a concert there to enable them to do so, but the lawyer failed to get them on the quota. They had to request an extension of their visitor's visas, and that led to troubles with the American Federation of Musicians (AFM).

Joe and Boris, who had had no trouble obtaining entry visas under the Russian quota and starting the procedure for becoming citizens, joined the union in 1939. The Schneiders could not do so because they were not eligible until they had their first papers. Learning that the Quartet was scheduled to perform as well as make recordings in the summer of 1940, James Petrillo, head of the AFM, wired Roismann that "unless all instrumentalists are members . . . no member of this organization will be permited [sic] to perform."[29] The Schneiders pleaded with Petrillo to make an exception "for us."[30] They now expected, they said, to reenter the United States on the Polish quota through Canada in August 1941. Petrillo relented, saying he would accept the Schneiders before they had their first papers as long as they paid their initiation fees and dues in advance, which they promptly did; however, this incident was not the last run-in that the Quartet would have with the musicians' union.

The Schneiders finally flew to Toronto in 1942, picked up their immigration visas, and flew back to the United States the same day. While waiting for their plane's departure at the Toronto airport, Mischa, ecstatic, had gotten drunk. When he reached New York he went to the Russian Tea Room and, sitting there, thought, "At last I am going to be a called a citizen. I will belong to a country."[31]

Once World War II broke out, the Schneider brothers' new status created somewhat of a problem. Sasha, then thirty-two years old and the youngest of the group, was now eligible for the draft. He wrote to

Spivacke at the Library, asking whether there would be any way he could get into the Navy Band if he had to serve.[32] The question was moot, because when Sasha was called for a physical examination, he was told that injuries to his leg caused by a boyhood case of tetanus made him ineligible.

Grateful to be on their way to becoming American citizens, the members of the Quartet began playing for war-relief benefits and at military camps, both in the Washington area and in Colorado and California. Several "colored soldiers," a sergeant reported with some amazement, walked more than a mile to hear them perform at a service club in Camp Lee, Virginia, and the entire audience rose as "one man and applauded vociferously" as the four musicians went down the aisle after playing. The sergeant said the evening was "very hot" but the Quartet members, ever sticklers for tradition, refused to take off their coats "but felt they should keep them on."[33]

Ordinarily, the Quartet chose easy-to-listen-to, melodic pieces to play for military audiences, avoiding Beethoven or Bartók, for example; but even so, sometimes the result was less than desirable. At performances at a hospital in the Presidio in San Francisco and at Dibble Hospital in Palo Alto, California, they played Mozart's "Hunt" Quartet, two movements of Debussy's Quartet in G Minor, the Andante Cantabile from Tchaikovsky's Quartet in D Major, and the finale of Haydn's "Lark" Quartet. At each hospital, Luther Marchant, who was responsible for bringing the Budapest to Mills College, spoke to the audience beforehand, explaining the works to be heard. But both times, Mischa wrote to Spivacke, "soldiers came[,] listened for a few minutes and left the hall after a few minutes, only a very small group remaining until the end." The audience at the Dibble Hospital was "entirely undisciplined so that Marchant had to tell them that if they don't want to listen to the music they could leave the hall only at the end of a movement." Maybe, Mischa speculated, "chamber music is too high brow an art for the majority of soldiers."[34] Spivacke thought otherwise. He suspected the special services officers had not announced the concerts "properly."[35]

The members were more hurt by the unjustified criticism of Glenn Dillard Gunn of the Washington *Times-Herald.* The Quartet had asked composer Roy Harris to arrange "The Star-Spangled Banner" for string quartet, so that they could play it at the opening of a recital. Hearing it performed at the Library in early 1942, in a concert in tribute to the Pan American Union, Gunn blasted the "Hungarian version" and suggested that the "European newcomers" had done injury to the national anthem. They were so incensed by Gunn's remarks that Mischa wrote a letter to him on behalf of the Quartet, pointing out that Harris was "a very eminent American composer whose native characteristics have often been pointed out." The Budapest, he added, "hope you will give us the courtesy of a correction in your column."[36]

They were very proud of becoming American citizens. "Speak English," Mischa would call out if anyone at a rehearsal began talking in German or Russian.[37] They were all chagrined and embarrassed to learn that the Nazis had appropriated the Quartet's name during the war and that a Budapest String Quartet was playing in German army camps in Czechoslovakia.[38] They talked about changing the name of the Quartet—Hungary was a German ally—but the Columbia Recording Corporation talked them out of it.

Meanwhile, Joe Americanized his name—from Josef to Joseph, and from Roismann to Roisman. Mischa and Sasha—who were born with the surname Sznejder—were already the Schneiders to everyone but the immigration authorities. Boris never changed his name but began celebrating his birthday on June 23, arrived at by switching from the Russian Gregorian calendar to the westernized Julian calendar (though he made a mistake and added thirteen days instead of twelve days to the Gregorian's June 10).

The war did little to impede the Quartet's touring in America. If anything, they were more active than ever—"in one city on one night and in another the next," said Joe. "It is always a rush."[39] Annie Friedberg was frantic, trying to schedule their train and hotel reservations when both seats and rooms were scarce items. Mischa called a twenty-city, twenty-two concert tour during the winter of 1943 "the most strenuous we have had in this country. The trains were overcrowded, the hotels also. Mostly we had to sleep two in one room and that was not nice at all."[40] That tour began in New York, and then the Quartet went on to Pittsburgh, Buffalo, and Montreal before heading west to St. Paul and then south and west to Louisville, Columbus (Miss.), Dallas, Austin, Pasadena, Portland, Bellingham (Wash.), and Seattle; went back to Portland and then to Cheney (Wash.), Missoula, and Sioux Falls; and, finally, traveled back and forth between New York, Princeton, New Rochelle, New York, Buffalo, and New York. And that was only part of its expanding schedule. For the first time the Quartet played in New Orleans, in Newark (N.J.), at the Mormon Tabernacle in Salt Lake City, in the Ascension Parish House in Denver, in museums in Worcester (Mass.), Toledo (Ohio), and Detroit, for music societies as diverse as the Tuesday Musical Club of Omaha and the Woman's Club of New

Rochelle, and across the country on campuses that included Ivy League schools as well as Downer College in Milwaukee, Cornell College in Iowa, and Montana State University at Bozeman. Besides such tours, their regular schedule of concerts at the 92nd Street Y, Washington Irving High School, and the Frick Collection in New York and their fall and spring programs at the Library made the Quartet members, Mischa said, constant "commuters between Washington and New York."[41]

Everywhere, the critics raved. In New York, Virgil Thomson in the *Herald-Tribune* described a performance of Schubert's "Death and the Maiden" Quartet and Schönberg's "Verklärte Nacht" as "a delight to the ear."[42] Neil Straus of the *Times*, whom they credited for their success, thought they were better than ever, saying "the ensemble has enlarged its dynamic range of late and has added to its sonorities without losing any of its perfection of sound."[43] After one of the Quartet's programs of Beethoven at the Young Men's Hebrew Association (known as the 92nd Street Y), B. H. Haggin, the critic for *Nation* magazine, asked an aging chamber-music lover who had heard the Kneisel Quartet what he thought of the Kneisel after listening to the Budapest players. "He was silent for a few moments before he said: 'Don't ask me about them,' and was silent again before he exploded: 'Those wooden Indians!'"[44]

The reaction was the same wherever the Budapest performed. A Buffalo *Courier-Express* reviewer said, "many listeners must have uttered hopes that the fate of other excellent quartets such as the Kolisch and the Roth never will descend upon the Budapest Quartet."[45] A Dallas critic wrote, "Rarely before, or not since the heyday of the Flonzaleys, has quartet music been so communicative personally."[46] A Chicago critic could not get over their "magnificent teamwork, an amusing instance of which came in the Beethoven when Mr. Roismann, the first violin, came to a page turn in the middle of a trill. What happened? Just that Mr. Schneider, the second violin, reached over and turned the page for him, without dropping a note of his own performance."[47] The Budapest, said a San Francisco *Chronicle* reviewer, "closed the most successful chamber music series that has ever been presented in this community, at least in my time."[48] The critic of the Chicago *Daily Tribune* called the attendance figures at four Ravinia Festival summer concerts—7,594 concertgoers in all—"nothing short of sensational." (The attendance at six programs by the Pro Arte Quartet the year before had only totaled two thousand.) The success of Schubert's Cello Quintet in C with Dudley Powers was so phenomenal, he said—"Never in my experience has a chamber music audience burst into a tremendous roar of approval"—that a movement was repeated. "Stamping and cheers have been regular features of the audience's reaction at all four concerts. . . . Thousands of skeptical listeners have learned to enjoy it [chamber music] for the first time."[49]

By December 1943, the Budapest Quartet was receiving national attention. The first of many articles that would be published about them ran in a nationwide magazine, *Time*, that month. It talked about the number of bookings they had, the audiences they drew, their fees, the fact that they sold a staggering total of three hundred thousand recordings a year and, among other erroneous statements, that Roisman was the only member ever to have visited Budapest. "Their drinking habits," it went on, "are Roismann, tomato juice; Sasha, Burgundy; Kroyt, vodka, and Mischa, milk."[50]

In an amazing five years, at a time before hype and press agentry became a staple of the field of performing arts, the Quartet had achieved celebrity status. But how did they do it? How was it possible that four musicians whose psyches were so different and whose paths were so diverse came together, one by one, to share an unusual musical life? When the chance to join the Quartet came, Joe had been struggling, playing in cafés and in a cinema orchestra; Mischa was teaching, bored, and plagued by acute performance anxiety; Sasha and Boris were trying to flee Germany—Sasha suddenly confronted with an ominous whisper of what lay ahead, and Boris, who had lived happily in Germany for nearly thirty years, finally jarred into the realization that as a Jew his career was blocked and his life and the lives of his wife and child were for the first time seriously threatened. It was these four men who carried the Budapest String Quartet to fame. But, in fact, none of them was an original member. One by one, they took over another, earlier Budapest String Quartet, supplanting Hungarians with Russians and, more important, dramatically changing the entire musical approach of the ensemble.

The first one to become a member of the Quartet was Joe Roisman. His joining marked the beginning of a fateful change.

4

Allegro: *Joe*

Josef Roismann was, above all, Russian, a native of Odessa, which has probably nurtured more violinists than any other city in the world. Ever since a precocious Mischa Elman had left to make a name for himself throughout Europe—he first performed in Odessa at the age of eight—the mothers of other Jewish youngsters saw a career in music as the way out of the ghetto, social ostracism, and a life restricted by czarist decrees. Jascha Heifetz's subsequent meteoric rise fed this belief. You could buy a violin in Odessa for a few rubles, and for years upon years untrained, poor violinists played for bar mitzvahs, weddings, and even Gentile functions, as they do in Chekhov's *Cherry Orchard.* From Odessa came, among others, David Oistrakh, with whom Roismann's sister, Rosa, a pianist, performed. The term "Russian violinist" became as common as the term "Italian tenor."

Odessa was then a cosmopolitan melting pot, a bustling seaport of some four hundred thousand people that rose like a terrace around a circular bay—"the pearl of the Black Sea." On windy days, another musician from Odessa said, you could hear "the waves of the Black Sea—that was when I fell in love with the key of G minor."[1] The city was alive with music; the Odessa Opera was the stepping stone for singers, and all the stars—Battistini, Caruso, Ruffo, Shaliapin, Tetrazzini—sang there regularly. It was also a city of babel—of nouveau riche who tried to mimick Russian aristocrats by speaking French, of traders who spoke Greek, Italian, Bulgarian, and Romanian. Except for Russian, Yiddish was the most common language. One-third of the city's inhabitants were Jewish, most of whom lived

27

in the ghetto of Moldavanka, where flamboyant bandits ruled the streets.

Outside the ghetto area were substantial, ornate mansions shaded by huge acacia trees and public buildings in a smorgasbord of styles—the opera house in Viennese Baroque, the stock exchange in Florentine Gothic. One side of Primorsky Boulevard, above the port, was lined with sumptuous homes; the other faced a sweeping vista of sailing ships, fishing boats, and ferries. A dramatic flight of stairs led from the boulevard to the docks below—the steps made famous in Eisenstein's film *The Battleship Potemkin*, though the events of the 1905 uprising that the movie depicts actually took place some distance away.

Roismann did not live in the ghetto, though his family was by no means wealthy. His father was a haberdasher. Roismann was born on July 25, 1900, four years after his sister, Rosa. When he was six years old, his parents presented him with a violin and sent him to study with Pyotr Stoliarsky, the first teacher of Oistrakh and Nathan Milstein, another Odessa progeny. By the age of nine, Roismann had attracted the attention of a Mrs. Vissotzky, the wife of a wealthy tea tycoon, who was underwriting the education of more than thirty young Russians in various parts of Europe. It was common at that time for poor music students to be supported by a royal or rich patron; indeed, before modern times, when competitions and scholarships took their place as financial underpinnings, patrons not only subsidized musicians' educations but also purchased instruments for them, hired concert halls so they could give recitals, and often provided a stipend as well to cover their living expenses. Mrs. Vissotzky was already helping Rosa with her studies and intended to pay for Roismann's going to St. Petersburg to study with the most famous violin teacher of his time, Leopold Auer. But Rosa became ill, and then, traumatically, their father, only fifty years old, died of a heart attack.

The sudden loss of his father would affect Roismann all of his life. He, too, would suffer from a weak heart and, as a result, would be almost obsessive about his health, would avoid funerals, would become increasingly fastidious and involved in petty details, and would be rather superstitious. Leaving a concert one night, he asked a friend to retrieve his umbrella from backstage; he could not return himself, he said, because, "Don't you know it's bad luck to go back for something you've forgotten?"[2] As an adult, Joe gave the impression of being cold, detached, unimpassioned—"aloof" is the word that mostly comes to mind when people try to describe him. He was a short, slim man whose looks seemed to emphasize his apartness. Joe's brown hair began to recede at an early age; by his mid-forties, he was left with a tonsure that eventually turned white. The fringe of hair made him appear distinguished and aristocratic—and unapproachable. He was an inveterate pipe smoker and collected Meerschaum pipes; he had hundreds of them.

Joe developed into a compulsive creature of habit, up every morning at the same hour, napping every afternoon, the first to show up for rehearsals or a concert, and always at a train station or an airport an hour ahead of everyone else. He was also a very private person; friends were shocked when they learned that he once fathered an illegitimate child.

Instead of paying for Roismann to study with Auer, Mrs. Vissotzky arranged for Joe, his mother, and Rosa to go to Berlin so that Joe could study with a talented but dissipated violin teacher who had once taught in Odessa. His name in Odessa was, appropriately, Fiddleman. He now called himself Fiedemann—Alexander Fiedemann. Mrs. Vissotzky's only request was that the Roismanns take with them a young cellist named Boris Blinder. (He was the brother of Naoum Blinder, who was then studying in England and was later concertmaster of the San Francisco Symphony and the teacher of Isaac Stern.) With young Blinder in tow, the Roismanns moved into an apartment above the flat of another of Fiedemann's students who was also from Odessa, Boris Kroyt. While Rosa took lessons with Leonid Kreutzer, Joe studied with Fiedemann until 1914, when World War I broke out and the Roismanns were able to get exit visas to return to Odessa.

On Fiedemann's advice, Roismann continued his studies with Naoum Blinder, who had also returned to Odessa and had become a professor at the imperial conservatory. Joe acquired his first taste for chamber music by playing trios and quartets with him and rapidly developed a love for the literature. Joe had an unorthodox method of fingering. Though he did not have a big left hand, it was very flexible. Instead of employing the standard 1-3-5 positions on the fingerboard, he was able to extend his fingers out of one position without going to another, "creeping around," much as Itzhak Perlman does today. "He could do anything," a colleague said. "You could tell him anything and he would do it. Tell him, 'Joe why don't you take with this fingering or with that fingering.'"[3]

Joe graduated from the conservatory with the title of "Free Artist," which meant that he could reside even in St. Petersburg, where Jews ordinarily were not permitted to live. He chose, however, to remain in Odessa, and won the post of concertmaster with the Odessa Opera. But the war years in Russia were almost insufferable. There was scarcely any fuel for heat in the winter and little food to eat any time of the year.

One cold winter, Joe had to wear gloves with the fingertips cut off so that he could perform. Worse, though, after the war first the White Army and then the Red Army overran Odessa. The Bolsheviks conscripted Joe into a touring group of musicians to play at farms and in factories; they received sugar, salt, and potatoes in return, which Joe dutifully sent home to his mother. However, fed up with being forced to perform, his career at a standstill, one day in 1923 he took advantage of being in a town close to the Polish border. Together with several other musicians he slipped across.

Joe hid out for two weeks before feeling safe enough to make his way across Poland and into Czechoslovakia. In Prague, he was able to resume his studies with František Stupka, who had taught at the Odessa Conservatory and was now second conductor of the Czech Philharmonic. Stupka got Joe a job with the orchestra and also engagements in local cafés where, typically, many aspiring musicians played in order to earn a living. Some of the little six- or seven-member orchestras performed in the afternoon hours, others in the evening, either for pay or tips or, sometimes, just for what was left over on the diners' plates. There he was, decked out in full dress—the first time he had ever worn formal attire—a *primo geiger* (the lead soloist), standing up instead of sitting; playing gypsy music, waltzes, and popular tunes; eating leftovers; and relying on gratuities to pay for his rent and studies.

While in Prague, Joe met and married an attractive, dark-haired Hungarian woman, Pola Kvassy, who had come to Czechoslovakia to study. She was as quiet and as private a person as he was and was skilled with her hands; she could make her own dresses and hats, costume jewelry, and decorative pillowslips. The youngest of seven children, Pola—or Paula, as Americans spelled her name—was also a linguist. She could speak five languages, or rather six, for she and Joe developed an argot of their own, a hodgepodge of languages that no one else could understand. Speaking it insolated them from other people. They could talk together in public in total privacy. The two were wed on what was to Joe's superstitious mind a fortuitous day—a Friday the thirteenth—in February 1925. Joe was twenty-four; Pola, twenty-two.

Joe tried to contact his boyhood friend, Kroyt, who still lived in Berlin. He was anxious to move there himself. Kroyt received his letter but mislaid it. Nevertheless, Joe managed on his own to get to Berlin, where, fortunately, he ran into Kroyt on the street. Kroyt was then with an unusual eighty-piece symphony orchestra at the Ufa-Palast am Zoo movie house that was conducted by Erno Rapee (later the conductor at Radio City Music Hall in New York City). The orchestra not only played the background music for silent films but also performed classical music three times a day between screenings. Through Kroyt, who performed as soloist with the movie orchestra, Joe got a job in the orchestra as well as engagements in cafés. He was performing with the orchestra when he was located by members of a Hungarian chamber ensemble that was enjoying some measure of success in Europe. It called itself Budapesti Vónosnégyes—the Budapest String Quartet.

5

Budapesti Vónosnégyes

The Budapest String Quartet—the original one—was, as the title implies, very much a Hungarian group when it was organized in 1917 by four friends who met and performed together in Budapest. By the turn of the century, that city vied with Prague and Vienna for a position as the cultural center of central Europe, and much of the artistic life of the Hungarian capital in the years before World War I centered on the State Opera House, a neo-Renaissance building that was the most modern structure of its type when it opened in 1884. Little more than a block away was the Budapest Academy of Music, a breeding ground for many of the musicians who worked at the opera house or played in the symphony orchestra that performed on Monday nights, when the opera was closed. Aspiring musicians who used to bolt Hungary to study in Vienna, Prague, or Berlin no longer found it necessary to do so.

During World War I, the four musicians, all members of the opera orchestra, found themselves with time on their hands. They had been spared being drafted into the Hungarian army because of their positions in the orchestra, but the war limited the orchestra's activities and, as a result, their incomes. Their teachers suggested that they could earn extra money by forming a quartet.

Their teachers—"mentors" is a better word since the four were no longer students—were Jeno Hubay, a native of Budapest; and David Popper, who was born in Prague. They had themselves been members of a well-known, respected quartet in the 1880s and 1890s, Hubay as the first violinist and Popper as the cellist. Brahms was so enamored of the way they played that he often asked them to sight-read a piece he had just completed so he could hear what it sounded like.

Hubay had studied with the man considered the master violinist of the late nineteenth century, Joseph Joachim, who had succeeded Niccolo Paganini as the most famous string player in Europe. Joachim was also the leader of the most popular quartet of the time. Though he did not possess Paganini's extraordinary technical agility, Joachim was, nevertheless, a gifted instrumentalist whose tone, musical maturity, and intelligence were acclaimed.

Hubay and Popper organized an ensemble that abroad was called the Quartet Hubay–Popper; their performances were announced as "Hubay–Popper'sche Abende"—an evening of Hubay and Popper. For reasons of national pride, their quartet at home was called the Hungarian Quartet or, sometimes, the Budapest Quartet, a title that their four former students took as their own.

To a great extent, it was through the Hungarian, Hubay, and the Bohemian, Popper, that Budapest had become a center of musical education. Among the outstanding string players who studied under Hubay or Popper were Joseph Szigeti as well as a number of musicians whom they encouraged to form their own quartets—among them, Feri Roth and Sandor Vegh. The style of playing then was called romantic. It was extreme by modern standards—sliding from one note to another called *portamento*, extensive reiteration of a single note called *tremolo*, excessive vibratos that often hid poor intonation, and a tendency to wrench emotional values from a phrase rather than to adhere strictly to the written notes. That tendency—which sometimes led to a ripe, gushing sound on string instruments—dominated an era when solo performers took liberties to play up their particular talents. The same was true for pianists. One did not go to a recital to hear Chopin; one went to hear Paderewski perform Chopin.

The world of music was then on the verge of tremendous changes in playing and composition that first began around the turn of the century. World War I abruptly halted the creative innovations, but only temporarily. It was an exciting, innovative period—one that blossomed after the war was over, when ideas seemed, paradoxically, to burst like bombshells in the very cities in Europe that had suffered in the war and its aftermath. Such composers of the romantic movement as Schubert, Schumann, and Brahms were being overshadowed by composers working in new ways—impressionists such as Debussy and Ravel or experimenters such as Schönberg and Hindemith, who questioned the very basis of the seven-tone scale.

It was during this ferment of ideas that the four young musicians in Budapest began to think of forming a quartet—and, inadvertently, made an important contribution to this world of change and revolution. From the first, however, they decided to follow a seating pattern that a much-heralded American quartet, the Flonzaley, had adopted. There has never been any set rule as to how the four musicians in a quartet should position themselves so as to best project their sound. A mid-eighteenth-century engraving shows the cellist seated on the left while the other three players are standing, though it is not clear who are the violinists and who is the violist.[1] The usual pattern at the turn of the century was the one Joachim had employed. He had the cello on his left, the second violin opposite, and the viola to the second violin's right. The first American-based quartet of distinction, the Kneisel, which performed between 1885 and 1917, followed that arrangement. The Flonzaley, however, placed the second violin on the first violin's left, the viola opposite the first violin, and the cello on the viola's right—an arrangement that the Budapest chose and which almost all quartets have since followed.

The Budapest String Quartet made its debut in December 1917[2] but not, as might be expected, in the Hungarian capital. Instead, the members chose the medieval city of Kolozvar, apparently because of Hubay's association with it. Kolozvar was a center of Magyar culture on the Transylvania Plateau some 150 miles east of Budapest. (The city is now part of Romania and called Cluj-Napoca.) Hubay had received an honorary degree from the university there four years earlier. No program of that first concert exists, but it was probably held at the university, south and east of Piaţa Libertăţii, or a short walk west of it in an early nineteenth-century building called the Redoute, where Lizst had performed in 1846. The concert was evidently a success, because shortly after the new year, 1918, began, the members felt confident enough to perform for the first time in the Quartet's home base of Budapest, at the Urania Theater.

From the outset, the four young men decided to break away from several traditions in string quartet playing. For one thing, there would be no leader. Previously, and in many groups for many years afterwards as well, the first violinist was considered a quartet's leader; he chose what would be played and decided tempi, phrasing, bowing, the length of ritards, dynamics, and stylistic flourishes. He was, in effect, a dictator. The distinction between the first violinist and the other members was made quite clear when, for example, the noted German violinist–composer Louis Spohr performed; he stood to play while his colleagues sat. The great Joachim had three different quartets in various parts of Germany with which he performed when he was in each's respective area. Each of them was called the Joachim Quartet; the violinist simply told the local musicians how to play. When the "Joachim Quartet" went on tour to England, Joachim engaged three English players to perform with him there.

To some extent, the idea of the first violinist being the leader makes musical sense, for in almost all the pieces written during the classical and romantic periods of the eighteenth and nineteenth centuries, the first violinist carries the melody or major thematic line. So the idea of sharing decisions was revolutionary. Disagreements among the Budapest members about how fast a piece should be played, how loud, how soft, with what accents and pauses—any of the myriad questions that the notes on a printed page conjure up—would be decided by vote. Democracy would rule, and any member who disagreed would have to learn to live with the result. The rule would apply to business matters as well; and, in case of a tie vote, the status quo would prevail. The problem, of course, was what to do in the event of a tie vote over a musical disagreement. Impasses could lead to lengthy arguments, lobbying, and bitterness.

That the new quartet's first violinist would agree to such an arrangement was evidence not only of the members' friendship as compatriots in the opera orchestra but also of the first violinist's lack of assertiveness. His name was Emil Hauser. Hauser, a handsome, dimple-chinned man, was the youngest of the Quartet members—twenty-four years old at the time of its debut—which may partly explain why he was so reluctant to be aggressive. A native of Budapest, Hauser had studied with both Hubay and another of Joachim's students at the Budapest Music Academy and, afterwards, with Otakar Ševčík at the Pisek Art Colony near Prague. Just before the outbreak of World War I, Hauser was concertizing as second violinist with the Rebner Quartet and teaching at the Hoschule für Musik (the State Academy High School for Music) in Frankfurt, Germany. For a brief period, he served as second violinist in the Konzerthaus Quartet led by Adolf Busch (later one of the founders of the Marlboro Music Festival in Vermont) and second concertmaster to Busch in the Wiener Konsertverein. After the war began, Hauser returned to Budapest and was drafted into a military band, but he evidently was allowed to appear with the opera orchestra as a soloist.

All that is known about Alfred Indig, the second violinist, is that he was Hungarian, a member of the opera orchestra, and had apparently also studied at the Budapest academy.

The violist was 31-year-old Istvan Ipolyi, who was born in Ujvidek, Hungary. Like Hauser, he had graduated from the Budapest academy. A sad-eyed, glum-looking musician who sported a moustache, Ipolyi was also a serious-minded musicologist, interested in the principles of music making. He had once studied with French violinist and composer Henri Marteau, who succeeded Joseph Joachim as head of the Hochschule für Musik in Berlin. Ipolyi's wife was an Austrian who sang in the opera chorus.

The only member of the Quartet who was not Hungarian was the bespectaled cellist, Harry Son, though like Hauser and Ipolyi— and evidently Indig, too—he was Jewish. That is not surprising. Most leading string players in orchestras throughout Europe were Jewish, and at one time before World War II, all the leading violin virtuosos—Mischa Elman, Jascha Heifetz, Bronislav Hubermann, Fritz Kreisler, Yehudi Menuhin, Nathan Milstein, David Oistrakh, Joseph Szigeti, and Efrem Zimbalist—were Jewish, with one exception, the Frenchman Zino Francescatti. The oldest of the Budapest four—thirty-seven—Son was born in and studied initially in Rotterdam but at seventeen went to Budapest to study with Popper.[3]

At first, the Budapest members continued to perform with the opera orchestra, but once they had established a repertoire for concertizing, they all resigned their positions. Instead, they agreed to devote their entire time to rehearsing and performing together. None of them was to take a teaching position or to perform outside the Quartet, whether it be in solo recital or with an orchestra. Dedication to quartet playing was to be total—an unheard-of arrangement and one quite problematic. By the end of the war, one could count more than fifty quartets that were concertizing on the Continent and in England, yet, despite their proliferation, no ensemble could support itself on performances alone. Their members taught, either privately or in academies, and performed in recitals with other groups and with or in orchestras.

It was a calculated risk. Hauser, Indig, Ipolyi, and Son believed that denying themselves outside activities would enable the Quartet to travel anywhere at any time, without worrying about scheduling overlaps. To ensure that no one quit during the season to go off on his own, they all signed a one-year contract binding them to a winter concert season and the summertime beforehand, when they would prepare their repertoire. In another revolutionary departure from the standard practice of the day, they decided to share concert fees equally. Ordinarily, a first violinist received more money than the other members because he was the leader and because more often than not he arranged the bookings. The other three members earned more or less than one another depending on how long they had been in the group. As time went on, the Budapest members even went a step farther than splitting proceeds four ways: new members shared concert fees equally immediately upon joining the Quartet, no matter how long the other members had been together.

There was one other rule, a practical one, dictated by scandals common among small ensembles: there was to be no interference from wives or girlfriends. They were not allowed to attend rehearsals or to participate in discussions of Quartet affairs. The Budapest members had seen too many other groups broken up by spats and disagreements instigated or exacerbated by the musicians' wives. The wives of second violinists and violists, in particular, goaded their husbands into demanding a bigger share of concert fees, argued for or against playing in certain cities, were jealous of the first violinist's receiving all the public attention, and pressured for the playing of works in which their husbands had solo parts. In the Budapest Quartet, from its founding to the day it disbanded fifty years later, no wife of any member—nor any girlfriend—ever had a say in the Quartet's musical or business dealings.

A minor problem occurred in 1920 when Indig quit the Quartet after a little more than two years. Apparently, as was common with so many other frustrated second violinists, he wanted a more important career for himself. His departure was the first of nine shifts in personnel, involving eleven members, that the Budapest Quartet would experience over the next thirty-five years. Six of the changes involved the position of second violin. All the other positions changed hands only one time. Only once did a member graduate to another postion within the Quartet.

It proved relatively easy to fill Indig's chair. The new second violinist was another native of Budapest, Imre Pogany, who was then twenty-six years old, about two months older than Hauser, and who knew all the other members. He had also studied at the Budapest Academy of Music, both with Hubay and with composer Zoltán Kodály and was serving as the assistant conductor of the opera orchestra and soloist with the philharmonic orchestra.

By the time Pogany joined the Quartet, it had already extended its bookings outside of Hungary. It performed in Holland not long after its Budapest debut in 1918 and quickly expanded its performance schedule into Germany when the members, shaken by the strikes, demonstrations, and communist trends in postwar Hungary decided to move their base from Budapest to Berlin. It was a wise move.

Although Budapest had achieved some prominence in musical education, the center of culture in Europe remained—despite the outcome of World War I—Germany. So many chamber-music societies existed—every little town had its own quartet—that, according to one musician who performed there, "you could play as many concerts as you want."[4] And of all the German cities, Berlin was preeminent, whether in music, architecture, painting, or the new art of film. The city lived a schizophrenic postwar existence—wracked by spiraling inflation and torn by bloody street fighting between radicals and reactionaries, yet at the very heart of exciting new movements that drew to it, like a magnet, the greatest artists of central Europe: painters such as Max Beckmann, George Grosz, and Wassily Kandinsky; performers such as Boris Shaliapin and Isadora Duncan; writers such as Maxim Gorki and Vladimir Nabokov; playwrights such as Bertolt Brecht and Carl Zuckmayer; film directors such as Ernst Lubitsch and Sergei Eisenstein; composers such as Arnold Schönberg, Alban Berg, and Kurt Weill; and a veritable multitude of musicians, including such established concert artists as Artur Schnabel and Bronislav Hubermann as well as such young talents as Vladimir Horowitz and Gregor Piatigorsky.

After hearing Schnabel play a piano recital, Clifford Curzon, a native of London, decided that "the only thing to do was to start life again, in Berlin! And so I gave up everything and went and lived in Berlin for two years. And so in that way I started life again."[5] Another young pianist, Artur Balsam, who was from Warsaw, found Berlin "incredible."[6]

The Budapest String Quartet debuted in Berlin during the winter of 1921–22. By that time, the Quartet was active in all the major European cities and known, depending on what country they were in, as Das Budapester Streichquartett, Le Quatuor de Budapest, Ill Quartetto di Budapest, and El Cuarteto de Budapest. Soon thereafter, it was playing as many as 125 concerts each season.

The Budapest gained a reputation for, among other things, performing modern compositions, many of which the Quartet premiered across Europe. Before long, it could list sixty-five works, fifty-nine quartets, and four trios in its repertoire—from classics by Haydn, Mozart, Brahms, and Mendelssohn, as well as the sixteen Beethoven quartets and *Grosse Fuge*, to contemporary pieces by Italian, French, Scandinavian, and German composers.

Critiques were decidedly mixed and often contradictory. Reviewers criticized their crudeness of sound, their tendency toward ultra pianissimo, and their lack of "impetuousness." A performance of Béla Bartók's First String Quartet was panned in one city but received an ovation in another.[7]

In May 1925 the Budapest Quartet first performed in London and other English cities, and that month the members signed a recording contract with His Master's Voice (HMV), a division of Gramophone & Co., with whom they were to record for the next fifteen years. Their first recordings, made at HMV's Abbey Road studio in London over the next two years when they were in England on tour, were of three quartets—a Haydn, a Mozart, and what was then known as Dvořák's "Nigger" Quartet and later called the "American" Quartet.

By 1927, the Budapest Quartet had achieved great success—and was about to experience its first major crisis. After a series of concerts in Germany that January, the group returned to London for three concerts. Performances of works by Beethoven, Schubert, Giovanni Sgambati, and Percy Grainger ("Molly on the Shore," arranged for string quartet) prompted the *Times* critic to say that "among the foreign quartets that have visited this country, the Budapest quartet holds a high place," and though "their tone is a little keener than the silky quality of one of their rivals, their energy [is] more controlled than that of another and their chording is particularly good."[8]

Which rivals the critic was referring to is unclear. At an earlier concert, in Vienna in 1924, a local critic had compared the Budapest to the Triestino Quartet of Italy, which was well regarded in both Vienna and Berlin. He said that "it is difficult to establish which one of these two ensembles was the best in its profound comprehension of the spiritual values in its magisterial transfiguration of sound."[9] At the time, however, there were a number of string quartets that were even more prominent than the Triestino—the Brodsky and Griller of England; the Pro Arte of Belgium; the Capet and Lener of France (the latter made up of students of Hubay and Popper who had also been members of the Budapest Opera Orchestra); the Klinger and Guarneri of Germany; the Busch, Rosé, and Kolisch of Austria; and the Flonzaley, which was subsidized by a wealthy Manhattan broker and named for his estate in Switzerland, where its members had rehearsed before making their first public appearance in 1904.

Like so many other quartets, the Budapest was plagued by dissatisfied second violinists. Now, for the second time in seven years, the musician who held that chair was disgruntled, and this time, unlike when Indig left in 1920, the situation became acrimonious. After the

Quartet completed a tour of Spain in May 1927, Pogany left unan-
nounced for America to meet with a fellow Hungarian he had be-
friended many years earlier, Fritz Reiner, who was now conductor of
the Cincinnati Symphony Orchestra. Pogany went to apply for a
position with the orchestra. Reiner offered him the chair of principal
second violin, but Pogany hesitated to accept it, probably because it
was not the first violin position. He returned to Berlin to discuss the
situation with Hauser. Hauser was evidently very upset by Pogany's
overtures to Reiner, believing them a betrayal of the Quartet. Pogany
had not said a word of what he was thinking to anyone else and was
about to leave the Quartet in the lurch just when they were going to
spend the summer preparing their next season's repertoire. During
the heated discussion, Pogany quit.

Hauser quickly tried to fill Pogany's chair. He spread the word in
musical circles in Berlin, hoping to find a replacement before the
annual round of summer rehearsals for the next concert season began. Erno Rapee heard about the opening. He could, indeed, recommend a violinist to Hauser, a man who was the third assistant conductor of the Ufa movie orchestra. He was a Russian named Josef
Roismann.

Joe was not sure he wanted to join the Budapest. He auditioned
for it that spring and was offered the post of second violin, but he
hesitated to accept it. He was already earning good money with the
Ufa orchestra—it paid better than the Berlin Philharmonic—and in-
cremented his salary by playing in cafés. He was reluctant to take a
chance with a quartet whose members' incomes depended totally on
the concerts they played, the number of which varied from concert
season to concert season. On the other hand, he was primarily interested in chamber music and especially in performing string quartets.
Pola decided the dilemma for him. Aware of Joe's predilections, she
convinced him to join. It was, he later said, the "best advice" he ever
had.[10]

Joe's training was a turning point in the Budapest Quartet's for-
tunes, though at the very beginning he found himself questioning
the wisdom of his decision. As the first "foreigner" to join the
Quartet—the Dutchman Harry Son, a founder, was not considered a
stranger—he was treated differently than any of the others had been.
He was to share in concert fees, but his 25 percent was put in a bank.
If he did not stay the full year of the contract that he signed, the
money was forfeited. If he did stay, he would receive the money, and
all four members would then sign a joint three-year contract.

Roismann signed, but the ordinarily unemotional violinist soon bristled when he ran into a more serious problem, the other members' musical limitations. But he had committed himself, and there seemed no possibility of getting his job back in the movie orchestra. He was not a happy man.

On the surface, the Quartet appeared to be making a name for itself. After a summer of rehearsals, Joe made his debut on September 17, 1927, in Oslo in a program of three Beethoven quartets—the Quartet in A, Opus 18, No. 5; the Quartet in F, Opus 59, No. 1; and the Quartet in D, Opus 18, No. 3. No review of that concert survives, but, two months later, when the Quartet performed an all-Schubert program in Berlin, the critic of the *Berliner Tageblatt* remarked that the Budapest "played with an intensity of expression that we have not heard from any of their rivals."[11] A London *Times* critic wrote about the same Schubert program the following March, saying that the members "gave full value to the dramatic passages which come so surprisingly from the most poetical of composers."[12] That year, while in England, the Quartet recorded eight quartets in six days.

Internally, the Quartet was wracked by a bitter quarrel. Joe found himself being pressed to side with one or the other in disputes over both the music and business affairs—"besieged for such partiality" was the way he put. Both Hauser and Son constantly pressured Joe to take their side when a vote was taken. Ipolyi was noncommittal, hoping "to serve the music without regarding anything."[13] The somber violist always tried to suppress "everything in myself wich [sic] could offend the others and disturb our work," but, he complained, "there has seldom been that right atmosphere of sacrifice and humble devotion without wich you can well make money but you cant never [sic] reach the highest ideals."[14] Neither Hauser nor Son, however, felt constrained to approach Joe for a "personal favour to vote for them."[15]

Joe was beside himself because he did not agree musically with either man. For one thing, Hauser and Ipolyi did not play spiccato in the customary way of bowing. For some reason, despite all their schooling, they had trouble with their wrist action. They were unable to manipulate the middle of the bow to create the staccato needed for the execution of fast passages of notes of equal length—as in the scherzo of Beethoven's Quartet in F, Opus 59, No. 1, one of the first quartets Roismann performed with them. Other musicians were able to play spiccato with a skipping bow. Hauser and Ipolyi could only do it by very short, incisive strokes with the tip, or point, of the bow, which had the effect of blurring the tempo. That technique had earned them the sobriquet *Das Spitzenquartett*—the Point Quartet—in Germany.

The title was not a compliment. The lack of such technique continued to hamper the Quartet for almost a decade more. All the members practiced individually as well as together, but Joe found he had to practice more than the others, in order to master *spitzen*. He soon became exhausted. *Spitzen* seemed to work only if it was not exaggerated. Joe despised the *spitzen*, found Hauser a mediocre violinist, and deplored the exaggerated sliding and excessive vibratos. He himself represented a new generation of violinists—with a rapid and sometimes continuous vibrato, a greater rhythmic incisiveness, and, perhaps what he was best known for, a natural elegance and brilliance.

Joe made no secret of his complaints about the shortcomings of the others, grumbling about them all the time. The crisis came to a head after the last of a round of German recitals were over in the winter of 1930 and on the eve of the Budapest's first tour outside of Europe, which was to include concerts in Indonesia as well as the United States. Son announced that he was quitting. The Dutch cellist, who was just shy of his fiftieth birthday, gave no reason, but evidently the strains of the disagreements within the Quartet were too much for him to endure.

The man chosen to succeed Son was recommended to the Quartet by the mother-in-law of one of the leading young cellists in the world, Emanuel Feuermann. Feuermann had studied with him in Leipzig, when both were students of the noted cello teacher Julius Klengel. The young cellist's name was Mojzesz Sznejder, but, like many Jewish musicians, he had changed his last name to a more Teutonic name, Schneider. Legal documents gave his new first name as Michael, but he called himself what his family called him, Mischa—Mischa Schneider.[16]

Schneider auditioned for the Budapest in the music room of Feuermann's in-laws and, once accepted into the Quartet, began rehearsals with them in April 1931, in Copenhagen. Again, as in Roismann's case, the Quartet chose well. Mischa would eventually be hailed as the greatest cellist in chamber-music history. And, perhaps just as important, because of him, his brother Abram Sznejder—Alexander (Sasha) Schneider—would one day join the Quartet as well.

At first, though, Mischa, like Roismann, was in for a shock.

6

Thème Russe: Allegro: *Mischa*

Mischa wondered what he had become part of. The rehearsals in Copenhagen seemed endless. They talked and talked and talked, hour after hour after hour, accomplishing little. "I thought we would never stop talking and get down to playing."[1] Hauser, now thirty-seven years old, was neurotic, vain, too "full of ideas"—"a mystic," Mischa said. The violinist, he felt, was a bit free in his *portamento*, though stingy in his use of vibrato. Hauser was also so nervous that his brother, a psychologist, would send him little notes of encouragement before a performance. The violinist would take them from his pocket to read and, closing his eyes, meditate on what they said before going out on the stage.[2]

Mischa found the rule about voting to decide musical questions so unworkable that he wanted to quit. "We were arguing so much, you know. We would sit in a rehearsal and spend most of the time arguing who is right and who is not right—one wanted it this way, the other wanted that way."[3] Ipolyi took him aside, to explain how important it was to respect each others' opinions. "Mischa," he said, "if three people tell you it is better to play a certain way, I think you should give in."[4] Mischa relented, though he thought that Ipolyi, now forty-four, graying, growing a pot belly, and absent-minded, was not a very good violist.

Roismann looked down his nose on both Hauser and Ipolyi as well, and soon a division formed. Roismann and Schneider—"the shortest" and "the tallest," Mischa wryly mused—discovered that they had a lot in common. Besides being Russian, they both liked to play roulette, adored café life, and had the same views about chamber music.[5] They quickly became friends, though they never addressed each other by first name. It was always "Mr. Roismann" or "Mr. Schneider" or simply "Roismann" and "Schneider."[6] Soon it became Roismann and Schneider versus Hauser and Ipolyi. The young against the old. The Russians against the Hungarians.

The animosities intensified as the Quartet prepared to go on an extensive East Indies tour sponsored by a society of Dutch plantation owners. Mischa, then twenty-six years old, considered himself a pacifist, perhaps in reaction to a stormy childhood dominated by a strict father. By chance, he was born in Vilna, though it might very well have been New York. His father, Izhok Sznejder, a locksmith by profession, sailed in 1902 to America, where two of his brothers and two of his sisters had already emigrated. He planned to summon his wife and daughter, Manya, once he was settled in Manhattan. But Sznejder was soon disillusioned with the New World, and when a pickpocket lifted his watch, he decided he had had enough of it and returned to Vilna, where Mischa was born on February 5, 1904. The city, now Vilnius and part of Lithuania, was then part of Russia and almost as famous as Odessa in terms of its cultural life and the number of string players it bred—above all, Jascha Heifetz, who was born there. Because of its large Jewish population, it was known as the Jerusalem of Russia.

Although not in any way gifted, Izhok played a wooden flute and worshiped music. He made his children take up instruments. Mischa was still in bed on the morning of his ninth birthday in 1913 when his father entered the room, lugging an instrument case. "Here is a cello and you are going to study it" is all he said. "There was no questions asked," Mischa later recalled. "I just looked at it—such a big thing."[7]

Manya had already taken up piano—the Sznejders owned an upright. When Abram (Sasha) was born later, he was given a violin. Only Gregor (Grisha), the second of the Sznejder sons, who had no talent for music whatsoever, was spared.

Mischa began studying the cello with a friend of his father's, Efrem Kinkulkin, a former student of Julius Klengel of Leipzig. Three years later, at the age of twelve, Mischa had advanced enough to join the local opera orchestra, though he hated it—all the male singers were German army personnel, and all the female singers had been imported from Germany. The German occupation, however, did provide him with a memorable experience, one that haunted him for the rest of his life: it was the first time he played in a quartet.

The occasion was a Christmas celebration in an overheated army barracks in Vilna, the sweltering atmosphere due, in part, to a thousand candles burning brightly on an enormous decorated evergreen that towered above Mischa's chair. The audience was an infantry company of the Kaiser's Army; the string players, all German soldiers except for Mischa. They played Haydn's "Kaiser" Quartet, which was the German national hymn, and the slow movement of Mozart's "Dissonant" Quartet. In all his years of concertizing afterwards, whenever Mischa played those pieces again, the image that immediately came to mind was "of that night and that barracks room filled with light and faces smiling over uniforms."[8]

Mischa was "paid" with food after the concert was over, a welcome recompense for his family, which often had to fast for entire days because of shortages. For Mischa, though, the experience provided another kind of reward. He was so excited by playing chamber music that he dreamed that one day he would "play with a famous quartet."[9]

The family survived the war but found its aftermath just as difficult. Bolshevik troops took over Vilna for a while, and when they evacuated the city, the Poles returned and instituted a pogrom. The Sznejders survived that, too, chiefly because they lived in a large apartment complex outside the Jewish ghetto that was barred shut every night. For Mischa, it was a time of maturing. While the Bolsheviks occupied Vilna, an officer and his wife were assigned to the Sznejder home. When the officer was away, the wife seduced Mischa. He had never seen a naked woman before. The two were lovers until the Red Army troops left.

Mischa's parents were evidently unaware of his liaison with the officer's wife. His father would certainly never have tolerated it. Sznejder was a stern disciplinarian. His children had to study every day, and at suppertime, he questioned them rigorously about the time they had spent with their instruments. If not enough time had been spent practicing, up went Manya's skirt, down came Mischa's or Sasha's pants, and off came the underwear, and he whipped a bare bottom with a twisted towel. "Father was tyrannical about practicing."[10]

The resentment caused by such intimidation split the family. Finally, one day, when he was fifteen years old, Mischa could not take it any more. He was terribly upset when his father again punished Sasha for skipping practice. "If you touch Abrasha again, if you hit him once more, I'll hit *you* and leave this house," Mischa said. His father abruptly left the room, and he and Mischa did not speak for months.[11]

Mischa, the big brother, would always defend Sasha, though he was also the first to chastise him when he acted up. A strict moralist, Mischa was once so upset many years later when Sasha brought a mistress to a friend's home, where there were children present, that he did not communicate with Sasha for a year.

Mischa's great gift while growing up, one that everyone always commented upon, was his own paternal qualities, a sharp contrast to his father's. He exuded warmth. He loved children, all children, and they flocked to him. His great despair was that all the traveling he did with the Quartet took him away from his family. People who came to know him found him a gentle, soft-spoken, giving person who was never short-tempered and a good listener. Misha was intro-spective, but he could also be very stubborn—especially when it came to discussing politics or, as more than one colleague found out, when he was not sure of a musical idea but, nevertheless, defended it. He was literal minded as well, and sometimes did not realize when someone was teasing him. A wife of one of the Quartet members, for instance, once kidded him about the difficulty the musicians had when looking for a place to eat after a late-evening concert; she suggested that the Quartet only play in cities that had delicatessens. "Who asked you?" a serious Mischa retorted, ever determined to protect the Budapest's rule against wifely interference.[12] He took umbrage when someone else as a joke chided him for not liking a particular Mendelssohn piece, suggesting that he was anti-Semitic.

In 1920, a year after his run-in with his father, Mischa left home. He was sixteen years old and wanted to study with Klengel at the Leipzig conservatory. He was too poor to hire a hack, so he set out on foot, carrying a straw trunk on his back and his cello in his right hand. Because the Polish Army then occupied Vilna, he had to walk to a neighboring town where he could catch a train to Germany. His mother and brother Grisha accompanied him to the outskirts of the city. After a "heart-breaking goodbye," Mischa started off, every so often turning until his mother and Grisha became so small that he "lost them on the horizon."

Many years later, Mischa added up all his traveling—sixteen times across the Atlantic between Europe and America, eight times around the world to Australia and Indonesia, hundreds upon hundreds of times he left home on tour—but, he said, he never forgot "the loneliness of that moment" as he walked away from his mother and brother in Vilna.[13]

As it was, Mischa almost did not make it to Leipzig. Crossing the border into Germany in the dark, he stumbled and fell on the road, dropping his cello. The instrument broke on impact, and for a time Mischa worried that he might never get to play cello again. Luckily, he was able to find some odd jobs in the area, and after many days of working, earned enough money to have the cello repaired.

When Mischa finally reached Leipzig, he discovered that he was one of an auspicious assemblage of young musicians. Emanuel Feuermann was already a student of Klengel's. Gregor Piatigorsky would soon join them; Benar Heifetz, too. The experience was exhilarating. There was an annual Bach festival in Leipzig. One night, Mischa went to hear Pablo Casals play unaccompanied sonatas. He promised himself afterward that he would someday go to Paris to study with Casals's assistant, Diran Alexanian. And he did in 1928.

Most of Klengel's students lived in the same boarding house, where there was always the sound of a cello playing. They talked music, played chess, drank beer, and, when they had money, went to a brothel. To earn money, Mischa worked in a theater orchestra, then got a job as first cellist with the Grotrian Steinweg Orchestra. Mischa soon became "enamoured of everything German—music, art, history, philosophy, science, hygiene." He could imagine murderous Russians or Poles instigating a pogrom, but never the Germans. "How well the Jews have been assimilated in Europe," he would write in a journal in 1930. "But in 1930, even more in Leipzig in 1920, we *felt* assimilated. We not only admired the *kultur*, we kept it alive with our playing of the masterpieces of the great German composers. . . . Germany seemed so civilized. One of the most civilized nations in Europe."[14]

Over his parents' protests, Mischa married a blonde, blue-eyed German girl as soon as he turned twenty-one, in 1925. "With so many nice Jewish girls in the world, you can't find one?" his mother asked. Mischa could not explain to her that he was never attracted to Jewish girls. "To make love to her, a girl had to be blonde."[15] His bride was Lotte Nitschke, the daughter of a teacher with whom Mischa was now boarding. Lotte was the first of three women Mischa married, all of them blonde Protestants.

After he received a diploma from Leipzig, Mischa and Lotte moved to Frankfurt, where he had been offered a job teaching in the music conservatory. Their daughter Natasha was born in 1927. Mischa, meanwhile, wondered about the direction his career was taking. He hated playing solo. "It's a question of nerves versus ego, I think," he wrote in an autobiography he once began. "With me, nerves always won." His anxiety was fed by some troubles with technique that he had to overcome: problems with rapid staccato and a third-finger trill that was so difficult for him that he had learned to do it with his first and second fingers. Before a recital, he would be feverish, pace back and forth, and could not hear or see anything—or so it seemed. "I'd sit in the dark trying to concentrate but thinking all the time that soon I would be out on a stage alone with my muscles tightening and the perspiration covering me and all those people in the audience staring."

Mischa's first terrible experience with solo playing had occurred during a recital of young cellists in Vilna. He had gotten such cramps in his right leg that he had had to stand up and wait until the knots relaxed. "Then I played in a delirium, with no idea whether the performance was good or bad. What a nightmare! And I never outgrew it." Later, when studying in Leipzig with Klengel, a fellow student had advised Mischa to drink a glass of beer before playing to relax. He had done that, but had gotten so dizzy, he said, that "it was worse than playing sober." The low point, however, was one night in the 1920s, when the director of the Frankfurt Conservatory asked Mischa to play a cello sonata he had composed: "I was hypnotized with fear. All the difficult passages blurred and danced before my eyes."[16]

The answer, Mischa believed, was playing in a quartet. In a group of players, he did not become nervous. He had filled in as cellist several times with the Prisca Quartet, an unimpressive, conservative ensemble that considered him revolutionary when he suggested they perform a Hindemith, Bartók, or Schönberg quartet. However, when he heard that the cellist of the quartet had contracted tuberculosis and the quartet needed a replacement, Mischa applied and got the position. Even though his papers were not in order—he was stateless—Mischa had no trouble touring with the Prisca because the other members were blond and so obviously German. The quartet performed regularly in Latvia, Estonia, East Prussia, Switzerland, and Italy.

The only trouble was that the two violinists were married to each other and bickered constantly. The man had had an affair with another woman, and the wife knew about it and injected the husband's adulterous behavior into every argument they had, whether about music or personal. Their quarrels finally got on the nerves of both Mischa and the group's violist, and both quit. The experience taught Mischa a lesson about separating personal problems from a quartet's musical life.

While in Cologne with the Prisca, Mischa was often invited to play chamber music with two wealthy families. One of them lent Mischa a Seraphin cello. The other family, the Reifenbergs, had a daughter, Eva, who had married Feuermann. It was Mrs. Reifenberg, who had a keen interest in music and musicians, who brought Mischa to the attention of the Budapest String Quartet.

From the start—those lengthy, verbose rehearsals in Copenhagen and then daily practices during their month-long ocean voyage to Batavia, Java—Mischa's experience in the Quartet was unsettling. He debuted in Batavia with the Quartet on June 29, 1930. The program included Haydn's Quartet in G Minor, Opus 76, No. 1; the Beethoven Quartet in F, Opus 59, No. 1 of spiccato scherzo notoriety, and Mozart's Quartet in D Minor.

The next two months, as the Quartet traveled from one Indonesian town and island to another, were a curious mix of comic episodes and serious disputes. The humidity caused the rosin to melt and the strings to whistle; the instruments started to become unglued as well; mosquitoes plagued them during performances no matter how much citronella they poured over themselves; and lizards called titijaks croaked suddenly in the midst of a performance.

Sleep was always a problem. The heat made everyone testy, especially Hauser and Roismann. One afternoon, in a hotel, they got into a loud argument when Hauser started practicing just as Roismann went to take his nap. "You don't rehearse now when I am trying to sleep," he yelled at Hauser.[17] The two hardly spoke after that during the rest of the tour. Mischa, too, got angry with Hauser after the violinist told a local music critic that the Quartet had been unable to rehearse before a recital because of the hot weather. Mischa was "categorically against divulging such things" and was extremely upset.[18] And there were little annoying things, too, petty peeves blown out of proportion by the hostilities: the time a performance was delayed when Hauser lost the key to his violin case and had to break it open; Ipolyi forgetting his music at a concert; Hauser accepting the invitation of their Dutch hosts to stay with them rather than book into a hotel as Roismann and Mischa preferred; and Ipolyi's habit of exaggerating everything in a conversation.

By the second week of July, Mischa's morale was "very low," and the schism between the Russians and the Hungarians was widening.[19] Roismann was now openly mad at the way Hauser played. At one concert, Hauser ran his bow between the strings, which caused a lot of commotion in the audience. It got so bad that when the members rode the train between concerts, someone always suggested that they all keep their tempers in check. But the split continued at rehearsals and even about rehearsals. Mischa was furious when, despite little sleep, he got up for a scheduled run-through only to be told by Hauser that it had been cancelled. Later, when Roismann complained to Hauser about not having rehearsed, Hauser shot back, "It's you who will have to look after my wife and children if my hands are ruined." Roismann answered in Yiddish, "Save the Jews." Ipolyi just shook his head.[20]

At a rehearsal sometime later, the Quartet was working on the last movement of a quartet by Max Reger that called for *spring-bogen*—that is, spiccato playing. Hauser, as usual, wanted to play on point. Mischa was against it. Ipolyi, however, insisted that spiccato playing sounded scratchy, that *spitzen* was better. Roismann gave in to point, saying that otherwise the Quartet could not play the piece properly. "Such arguing about our music during those rehearsals!" Mischa wrote in his diary. "We all talked at once—'through each other.'"[21]

The only good that came of the arguments was the adoption of a new rule to resolve tie votes in disputes over music. Henceforth, in deciding how each piece was to be played, one member would have two votes instead of one. Who would have the second vote was a matter of chance. Before rehearsing a quartet, the four musicians took out four matchsticks. They broke three of them in half, but left the fourth intact. One of them held the matchsticks in his hand, so that they all appeared equal in length, while the others chose. Whoever picked the whole match received the second vote to cast whenever a deadlock occurred over a musical point in the work—a vote that theoretically was cast for the composer. They kept track of who held the deciding vote by putting the person's initials on the first page of that quartet's music. No one, however, tallied up how many pieces any one of the four members held the deciding vote for. The random division of the deciding factor in disputes was passed along in time to new members—a new second violinist inherited the previous second violinist's voting rights; a new violist, those of the violist he was replacing. The rule ensured that the Quartet's democratic character would survive the constant wrangles that every ensemble experiences.

The Quartet reached New York after New Year's Day 1931. The city was alive with music—Arturo Toscanini conducting the Philharmonic Symphony Orchestra, Serge Koussevitzky with the Boston Symphony, Jascha Heifetz at Carnegie Hall, and tenor Beniamino Gigli and baritone Paul Robeson in recitals there, too—in all, thirty-five musical events in one week.

The Budapest's first appearance took place on Sunday afternoon, January 4, at the Art Centre on East 56th Street off Madison Avenue, as part of a mixed-bill program that included Aaron Copland playing his recently composed Piano Variations. The concert, under the auspices of the League of Composers, opened with a brief talk by English conductor Eugene Goossens, who spoke on the subject of modern music. The Budapest played a Hindemith quartet before Copland performed and a Kodály quartet afterwards. The critic of the *Herald-Tribune* was especially taken by their rendition of the Hindemith work, saying the "often poignantly beautiful though somewhat attenuated slow movement gave the four players opportunity to prove themselves artists of profound and subtle insight."[22] The *New York Times* reviewer was less magnanimous. He did not care for either of the two works the Quartet played—their composers, he said, were "extreme modernists"—but he found that the "playing of the new quartet was sincere and musical, and its future appearances may be awaited with interest."[23]

Once outside of New York, however, the Quartet's reception was less than enthusiastic. An Ithaca critic found little to praise when the Budapest performed for the first time entirely on its own at Cornell University four nights later in a concert that is sometimes incorrectly labeled their American debut. Their program consisted of quartets by Haydn and Smetana and, again, Beethoven's Opus 59, No. 1. The violins, the critic said, "did not bear out the roundness of tone of the other instruments, the first violin being offensively whining at times and occasionally squeaky." The first movement of the Haydn, he said, "was run through and finished before either the musicians or the audience were wholly prepared for the evening's program." He thought "Mr. Hauser faltered a trifle in the trio section of the Menuetto." Anyway, he added, "the Quartet conducted itself rather informally, commencing movements rather suddenly and pausing for considerable intervals between."[24]

Undaunted, the Quartet went on to Buffalo to play the first of two recitals sponsored by the Buffalo Symphony Society and then returned to New York to play in Town Hall for the League of Composers. This concert was hailed as their first New York recital, their performance on January 4 notwithstanding. The program included a late Beethoven quartet, Bartók's Opus 7, and Schubert's posthumously published Quartet in D Minor entitled "Death and the Maiden." Hauser had just gotten over a cold, which perhaps explains the problems he had had in Ithaca and why, this time, the *Times* reviewer was so negative. "Each man," he wrote, "manifestly felt every note they played," but the result was "not well balanced."[25] And while the *Tribune* critic praised Mischa's "tonal fullness and polish," he damned Hauser for "somewhat lacking in smoothness and roundness."[26]

The Quartet returned to Europe in February 1931 perhaps wiser but not much richer. All their American concerts had been arranged by Annie Friedberg, a native of Germany who had studied at the Frankfurt Conservatory and later had had her own singing career. Her brother Carl, a pianist, was among a number of notable musicians whom she represented in the United States from her office on West 57th Street in New York, including, at one time or another, pianists Vladimir Horowitz and Myra Hess, conductors Erno Rapee and Sir Adrian Boult, violist William Primose, and the Pro Arte Quartet. Sometimes, when Friedberg could not get a musical society or association to sponsor a recital, the Quartet had to rent halls for as much as a thousand dollars a night. After paying Friedberg her agent's commission and doling out cash for food, hotels, travel, and newspaper ads, the Quartet members returned to Europe from that first trip to America with only thirty dollars each. "Who made money?" Mischa asked rhetorically. "The manager made money, the hall made money, the newspaper made money."[27]

Meanwhile, the new rule designed to settle musical disputes did little to settle tensions within the Quartet. The situation escalated the following year, 1932, when Hauser asked the other members to allow him to concertize, whenever the Quartet was not busy, with a woman he was courting, harpsichordist Alice Ehlers, a pupil of Wanda Landowska. All of them said no. They evidently felt they could not afford the scheduling conflicts that would inevitably arise. Without regrets, Hauser, then thirty-seven years old, resigned and began a duel-career with Ehlers. His resignation was probably no surprise, considering all the turmoil in the Quartet.

There was no question in the minds of either Mischa or Ipolyi as to who should succeed Hauser as first violinist. Roismann was the obvious choice, though Joe, now thirty-two years old, did not lobby for the position. In fact, he was diffident about accepting it. He shared with Hauser an aversion even to being a nominal dictator. However, Mischa and Ipolyi pointed out the difficulties of trying to find and agree on someone to take over the important first chair, never mind the fact that they would all be in for long hours of practice with any new member until he learned their repertoire. In the end, they prevailed on Joe to accept the promotion. They "literally forced the issue that I should take over," said Joe.[28]

There was even talk about changing the name of the Quartet. Now that all but one of the founding musicians were gone, the name was no longer accurate. Someone suggested it be the Roismann Quartet, but executives at His Master's Voice felt a name change would lead to confusion with regard to recordings being sold under the Budapest title. Interestingly, though, old files at HMV's American partner, RCA Victor, are labeled "Budapest String Quartet (Roismann Quartet),"[29] and at first, in Europe, the parenthetical "(Roismann Quartet)" appeared also on concert-hall programmes.[30] Anyway, Joe, who was never a self-promoter, demurred about calling the Quartet after himself.

With the Roismann promotion, the critical question became who would fill Joe's chair as second violinist.

Mischa happened to visit his brother, Sasha, in Hamburg while on his way back to Berlin and mentioned that Hauser was leaving. He asked whether Sasha could recommend anyone to take over the second violinist's post. Sasha was then concertmaster of the Norddeutscher Rundfunk, a radio orchestra in Hamburg. It was already clear to him that Jewish musicians were becoming anathema in Germany. A couple of days later, the director of the orchestra confirmed his worries. At this point, Sasha telephoned Mischa.

"I have found a violinist for you," he said.

"Who?" Mischa asked.

"Me."[31]

7

Allegretto Vivace e Sempre Scherzando: *Sasha*

Of all the members of the Budapest String Quartet, Alexander Schneider was without doubt the most complex. He was at one and the same time a hail-fellow type greeted by smiles and kisses wherever he went and a mocking cynic who raised hackles, insulted people, and lost friends. He could be thoughtful and supportive, and he could be mindless and destructive. Everything positive about him was matched by something negative, or so it seemed when talking to his friends and musicians with whom he has performed. He was aggressive, ambitious, energetic, an inspiration to young musicians, helpful, willing to experiment musically, and a self-professed lover of wine, women, good food, and life in general. But he was also selfish, bombastic, and brash; liked to be the center of attention; could cripple young musicians with his sharp tongue; and where other members of the Quartet were earthy, he was often vulgar. "A fireball" who gave the Quartet "paprika" and "chutzpah," said one friend, but "a little boy who needs spanking" wrote another. "A dynamo," said a third; but "volatile and capricious," still another. "An explorer"—but "unbelievably stubborn." "The ultimate musician"—but "dogmatic." "A Maurice Chevalier"—but "a bon vivant with bad taste."[1]

Above all, Sasha was a rebel. His upbringing made him that. For one thing, he discovered that his mother, Chasia Sznejder, tried to abort him several times by taking hot baths and jumping off a high table. He was born, his mother insisted, sometime around

Christmas 1908, but a rabbi who issued a birth certificate several years later when he needed one listed the date as October 21.

One day, when Abrasha—as his family called him—was five years old, his father brought home a violin teacher who had with him a half-size violin that he claimed had belonged to Heifetz. "Every father wanted his son to be a Heifetz," Sasha later wrote in an autobiography he self-published.[2] Evidently, Sasha's father did, too, and it became one of Sasha's drives as well, a subconscious one; he never admitted it to himself, but it was apparent later to many musicians who heard him or with whom he performed. As a youngster, though, playing the violin was the last thing in the world he wanted to do. He preferred to play soccer.

Because of World War I in Europe and the constant back and forth of opposing German, Russian, Bolshevik, and Polish armies, Sasha never went to public school. His grandfather taught him Yiddish, and a tutor coached him in Russian. He was supposed to practice four hours a day, but as a young boy he rarely lasted more than thirty minutes with the violin before he ran out of his home to play. As a result, his father whipped him regularly.

Despite all the perils and hardships the family confronted as one army after another marched through Vilna, Sasha managed to escape any real danger. But after the war, a minor accident almost killed him. One rainy day in 1921, when he was thirteen, Sasha slipped and fell, splitting open the skin on his left knee. He was taken to a hospital but the wound was not properly cleaned, and he developed a raging fever, convulsions, and lockjaw—all symptoms of tetanus. The doctors shrugged and gave up on him, but fortunately a young medical student did not. He injected Sasha with an antitoxin ordinarily given to horses. The teenager recovered, but his bones were so affected by the convulsions that his arms, legs, hands, and feet had to be stretched. The procedure was extremely painful. Sasha received morphine injections every day, and there was doubt that he would ever walk again, much less play the violin. The incident, he later said, "gave me the discipline necessary to get somewhere and to be grateful for being alive."[3]

As a young boy, Sasha admitted, his "only enjoyment" besides children's games was to crawl under the table when guests were in the house for sabbath dinner and look up under the women's skirts. "I have never stopped being attracted by beautiful breasts," he said.[4] Sasha experienced his first sexual encounter when he was thirteen years old. He played the violin well enough by then to start performing in a trio in a hotel restaurant and sometimes played alone in one of its private rooms to create a romantic mood for a guest and his "girlfriend." One day he followed one of the girls home. She was putting a condom on him when he ejaculated. "I was dazzled," he said.[5]

Sasha never had any inhibition about talking, if not boasting, about his sexual conquests. A favorite word of his, one he coined, was "Schmockadores," which he spelled in a variety of ways and which he used variously as a noun, verb, or adjective, but always with a sexual connotation. The word embodied his open attitude about sex.

By the age of thirteen, Sasha was also playing in a movie theater, with a young pianist named Nadia Reisenberg, and at the age of fifteen he began studying with Ilya Malkin, a former pupil of Leopold Auer's who had taught Heifetz and introduced him to Auer. That year, while playing in the Vilna opera orchestra, Sasha was invited by a Soviet officer to play string quartets with him as second violin. The very first quartet he ever played was Ravel's Quartet in F.

Sasha did not become a serious violin student until he left Vilna the next year, 1924, and went to Frankfurt, where his brother Mischa and sister-in-law Lotte lived. Mischa, then teaching at the conservatory, arranged an audition for Sasha with its principal violin teacher, Adolf Rebner—with whom Emil Hauser had played. Sasha won a scholarship to study with Rebner. To earn living expenses, he landed a job in the last stand of the first violin section of the local symphony orchestra. The salary was meager, only fifty marks. On Saturdays, Sasha also performed in a trio at a sanitorium, each week playing the same pieces, a Franck violin and piano sonata and a Tchaikovsky trio. He received fifty marks for that, too, but was fed as well, and that was an important fringe benefit. It was a treat when he could afford to eat two frankfurters with sauerkraut and potatoes once a week. He lived in a maid's room, a cramped chamber without any plumbing, under the sloped roof of a house.

That summer Sasha became concertmaster of an orchestra attached to a spa at Bad Homburg, which performed every morning for guests. He also joined a piano quartet that played in a café there, and when it closed, he was able to return to his job in the Frankfurt orchestra. But the conductor was outraged when Sasha, instead of paying attention to him during a rehearsal of Beethoven's "Missa Solemnis," flirted openly with the lead soprano. He was summarily fired.

Though his life was a struggle, his spirits were, nonetheless, high. Like Mischa, he was enthralled with the "incredible experience" of being in Germany. "It was really a democratic country and there was a great sense of freedom in the air," he said. "I thought it was the greatest country in the world."[6] That, of course, was in 1924, during the Weimar Republic. For a time, when he was eighteen, he lived with a Belgian girl named Kitty, who, among other things, taught him to appreciate and dance waltzes. He wanted to marry her and wrote his father for permission. "If you want permission," Sznejder replied, "come to Vilna, put the chair in the middle of the room, hand me the belt, take down your pants, and I will give you permission to marry."[7]

Sasha, "a little Jewish boy from Vilna," was even able to perform for his idol, Heifetz. He had heard Heifetz play—so beautifully that it made him cry—and was able to wangle an opportunity to perform for him when Heifetz was again in Frankfurt for a recital. Heifetz accompanied him on the piano. In a typical display of audacity, Sasha, still a teenager, chose to perform Saint-Saëns's "Rondo Capriccioso," which was one of Heifetz's trademarks. Afterwards, Sasha was not certain "how badly" he had played, but it could not have gone very well.[8] Nothing came of the audition.

Sasha soon discovered that being both a foreigner and Jewish were drawbacks in Germany. In the fall of 1927, he was accepted as concertmaster of an orchestra in Saarbrücken, then a free city between Germany and France. The job, however, was a state one. The director wanted to hire him but was loathe to do so because he was not German. He suggested, however, that the problem could be solved if Sasha changed his name. Mischa's choice, Schneider—"a *goishe* name in Germany"—seemed appealing, so Sasha changed his to Schneider, too, and took a new first name as well. Abram Sznejder was now Alexander Schneider.[9]

Sasha remained in Saarbrücken for two year and a half years, occupying himself outside the orchestra by taking French lessons, going to brothels, and becoming an obsessive chess player. He applied for the concertmastership in a Dortmund orchestra, and when he did not get it, he was sure it was because he was Jewish. He wanted to take part in the Bayreuth Festspiele, but as a Jew he was not welcome. He was, however, successful in 1929 in winning the post of concertmaster in the Norddeutscher Rundfunk in Hamburg. In time, he became its program consultant, too, and tried, unsuccessfully, to substitute quartet movements for the marches and waltzes the radio orchestra regularly played. The orchestra was admittedly the worst of three orchestras in the city, but it paid the most. Sasha apparently spent most of the money he earned and his free time in the city's red-light district, smoking opium for days on end.

Sasha was performing with the radio orchestra when, in September 1930, the Nazi party won enough seats in a national election to make it the second largest party in Germany. The Nazis received six and a half million votes, nearly eight times more than they garnered in the previous election. Listening to election returns on the radio on the night of the voting, conductor Bruno Walter turned to cellist Emanuel Feuermann and said, "It's all over with Germany; all over with Europe."[10]

Walter's prophecy came true in stages. Less than two years later, in late January 1932, Hitler was named chancellor. On April 7, the Ministry of Interior issued the first of a series of anti-Semitic decrees dealing with the nation's educational system and civil service: "Officials of non-Aryan origin are to be retired."[11] Arnold Schönberg, a professor at the Academy of Music, was in Paris working on an opera when he learned that he had been dismissed. That same April, Artur Schnabel, who had already performed all thirty-two of Beethoven's piano sonatas over the Berlin radio and was supposed to repeat the cycle, had finished only four of the seven concerts when he was cut off the air. Ironically, the last sonata that was broadcast was the one in E-flat known as "Les Adieux." A piano quartet composed of Schnabel, Bronislav Hubermann, Paul Hindemith, and Gregor Piatigorsky—all but Hindemith were Jews—was scheduled to participate in a Berlin festival honoring the one hundredth anniversary of Brahms's birth, but the city's cultural office suddenly began to demur, and the recital never took place. A brave Adolf Busch, who was not Jewish, played a recital in Stuttgart at which a man in the audience stood up and gave the Nazi salute. "Put your arm down," shouted Busch, who then returned to playing when the man resumed his seat. When in Hamburg, Busch was informed by mail that Hitler was going to attend a concert of his quartet but that he had to find a different violist and a different cellist; the violist was Jewish, and the cellist was married to a Jew. Busch protested, saying that he would not change the membership of his quartet and describing the salutation at the end of the official letter—"Heil Hitler"—as "an insult to any decent German." His German citizenship was thereupon revoked.[12]

That May, bands of Nazi youths in Berlin broke into libraries, grabbed books that Propaganda Minister Josef Goebbels despised, and burned them in bonfires on Unter den Linden. Soon, Jewish newspaper publishers were forced to sell out to Aryans. Storm troopers raided and closed down the Bauhaus—a front, they said, for Communist propaganda. Down from the walls of the State Museum came the works of Jewish artists as well as of painters, like Van Gögh, who were considered degenerate. The *Berliner Tageblatt* published a cartoon in which the arms of a swastika were in the shape of fists holding pistols and a pitchfork. It was titled *"Juda verrecke"*— Jew croak.[13]

Amidst all these ominous signs, Sasha was still with the radio orchestra in Hamburg when, in mid-May 1932, Mischa told him that Hauser was leaving the Budapest String Quartet. A day or two later, the director of the orchestra asked to see him. The director was Jewish, too, but he hid the fact, wearing a Nazi brown shirt to disguise himself. He told Sasha that being a Russian and Jewish to boot, he would undoubtedly lose his job. He suggested that Sasha write a letter requesting a leave of absence but also agreeing to play six solo concerts with the orchestra during the year he was on leave. If he did, the director would guarantee his full annual salary.

Sasha wrote the letter, but then had second thoughts. The director's offer finally persuaded him that the situation for Jews in Germany was worse than he realized. He picked up the phone and called Mischa.

Sasha's joining the Budapest had an immediate effect. "Since its concert here two years ago," wrote a critic in Ithaca, New York, when the Quartet returned to Cornell University in February 1933, "the quartet has made enormous strides in the perfection of its ensemble art."[14] Howard Taubman, in the *New York Times*, called their recital in Town Hall that March "one of the most brilliant performances of chamber music of the season."[15] The Buffalo Chamber Music Society credited the Budapest with saving the young organization through the enthusiasm they created at a concert in the Hotel Statler Ballroom the following February.

Another tour of the Dutch East Indies in the fall of 1934 was so successful that the Quartet was asked to return the following year. Before that 1935 visit, they spent three months touring America; following it, they traveled seven months in Australia and New Zealand. The Australian tour was made under the auspices of the Australian Broadcasting Corporation. It was the first time any quartet had ever performed on the continent and it was received so well that the ABC offered a guarantee of six months of concerts yearly if the members settled in Australia.

No one in the Quartet wanted to remain in Australia, especially Sasha. In a typically rash act, the day before the Budapest had left for Australia, he had married a young blue-eyed German blonde whom he hardly knew. Her name was Gerte, and she worked for an oil company. He met Gerte in Paris through her cousin, spent all of a long walk home to her hotel with her, and then corresponded with her over the next several months. The two did not see each other again until the eve of their wedding in London in June 1935. They spent their honeymoon on board the *Barabool*, a miserable steamer with cabins so small and beds so narrow that even though the couple had the best stateroom available, they slept on the floor. The marriage barely survived the boat trip.

Meanwhile, the praises the Budapest was receiving again masked the real truth. Sasha bridled at knuckling under to the Quartet rule about musical decisions. He was incensed when, during the rehearsal of a Beethoven quartet, he was outvoted even though he held two votes. He had an "absolutely different musical idea than my three colleagues." Sasha was so "terribly upset" that he "couldn't accept this decision easily." He felt he "could not continue as a member of the quartet and wanted to resign." Ipolyi had to play the role of pacifier, as he had done with his brother Mischa. He explained to Sasha "how difficult it is and will be to work the democratic way which was so perfect in the Budapest String Quartet— without any dictatorial power and with complete respect for each other's point of view since, luckily, we all had the same musical direction."[16] So Sasha stayed, his rebelliousness under control, but only temporarily.

Ipolyi himself began displaying all the signs of mental collapse and was playing erratically. Mischa was in the process of divorcing Lotte and marrying again. The Quartet was struggling to stay alive financially. And by 1934 the situation in Germany had deteriorated. Jewish musicians were expelled from all orchestras, and the music of Mendelssohn and other Jewish composers was banned. But oddly, the Quartet had not yet experienced any difficulties performing in Germany. They guessed that was because of the name Budapest. Then one night when they came on stage to perform, they saw uniformed Nazis in the hall, and after the concert a number of Nazis came backstage to congratulate the "Hungarians." The four Jews all felt a chill run down their spines. That night, they decided to abandon Berlin and move to Paris. They never set foot in Germany again.

The musicians were no strangers to Paris. The Quartet had already played its first Beethoven cycle—all sixteen Beethoven quartets and the *Grosse Fuge*—in April 1933 in six different mansions in Paris. The concerts had been arranged by Count Fitz James Miramon, who helped the Budapest to get established. The prestigious

Salle Gaveau subsequently booked them to play the cycle every year in the French capital.

Though the Quartet established a reputation in Paris and was able to concertize in Holland, Belgium, Italy, England, and the United States, it was a hard life. Mischa's first wife, Lotte, had not been able to abide the constant traveling, or being alone with her daughter Natasha when she did not accompany him. Mischa's second wife, a Danish woman named Dorthe whom he met while still married to Lotte, would experience the same sense of abandonment after giving birth to his second daughter, Grit.

Wherever they were, the four musicians lived in the cheapest hotels. Sasha carried a portable burner in his suitcase so he could cook his own meals. The rule about any member playing outside the Quartet was relaxed so that Joe could return to playing in cafés to make ends meet. Lunch breaks during rehearsals meant a bowl of soup and as many free *broetchen* as they could eat. Even though their Beethoven cycles in the Salle Gaveau played to sold-out houses, they only made enough money from them to pay their hotel bills and to sit down together for one good dinner.

When on tour in America, the musicians traveled by Greyhound bus, often had to share bedrooms, never stayed in one place long enough to get their laundry done, and were always overburdened with instruments and suitcases. To lighten his load, Roismann would tear out and throw away each page of a book as soon as he finished reading it. A cousin of the Schneiders' drove all four to Indianapolis during a Depression-inspired bank holiday when they could not get cash for a train. They were so cramped for space in the tiny Chevy that Sasha spent the trip on the floor with Mischa's cello on top of him. As uncomfortable as he was, he was able to fall asleep.

In New York, the Quartet always stayed at the Great Northern Hotel (now the Parker Meridien) on 57th Street between Sixth and Seventh avenues. Rooms cost $2.50 a night, $12.50 for the week. The hotel was down the block from the Russian Tea Room, but, being careful not to overspend, they could only afford to eat in the Horn & Hardart automat a few doors away—paying fifteen or twenty cents for breakfast, twenty-five to forty cents for lunch, and anywhere from fifty to seventy-five cents for supper. They were getting between two hundred and three hundred dollars a concert—minus agent's commission, minus bus and train costs, minus hotel expenses, minus food outlays, minus newspaper ads, minus the cost of promotional broadsides, minus the cost of publicity photos, with the balance split four ways. And they had to pay, of course, for the trans-Atlantic back-and-forth trips, too. "We made very little money," said Sasha.[17]

The hardships of travel were one thing—the discomfort and difficulties were bearable. Even being homesick was tolerable as long as they could at least count on getting engagements. But Ipolyi's state of mind was another matter. He was having a nervous breakdown. "He couldn't continue playing," Joe explained. "We were all nervous about him on the platform; never knew what he was going to do."[18] It is not clear what the problem was, whether it was all the traveling, the heated disagreements, worry about conditions in Europe, or feeling like an outsider in the Quartet now. The others were all Russian, he was Hungarian. Although all four of them spoke German, the Russians sometimes lapsed into their own language. Roismann once confided that he and the Schneiders wanted to speak Russian all the time but could not because of Ipolyi, so they wanted to get rid of him.[19] Besides, they were all eager to get away from *spitzen*, as well as other predominantly romantic ways that Ipolyi played. On one visit to New York, they had gone to hear Toscanini conduct and were overwhelmed by the clarity and precision of his interpretation. Roismann and the Schneiders were already inclined to avoid the excesses of other instrumentalists. They now wanted Toscanini's approach to be their approach. The fifty-year-old violist, Ipolyi, undoubtedly felt isolated and unwanted. And apparently his resignation from the Quartet in 1936 was not voluntary. "We had to give him up" was the way Joe put it.[20]

Ipolyi was the last of the original Budapest members to leave. What happened to the first to quit, second violinist Alfred Indig, is unknown. He left the Quartet in 1920 and went on to perform as a soloist with the Concertgebouw Orchestra of Amsterdam and in 1931 became concertmaster of the Berlin Philharmonic. When the Nazis came to power, he fled Germany and was last heard of performing as the head of his own quartet in Paris in 1934. His successor as second violinist, Imre Pogany, emigrated to America in July 1927 to join the Cincinnati Philharmonic Orchestra, then conducted by his friend Fritz Reiner, and to teach at the College of Music in that city. Two years later, in 1929, he joined the New York Philharmonic Symphony Orchestra, conducted by Arturo Toscanini, as principal second violinist and was the second violinist in the orchestra's quartet. He stayed with the Philharmonic for thirty years, retiring at the end of the concert season in 1958 to live in Miami, Florida, where he died on August 25, 1975, at the age of eighty-two.

Cellist Harry Son, who left the Quartet in 1930, emigrated to Palestine, where he resumed concertizing and toured abroad. Sometime before World War II broke out, he returned to Rotterdam. He was there when the Germans occupied Holland. Both he and his wife were arrested by the Gestapo and never heard from again. First violinist Emil Hauser, who resigned from the Quartet in 1932, enjoyed a lifetime of musical activities. He emigrated in 1933 to Jerusalem, where he formed a quartet and also founded the Palestine Music Conservatory. He helped violinist Bronislav Hubermann rescue scores of Jewish musicians from Austria, Czechoslovakia, and Germany in the late 1930s and was instrumental in the founding of the Palestine Symphony Orchestra. For his efforts, he was awarded the Order of the British Empire. In 1940, he moved to the United States, to teach chamber music at Bard College in upstate New York, and later at the Juilliard School of Music. Hauser returned to live permanently in what was now Israel in 1960 after contracting Parkinson's Disease. He died in Jerusalem on January 27, 1978, at the age of eighty-four.

Violist Istvan Ipolyi settled in Norway, where the Budapest had spent many summers rehearsing before each concert season. During the German occupation of that country, he was arrested and placed in a detention prison, awaiting deportation to a Nazi prison. It was a nightmarish experience. "Every night, going to bed," Ipolyi later said, "I am remembering the horrible feelings I had on the evenings in the concentration camp, never knowing what the next day will bring."[21] Through the personal intervention of Count Bernadotte, head of the International Red Cross, Ipolyi was freed. He fled to Sweden and remained there for the duration of the war. On his return to Norway, he became a Norwegian citizen, mentor of a quartet in Bergen, and a professor. He and his wife lived what he called "a rather secluded life." He loved teaching, he wrote Sasha, who sent him food packages after the war—"I feel drunken when working with my favourites. And particularly with the quartet."[22] Mischa saw to it that he received the royalties due him from record sales. Ipolyi wrote several books, claiming to Sasha that he had "found an entirely new theory of the origin of music."[23] He died in Bergen on January 2, 1955, at the age of sixty-eight.

Ipolyi's departure initiated another crisis in the Quartet's history. Even before he left, a major financial opportunity presented

itself when the Australian Broadcasting Corporation again engaged
the Quartet for a twenty-four week tour that would start in May
1937. They were to give four performances a week and were given
the option to appear ten weeks in New Zealand as well. It was an
offer the Quartet could not afford to reject. In addition, they still had
to fulfill their regular round of engagements in Europe and America.

Roismann immediately contacted a fellow Odessan he had
played with as a child, Edgar Ortenberg. They had last bumped into
one another in Berlin in 1926. Ortenberg was an experienced first
violinist and now had his own quartet in Paris. They met at a café,
where Roismann asked him whether he would be willing to switch
his instrument from violin to viola and join the Budapest. Ortenberg
agreed on the spot, but when he returned home to tell his wife,
Tamara, she was aghast. "I married a violinist and I want to be the
widow of a violinist, not the widow of a violist," she announced.[24]
Ortenberg had to telephone Roismann and withdraw his acceptance.

Roismann had another idea. There was another Odessan he
knew who was no stranger to the viola, his teenage friend from
Berlin, Boris Kroyt. Joe set about trying to track down Boris.

8

Adagio Molto e Mesto:
Boris

Kroyt was in Berlin. He had lived in that city since 1907, when, at the age of ten, he had gone there to study with Alexander Fiedemann. Although he had lived in Berlin for twenty-nine of his thirty-nine years, he had never renounced his Russian citizenship. He was, however, in the post-czarist Soviet era, stateless and for once worried about the political situation in Germany. Boris never considered himself German, but he had taken Germany's side during World War I; he thought the country was the victim of aggression by other European nations. He did not start to entertain thoughts about leaving Germany until the mid-1930s, when it became all too clear that it was no longer possible for a Jew to pursue a musical career, or even to live safely in the city.

So many others had by this time reacted to the growing totalitarianism of the Nazi regime that a veritable exodus was taking place—artists, writers, composers, and musicians fleeing to Paris, London, Switzerland, and, in particular, the United States and enriching the cultural life wherever they went. Kroyt used to say that he realized how ominous the future was when friends he had had for years, who never before had broached the subject, suddenly seemed obsessed by the fact that he was Jewish. He found himself without engagements, permitted to play for Jewish groups only. Previously on a busy concert schedule, Boris was now lying around his apartment all day with little to do, having a wife and small child to support, and, worst of all, in serious danger. After some searching he found what he thought was a way out. He signed a contract to join an all-Jewish orchestra in Tel Aviv. But at almost the same moment, his old friend Joe Roismann located him through Sasha's father-in-law.

The two Odessans, Joe and Boris, made an odd couple; they were as different as the two Schneider brothers were. If Joe seemed locked up inside himself and unapproachable, Boris was an extrovert, easy to get along with, and fond of jokes and joking. He was what some musical colleagues called "a genial Rover boy" and the "sweetest" of all the Budapest members, a "bon vivant with good taste"—the "Coca Cola" of the group because he mixed so well, held the Quartet together, and kept its turmoils under control.[1] His love of gadgets—he could not pass a hardware store without going inside—and his affection later for Lincoln town cars seemed childish to many. Though short and, in time, chunky-looking, he was vain about his appearance—wore a hair net to bed to keep his full, curly hair in shape; sometimes used elevator shoes to increase his height; and powdered his face with talc before going on stage. His grammar was never as good as the others' was, so the duties that Ipolyi had exercised as the Quartet's correspondent and quasi-recording secretary, and which Boris had been expected to assume, fell to Mischa. As a violist, however, Boris was virtually unsurpassed. He "sang" on the instrument, musicians said.[2] No quartet, one declared, "could compete with the Budapest, particularly after Boris joined."[3]

Kroyt's one great failing was that he did not like to practice; he was, he admitted, lazy about it. He did practice before the start of a concert season, but once the recitals began, the most he would do individually was run his fingers up and down the fingerboard or skim through a violin concerto on the viola to warm up. Fritz Kreisler had told him, he said, never to practice on the day of a concert. "He told me to take the instrument and improvise a little instead. It's bad enough to rehearse on the day of a concert, but I'm really sorry for those poor devils who are so nervous they have to practice up to the very last moment."[4]

Boris's getting away with such little personal practice was the legacy of being a child prodigy, so natural a player that he did not have to spend hours maintaining his technique. He was like that from the very start, and his years with Fiedemann—the worst of role models possible—encouraged his lack of enthusiasm for practicing. He learned what he could get away with from the moment he started studying with the teacher. He showed up for his lesson all prepared, only to be scolded, "You didn't practice, you stupid boy," as

Fiedemann, in a terrible mood that day, threw his music on the floor. Boris was "terrified." So the next time, he did not bother to go over the music and, instead, sight-read his lesson for Fiedemann. "Ah," the teacher said, "you must have practiced." Boris thought, "If I can fool him this way, why should I practice?"[5]

That he got away with such lack of discipline Boris credited to innate fortune. He was born lucky, or so he believed. At his birth— on June 10, 1897—he was still in the placenta, "born in a bubble," which was considered special, particularly since two brothers had already died in infancy. His mother kept the afterbirth, often showing it to Boris and telling him that he was a blessed child. "Somehow," he said later in the fractured English that was his hallmark, "I have always believed it. I am a person which brings very much luck to everybody which is near to me. I never had a bad day in my life."[6]

Boris's mother, Cecilia, was the second wife of Osip Kroyt, a former estate supervisor and tobacco merchant born near the Russian border with Austria who had settled in Odessa as a salesman. His first wife was barren, so Osip divorced her. Cecilia was Austrian and had trouble speaking Russian, a factor that would have an enormous influence on Boris's musical upbringing.

The Kroyt family—there was an older sister, Bertha, and later a younger brother, Miron—lived at Uspenskaya Ulica 78, a huge apartment house with a courtyard and a cow outside the Jewish ghetto in Odessa. They had five rooms, one of which was ordinarily rented to a student. The apartment itself was a rendezvous for radicals— including the Bronsteins (one going by the name of Trotsky), who were cousins. Clandestine meetings were held in the living room by candlelight, bombs were made in one of the bedrooms, and revolutionaries hid out there periodically. The apartment was just below the roof, a handy escape route when czarist police came, and it seemed that they searched the Kroyt quarters almost every week, always without success.

One of the Kroyts' student boarders was a young artist, who would sit in his half-dark room at sunset, playing the violin by ear. Only four years old, Boris took to trailing after him, imitating him and singing in exact pitch. The young man was so taken with young Boris's ability that he fashioned a small instrument out of drawing board for him to play on. It was Boris's first violin. The artist tried to convince Cecilia to buy Boris a real violin but both she and her husband were against Boris's becoming a musician. So the artist went out and for five rubles purchased one for him and started to show Boris how to move his fingers. Very soon Boris was playing better than his teacher, who then arranged for a student friend from the Royal Academy to give him lessons. Boris progressed so rapidly that after eight months, Boris's mother reluctantly gave in and agreed to engage an experienced teacher.

It just so happened that Alexander Fiedemann—he was Fiddleman then—lived a few doors away. Cecilia connived for Boris to play a Haydn trio with two other youngsters one afternoon in a room next to where Fiedemann was playing poker with some colleagues from the conservatory. Hearing the music and intrigued, Fiedemann came into the room and started conversing, in German, with Cecilia. A handsome man, a Don Juan by reputation, Fiedemann quickly ingratiated himself with her. Cecilia felt an immediate rapport with him, especially because he could speak German. He advised her to send Boris to the Royal Academy so that he could study with František Stupka, with whom Roismann studied many years later in Prague. In a uniform two sizes too big for him—so he could grow into it—Boris entered the academy.

His next teacher was Fiedemann's brother Max, who had studied in St. Petersburg with Leopold Auer. With Max on the piano, Boris made his public debut in Odessa in 1907 at the Officers' Club. He was ten years old and already used to the idea that he would be a musician. He often played in the Bronstein kitchen for Trotsky's mother, who would award him with a radish coated with butter. Both of Boris's parents, resigned now to the idea of his being a violinist, pushed him to practice and to play in society, especially for rich merchants who might contribute to his education. Max suggested that Boris study with Auer, but because of the relationship Cecilia had established with his brother Alexander, she decided he would be a better choice. After all, he spoke German. She felt she could entrust her son to him.

Fiedemann was now living in Berlin, so as to pay for his travel there and living expenses, Boris played a fund-raising concert in Odessa before he left. The concert drew a thousand persons and netted him about fourteen hundred rubles—seven hundred dollars. Boris would return to Odessa only once—and for the last time—in the summer of 1910 to be bar mitzvahed and to play at the Odessa World's Fair.

The train trip to Berlin was uneventful. A medical student on his way to the German capital accompanied Boris there, but as soon as their train pulled in, he left him all alone in the station. The youngster looked around for Fiedemann, but he was nowhere to be seen. Just then, a boy his own age approached him and introduced himself.

He was Mischa Violin, a student of Fiedemann's. In typical fashion, the irresponsible Fiedemann had sent a child to meet a child. Fiedemann was out looking for work, so distracted, in fact, that it was several months before he even asked Boris to play for him. Instead, Boris sat alone in his room most of the time or went for walks with Violin, awed by the electric streetcars, busy thoroughfares, and shops of the German capital. He soon became familiar with the entire city—the forest-like Tiergarten, the broad Unter den Linden, the Opera House, palaces, the massive Royal Armoury, and the sluggish river Spree. It was the time of *Kaiserzeit*, when "there was peace and order, and a respect for traditional values."[7] Young Boris, however, was homesick.

Fiedemann finally landed a job at the Stern'sches Conservatorium through the influence of one of his former pupils, Mischa Elman. He paraded both Boris and Violin before its director, Gustave Hollander, and got them accepted as students there, too. He also persuaded the banker Franz Von Mendelssohn, a relative of the composer, to provide Boris with an annual stipend of six hundred dollars and to finance concerts for him, renting the hall and hiring the orchestras. Mendelssohn presented Boris with a violin made by the eighteenth-century Italian luthier Lorenzo Storione; there was no question of repayment.

Fiedemann was a talented musician, had studied with Adolf Brodsky in England, had himself debuted at the age of ten with the conductor Artur Nikisch, and at age eighteen had joined the faculty of the Royal Academy in Odessa. But he was incorrigible. He drank, he gambled, and he chased women; in fact, it was bandied about that he had had to leave Odessa because of an affair with a rich man's wife. He was a charlatan as well; he would threaten to commit suicide if not given money or would arrange a recital for himself and then back off at the last minute and expect Boris to fill in for him. Once he took the money Boris had raised for a future concert and paid off his gambling debts with it; the youngster had to cancel the performance. Fiedemann also took to dragging Boris around with him on his daily rounds to cafés. Soon the boy became an expert billiards player, so good at it that many years later, after winning a game from Artur Schnabel, the pianist remarked, "You must have spent a lot of time in cafés instead to practice."[8]

For all his faults, though, Fiedemann was actually an excellent teacher, willing to let students develop their own style of playing rather than turning out a group of sound-alike automatons. In Boris's case, he recognized that the young boy wanted to "know more than a

virtuoso" who "only knows his instrument and how to show off."
Heifetz was archetypical—"unique, an Olympic violinist," Boris explained, "but for me he doesn't say anything. Five minutes after his
concert, I have already forgotten what he played, what he has created, because for me he has created nothing." Instead, Boris wanted
to be "a serious musician. Too many of the great violinists know
very little of the entire musical literature." Besides which, Boris
"always" wanted to play chamber music; it "fascinated" him.[9]

Despite his dissolute habits, Fiedemann, whose own son had
died of pneumonia, unofficially adopted Boris and encouraged him.
Boris heard the aging Joachim play, attended recitals by the Capet
and Rosé quartets, and went to concerts conducted by Nikisch, Fer-
uccio Busoni, and Richard Strauss. One memorable night, he met
the widow of composer Edvard Grieg. Busoni was there for the occasion and played a Beethoven trio, while Adolf Brodsky, who had
come especially from England, played a Grieg violin sonata with
Leonid Kreutzer. "These were our teachers, the men who influenced
us and whom we worshipped." Boris never forgot that night. "The
cafés where we gathered, where we talked over our ideas, the homes
where we played stimulated and excited us."[10]

By that time, Boris was living in a boarding house that his so-
called guardian, Fiedemann, had found for him, and after about a
year there, he moved to a pension run by a Viennese named Regina
Ernsweig, who became a surrogate mother for him. There were a
number of other young musicians living in her house, too. Among
them was Emanuel Feuermann's brother, who was so weak that he
had to practice with his elbow on the table. Mrs. Ernsweig spoiled
Boris so much that Fiedemann decided to send him to school. The
teenager found himself the only boy in an all-girls school. He performed in its orchestra, and as the lone male amongst all those
adolescent young women, he could not resist playing pranks. His
favorite was to fiddle a popular tune when the orchestra was in full
swing, blasting away in some symphony, so that only the girls sitting near him in the violin section could hear what he was playing.

Boris lived in boarding houses until 1912, when his mother and
his brother, Miron, a budding pianist, came to Berlin to live with
him. Mendelssohn agreed to continue his grant to Boris even though
he was no longer on his own. The following year, Boris's father and
sister joined them. They had an apartment in a section of Berlin
called Charlottenburg, near the zoo. Above them were the Roismanns, who had moved to Berlin so that Joe could study with
Fiedemann. Boris began spending a great deal of time with them,

often going to movies with the family and courting Joe's sister Rosa. That spring, Boris graduated from the conservatory with the Gustav Hollander Gold Medal. He was fifteen years old. School for him was over, though he still wore knickers, which caused a tizzy when he got a job as concertmaster with the symphony orchestra in Görlitz; the other musicians resented it.

For the next twenty-four years, before he joined the Budapest String Quartet, Kroyt was a concert artist, performing solo recitals, violin concertos, and chamber music. One summer he conducted the Berlin Philharmonic. He always wanted to compose and started a number of pieces, including a quartet, but he never really worked on them. He was especially fond of quartet playing because he felt that the solo repertoire for a violinist was so limited that he had to play the same concertos over and over again.

It was Fiedemann who introduced him to the viola—rather, forced him into playing it. One day, when Boris was still a teenager, Fiedemann, who had his own quartet, informed Boris that his violist was ill and that he would have to take over his part. It was an order. Fiedemann was imperious that way. "I never saw this instrument in my life," the youth complained.[11] Boris had only three days to master the viola and learn his part. That was no small feat. For one thing, because the viola is larger than a violin and has a longer fingerboard, the fingering is different; the fingers have to be spaced wider apart, and even the string on which the middle C is played is different. Then, too, the music itself is in a different clef, requiring a player to recognize while reading a musical part that what is a B on the middle line of the violin clef is the middle C on the viola's alto clef. That can be confusing in itself. Brahms, for one, made it more so with sudden departures into the violin clef and corresponding returns into the alto. And lastly, the viola requires a different approach to bowing that will bring out its deeper musical colors. The viola's sonority is undoubtedly what attracted not only Brahms to play the viola himself but also Mozart, Beethoven, Schubert, Mendelssohn, and, in the twentieth century, Paul Hindemith and Quincy Porter. Boris adapted so well and could switch from one instrument to the other with such ease that one night, with Leonid Kreutzer conducting, he performed on the same program both a Wieniawski violin concerto and played the solo viola part for the concerto-like "Harold in Italy" by Berlioz.[12]

While the Roismanns decided to return to Odessa when World War I broke out, the Kroyts saw no reason to do so, although they had czarist passports and were considered enemy aliens. They chose to

stay put in Berlin—and almost immediately regretted that decision.
Just three days after war erupted, several police officers came to the
Kroyt apartment and arrested Boris. As they took him away, a lieu-
tenant paused in the doorway, turned to Cecilia, and brutally told
her, "You'll never see your son again!" Boris never forgot the look of
desperation on his mother's face.[13]

Joe Roismann was watching from his apartment as Boris was
dragged away. It was a terrifying moment. Boris's mother had no idea
where to turn to for help.

Boris was taken to the neighborhood police station, three blocks
away, where his papers were on file. He was scared but kept his head.
In an arrogant tone that he had learned to adopt in Germany, he
threatened the police. They would be in deep trouble if they did not
release him immediately. He had influential friends, and he dropped
the name of a particularly powerful Prussian count who was one of
his admirers. The police were duly intimidated and reluctantly released him.

Life in Germany for Boris during the war was almost as harsh as
Joe and the Schneider brothers experienced in Russia. There were
shortages of everything but, oddly, caviar. What was available was
ersatz. For a long while, Boris was not permitted to concertize, and
he had to be home before dark each night or face arrest for breaking
the curfew. Eventually, however, amidst the craziness of the war,
Boris was allowed out of Germany to perform in Holland—though
he had to promise to return and was always strip-searched when
crossing the border. As Artur Balsam put it, "The Germans during
the first world war were gentlemen."[14]

While the period before the war was *Kaiserzeit*, years of tran-
quility, the period afterward was *Die goldenen zwanziger Jahre*—the
golden twenties.[15] Somehow a musician in his twenties could ignore
the soaring inflation, strikes and riots, unemployment and bank-
ruptcy, and the Nazis and Communists fighting in the streets because there was that other side to Berlin's dual personality. The city
had three opera companies performing at the same time, one conducted by Bruno Walter, one by Otto Klemperer, and the third by
Erich Kleiber. Its philharmonic orchestra had a policy calling for
composers to conduct their own works, so to Berlin came Stravinsky, Ravel, Bartók, and Prokofiev. Busoni was dead, but Arnold
Schönberg came from Vienna to take over his master class in composition at the Academy of Art, thereupon establishing Berlin as the
center of modern music. "I have discovered something which will
guarantee the supremacy of German music for the next hundred

years," he said, describing his vision of the twelve-tone method.[16]

It was as though the war had not taken place, or as though Germany had not been defeated, a time of "renaissance," said impresario Sol Hurok.[17] Pianist Abram Chasins said the city was "full of life" and, Paris notwithstanding, had "the most beautiful girls in the world."[18] Berlin, declared music publisher Hans Heinsheimer, "opened its arms wide to everything that was new, young, daring, different."[19] It was, singer Lotte Lenya insisted, "the most exciting city in the world."[20] A more jaundiced view was taken by thirteen-year-old Yehudi Menuhin, in Berlin for a violin recital. "Berlin had a most advanced and neurotic society," he said. "Not the authentic society but a new society based on new money, and on extravagance, brashness, show. The neurosis was the clash of values, between the old and the new. Everything became possible. Everything became EXperience, with a capital E—and a capital X."[21] It was the kind of atmosphere that fostered the biting, cynical operas of Bertolt Brecht and Lenya's husband, Kurt Weill, and that made George Grosz express on canvas his "despair, hate and disillusionment."[22] At the same time, however, Albert Einstein, brought to Berlin by Max Planck (the physicist who was then teaching at the University of Berlin), attended Menuhin's recital and told him afterwards, "Today, Yehudi, you have once again proved to me that there is a God in heaven."[23]

The social whirl that bubbled from this froth of creative activity centered on the city's numerous cafés, many of them newly opened by Russian émigrés, an incredible assortment of monarchists, anarchists, poets, and businessmen. There was the Café des Westens, the Josty, the Schiller, the Monopol, the Romanische—the last, a huge barn across from Memorial Church that held a thousand customers and attracted expressionist painters. They sat to the right of the revolving door. In the balcony sat rows of chess players. The cafés, the head of the Associated Press bureau in Berlin reported, were "crowded with stylishly garbed ladies."[24] Cocaine was pushed everywhere—by girls in nightclubs and by one-legged war veterans on street corners.

Boris was caught up in the city's mad world. He was now living in a triplex apartment with a bedroom fitted with different colored lights—an *eingefleischt* (an irreformable bachelor). He had a valet, and he had a mistress, Mimi Hartmann, who was the wife of the leading paper manufacturer in Hungary and eight years older than Boris. Mimi underwrote the establishment of a music society dedicated to contemporary music that sponsored festivals and a quartet, the Anbruch (the Beginning). Boris was the first violinist. The society had a magazine and put on six quartet recitals and ten orchestra concerts each season. Mimi's friends were aristocrats, and she liked to arrange masked balls, to which she invited Boris and his friends. He never went to bed before three or four in the morning. It was at one of these parties that he met Richard Strauss, with whom he performed several times. Strauss offered him the post of assistant concertmaster to Arnold Rosé, the leader of the Rosé Quartet who was also with Strauss's orchestra in Vienna and expected to retire soon, but Boris did not want to leave Berlin.

One day, Boris was passing a café when he heard the sound of a beautiful, unusually played cello. He went in to see who it was. The cellist was Gregor Piatigorsky, who had fled the Soviet Union by swimming across a river in the dead of night, his cello held over his head, while border guards emptied their rifles at him. The two musicians became fast friends—a sort of Mutt and Jeff pair, the exceptionally tall Piatigorsky looming over Kroyt. The cellist was living in an unheated attic and was undernourished. Boris got him a job in a small recording orchestra he was leading that played tangoes and tunes from operettas. Unwilling to be identified on the label, Boris recorded under the name Tino Valerio. Later he, Piatigorsky, and pianist Carl Schroeder recorded more serious trios together. And it was Boris who, in the fall of 1923, suggested Piatigorsky for the premiere performance of Arnold Schönberg's "Pierrot Lunaire." "He is a very remarkable artist, most promising," Boris told Schnabel, who was joining instrumentalists from the Berlin Philharmonic for the concert.[25] Piatigorsky was subsequently hired as the orchestra's solo cellist.

In 1927 Boris joined the Guarneri Quartet.[26] He was its violist for seven years, until it broke up suddenly during a tour of South America when the second violinist suffered a brain tumor and died after an operation. By that time, Boris had surprised all his friends by getting married. He was thirty-five years old at the time and though already engaged to another women, broke with her to wed Sophie Blumin. Sonya—as she was called—was ten years his junior, a ballet dancer by training, and the daughter of a wealthy Jewish architect who had been allowed to live in Moscow. Her family fled from the Bolsheviks and was now virtually penniless. Like Boris, Sonya was outgoing, a charming woman who had a European flair for making friends easily. In September 1933, Boris and Sonya had a child, Yanna.

It was becoming increasingly difficult to support his family in

Berlin. Boris started a second Kroyt Quartet.[27] Its second violinist was a Romanian who had been expelled from the Berlin Philharmonic because he was Jewish. But they were only permitted to play for the Jewish Culture League. When the first violinist of the old Guarneri, Daniel Karpilovksy, finagled a concert in Holland for the Guarneri, even though it no longer existed, Boris and the cellist and the violist of the Kroyt Quartet went there with him and performed under the Guarneri name.[28]

Looking for an opportunity to leave Germany, Boris signed with William Steinberg—a German Jewish conductor who later conducted the symphony orchestras of Buffalo, Pittsburgh, and Boston—to go to Palestine with his family to join the orchestra Steinberg and Bronislav Hubermann were forming there. No sooner had he done so, in mid-May of 1936, than the message from Roismann reached him.

Boris went to Paris to speak with Joe. He was not eager to go to the Middle East to play in an orchestra, but on the other hand, he was skeptical about making a living just by playing quartets. No member of any quartet he knew, including his own, had been able to exist on the earnings from quartet performances alone; besides, he had heard the Budapest perform with Hauser as first violinist and was not impressed. When he mentioned the offer to musician friends, they thought he would be insane to join. Joe, however, told him about the Budapest's list of appearances already lined up—opening their next season with thirteen concerts in Norway; then twenty-two more in the United States, followed by a round of recitals in England, Paris, and Holland; and finally a minimum of thirty-six performances in Australia and New Zealand—close to a hundred concerts scheduled, maybe more if some late bookings came in. Convinced, Boris accepted and signed a one-year contract—the last contract any of the Quartet members would ever sign.

The first concert Boris performed with the Budapest in Norway, on August 31, 1936, was a disaster; not the performance, though—a Haydn (Opus 64, No. 5), a Beethoven trio (Opus 9, No. 3) and Smetana's Quartet No. 1 in E Minor ("From My Life"). That evidently went well. But they earned only sixteen kroner, or a dollar per man, just enough for each of the four musicians to buy a can of sardines. It was Kroyt's turn to be shocked. "Tell me," he asked Mischa, "is this the famous Budapest Quartet?"[29] He turned to Sasha, "Are these the fees the Quartet is making on concert tours?"[30]

Sasha felt sorry for him, but not because of the sixteen kroner. Boris spoke a different musical language, different even from Joe, although they had both studied with the same teacher. Boris had studied much longer with Fiedemann and, as a soloist, had picked up the emotion-charged playing characteristic of virtuoso performers then. Sasha, for one, was worried about his adapting to the style of the others.

Boris joined the Quartet a day after his thirty-ninth birthday.[31] He was the oldest musician in the group—Joe was going on thirty-six; Mischa was thirty-two; and Sasha, only twenty-seven. Sasha had been only a still-flexible twenty-two-year-old when he had signed on. He knew that it would be "just as difficult for Kroyt as it was for me when I joined the Quartet," perhaps even more so. He spoke of his doubts to his former teacher, Adolf Rebner. Rebner, however, was optimistic. "It is the most wonderful thing that you have new blood coming into the Quartet and it will be better than ever before," he predicted.[32]

Boris, who was used to playing in quartets in which the first violinist decided matters, had other reasons besides the fee to be dismayed. "I sometimes wished Roismann would say, 'Now, play like this and don't spend so much time on these bowings. I will take all parts and I will write all the bowings.'"[33] But Roismann would not and did not take the lead about anything musical. To Mischa, that was a plus. "He would never impose his ideas. He would say, 'It would be good if you play it like that.' But if you said, 'No, it's difficult for me, I can't,' he would never insist."[34] Inevitably, there were disagreements. "We worked, we fought, we fought but we worked," said Mischa. "Even if we didn't agree, we worked. We knew that you had to work."[35]

The disputes were about tempos, phrasing, pauses—every subtlety that goes into a performance. They shouted at each other in Russian and German, shook their heads in anger, and leaned forward in their chairs, bows in hand like rapiers, to make a point in their arguments. But at the same time, a new era in the Quartet's life was developing, a mutual respect for one another's talents and musicianship. For the first time, all four members enjoyed performing together.

Rehearsals began with playing scales in unison for half an hour—Joe and Sasha playing the same notes, Boris an octave lower, and Mischa an octave lower than Boris—because, as Joe explained, "in public performances, you see, passages which are in unison are the most dangerous as far as intonation is concerned."[36] Boris thought the time well spent. "When I came to the Quartet, I never saw a collection of players which fit so badly together than these three together," he declared. "After many years playing they still played out of tune."[37]

Hours were also spent on practicing bowing together; "whether to play down or play up. We spent hours on such things," said Mischa.[38] Their fingering was coordinated so that they played "in exactly the same way," even in the case of the cello, Joe said, "so that the character of the phrase would be similar."[39] They "instinctively" adjusted the speed of their vibrato to one another.[40] "We worshiped the printed page," said Sasha. "There never was a quartet that paid so much attention to every millionth of a point. If we weren't sure whether it was a dot or a piece of dirt, we played the dot."[41] The Quartet even went so far as to mark the dynamics of every note in a crescendo—which Boris thought was "annoying and silly" because it "defeated the purpose of the crescendo and the individuality of the instruments. Every musician has a different crescendo. For an artist with a big tone, *piano* is one thing; for an artist with a small tone, it is something else. You can't go by the book, you can't rely on markings."[42]

Boris liked tempos to be faster than Joe or Mischa did. Joe believed a phrase played by one instrument and echoed by another should be played exactly alike. Sasha, who despised "homogeneity," said he did not "care to have another voice imitate" a "musical statement exactly" in "such a strait-jacket attitude."[43] Even bowings, he said, can be changed. Boris agreed with him:

> We would spend hours sitting down and writing the bowings—in a sense molding our four instruments into one. We sound like "one instrument," people would say. Is this good? Should a quartet sound like one instrument? Few people are really aware of the different quality of the instruments, particularly of the difference between the viola and the violin. There's the old saying, "When you play quartet, you have to lose your personality." But this is absolutely wrong.[44]

So there were loud shouting matches, with invectives hurled back and forth, until a vote was taken and the matter settled. It was true, Joe said, that sometimes their disputes got so rancorous that two members might not speak to each other for several weeks, "but no matter what mood we were in, once on the stage [there was] 100 percent cooperation."[45]

Boris, meanwhile, pondered his decision to join the group. In the back of his mind was the thought that he could always abandon the Quartet if the situation did not get better financially.

Things did improve. Some concerts brought in as much as a

hundred twenty kroner, and a radio broadcast in Oslo paid three hundred kroner, minus an agent's 10 percent fee and, of course, their expenses. Anyway, they explained to Boris, the first thirteen concerts in Norway were really try-out recitals, to perfect the Quartet's repertoire for what they considered more serious touring ahead. Their repertoire included about sixty pieces, from classics to what Joe called "ultra-modern"—among them, works by English composers Vaughn Williams, Edward Elgar, and Frank Bridge that the Quartet planned to introduce to Australia. They had spent the summer rehearsing them and still got together every day before concerts to run through their programs.

By the time the Quartet reached the United States in early November 1936—nearly two years before its famous Town Hall concert—Boris fit in so well that a critic in the New York *American* "wondered" if "any quartet now before the public approaches it in style and musical insight."[46] Another said that "when I say that the performance of [Beethoven's] Opus 132 was one of the greatest performances in all my experience, I mean that the thinking, feeling and working together of these four individuals gave to the sounds that reached my ears a quality and an organization, and through these a heightened significance, such as a great work of Beethoven has had when conducted by Toscanini or played by Schnabel."[47]

The U.S. tour included an odd assortment of appearances indicative of the formative stage of the chamber-music field in the United States. It began with a morning concert at a golf club in Westchester County, New York, followed by two more morning recitals at a private home in Greenwich, Connecticut. All three were arranged by Eddie Brown, who also hired the Quartet to perform on New York's radio station WQXR, which he was in the process of developing into a major classical-music outlet.

The Budapest also performed in a high school in Haverhill, Massachusetts, and at the Women's Republican Club in Boston. Fledgling chamber-music societies in Buffalo and Los Angeles had to rent hotel ballrooms to present the Quartet. The Coleman Chamber Music Association presented them at the Pasadena Playhouse. Their eight-week tour included performances at the Academy of Music in Brooklyn, at Columbia University, in Town Hall in New York City for the New Friends of Music, at Cornell and Princeton Universities, for the Bohemian Club in New York City, and at the Shrine Auditorium in Oklahoma City.[48] The Quartet performed for twenty-five cents a ticket at a Peoples' Symphony Concert at Washington Irving High School in Manhattan. In all, the Quartet earned a total of

$6,350 for its U.S. concert tour—minus the usual outlays—a better but not overwhelmingly prosperous eight weeks of work.[49]

The critical response everywhere, however, was positive. "The virtues of the Budapest Quartet loom large, while the faults are microscopic," a Buffalo critic said. "Individually and collectively the four players disclose tonal beauty and resonance, and the ensemble as an artistic entity takes its place in the front ranks of string quartets of the day."[50] The critic for the Ithaca *Journal* was enthralled: "At the conclusion of the recital one left his seat with the feeling that somehow he had experienced something great, and it is not unreasonable to imagine that the ensemble shared the same feelings with the audience." Sometimes, out of New York City, the Quartet played encores, but, the Ithaca reviewer said, "there was no encore, for there was no need of an encore."[51] Their concert in San Francisco brought accolades from the *Chronicle*'s reviewer: "The tone of Mischa Schneider's cello is a perennial marvel, Joseph Roisman and Alexander Schneider know a good deal more than a thing or two about the violin, and Boris Kroyt, the quartet's new viola player, is an artist of the first caliber."[52] A critic for the Los Angeles *Times* echoed the remarks, commenting on the "extraordinarily appealing tone" of Roismann and saying that "Alexander Schneider . . . [was] close in rank." Kroyt, she said, "plays the viola like a virtuoso of the violin," and Mischa, she said, "is an ensemble player of exceptional merit."[53]

Praise followed them that spring 1937 to Australia, New Zealand, and the Dutch East Indies. Audience attendance grew appreciably from their last appearance in Australia. Four concerts in Perth in ten days were all sold out. "The quality of the ensemble," said a reviewer in *Wireless Weekly*, "has been improved much by the new viola-player, Mr. Boris Kroyt. . . . In fact, it seems to me that the intellectual leadership of the quartet lies now in his hands. . . . Perhaps he is responsible also that the pitch of the Budapest Quartet, which was formerly so that people who, like the writer of these lines, are in the unhappy possession of perfect pitch, had to transpose everything by a semitone, has gone down by a few vibrations."[54]

Though the year of concertizing was a critical success, the future was uncertain. The Spanish Civil War had broken out in July 1936. The Quartet had once played as many as thirty recitals in one month in Spain, but now none were possible. Engagements in Italy, once numerous, were now few. "People are so busy with politics in some countries," Joe told a reporter, "that they have no money for us."[55]

Only Paris and London were still viable for an extended round of concerts.

A disagreement broke out among Quartet members about whether they should try to settle in Australia. Joe was appointed to find out if the earlier offer of the Australian Broadcasting Company, for the Quartet to become its quartet-in-residence, was still good. The Schneider brothers were now for emigrating there. Mischa even went so far as to formally apply for permission to do so and become a British subject.[56] Joe and Boris, however, were against it. An evenly divided vote meant, according to Quartet rules, that the status quo prevailed. Living in Australia was ruled out.

After returning to France and playing both there and in England, the Quartet made its fateful trip to New York in early March 1938 aboard the liner *Manhattan* to begin another tour of the United States, the sixth the Quartet had undertaken since 1931. It was to be the most important tour of their lives, though they certainly had no reason to suspect that it might be. After all, their previous tours of the United States had hardly been memorable economically. And then to be greeted this time with such bureaucratic obstinacy when they arrived in New York Harbor and to be shunted to Ellis Island in such a degrading way aboard a coal barge made them feel like poor peasant immigrants. They would have been skeptical if anyone had suggested then that almost overnight they were about to become the reigning stars of an incredibly expanding American chamber-music scene.

9

Twin Peak Number One

The outlook in America was unpromising that March of 1938. Despite the success of the previous year's tour, the number of bookings on the Quartet's schedule had actually dwindled, from twenty-two concerts to sixteen. As Joe was quick to point out in an interview, America did not enjoy the public acceptance of classical music that European countries did. The only thing America had going for it, he said, was enthusiasm.[1]

What amazed the Quartet members was how quickly their unpromising tour turned into a success, unleashing a wave of popular support and a veritable flood of engagements, sold-out performances, and radio broadcasts—ironic, indeed, when you compare Noel Straus's providential glowing review of that Sunday afternoon's Town Hall concert with their own, almost diametrically opposite, assessment of how they played. "If there is a finer string foursome in existence . . ."—his words alone, some of the Quartet members believed, were responsible for their subsequent success.

That reaction is even more surprising when you consider what many musicians think of critics. Many performers look down their noses at critics, deliberately ignore them, and refuse to read what they write. Critics, they believe, are, to use Sasha's words, "screwed up" musicologists. Sasha, for one, thought that despite all their knowledge about music, "anyone who is not a professional performer can ever really know what it is like to be on stage, completely exposed, trying to do justice to the music."[2] But such a view is simplistic. A good critic—and Sasha would be the first to admit that there are some good critics—feels "a responsibility to the musical

life of the community in which he lives to raise the musical standards of that community according to his or her perception by edu-
cating the public so they can make their own opinions about what is
good or bad music making."[3] Good critics inform their readers; they
understand the pressures a performer faces. And the truth is that
critics—whether worthy or shallow—can make or break a performer's career. They may be unoriginal in their thinking, oblivious
at times to subtleties of performance and sometimes arrogant, but
they are a fact of life. Too often they mimicked one another in
reviewing the Quartet's playing or misread a performance. Mischa
always thought that critics took too much credit for the Budapest's
success. "You come and play, you come and play, you come and
play," he said, "and suddenly they all start to say we made you. How
can anybody say that?"[4] But without those very same critics, where
would the Quartet have been? How many people ignorant of chamber music would have heard about them, gone to their concerts, and
learned the pleasure of string quartets?

Professional musicians may think that critics exercise too much
power or influence that way, but a good review does sell tickets. The
Budapest Quartet invariably got good press. Critics almost fell over
themselves trying to express in print the way they played, how they
sounded, and what insights they brought to the music. But no, it was
not just one review in the *New York Times* that launched the Quartet. The factors involved in their success were many and more complex than one favorable critique, or even a series of rave reviews.
After all, their performances the previous year in America had been
widely praised.

Even the reason Mischa offered—that the Budapest alone of all
quartets was willing to sacrifice family life to tour extensively to
concertize—is too simplistic. They were much more than just a
troupe of music-making performers willing to travel anywhere.
They were something special. To those who heard the Budapest
play, they were four virtuosos. Many remark on their unusual unanimity. "They breathed together," said critic Paul Hume. "They
vibrated together," said pianist Ruth Laredo. "They played like one
instrument," said recording executive R. Peter Munves. "You could
tell it was the Budapest String Quartet by the unanimity of expression and the composer's voice in different registers." Violist Walter
Trampler recalled standing in back of a hall when he first heard
them: "There was no little ratty entrance. It was on the button.
There was a chord—BOOM!" Every chord they played, said violinist
Felix Galimir, "was polished, absolutely together, absolutely in

tune, the balance perfect, elegant." The Budapest was, violinist Edgar Ortenberg said, "sixteen strings and one bow."[5]

When Joe Roisman was asked his opinion about what made the Budapest different from other quartets, he replied, "We were well attuned to each other. We were happy and 'uninhibited.' We were playing in strict chamber-music style and yet no other quartet had that style. We were carried away by our temperament, we let ourselves go. We played Debussy one way, Beethoven different, Dvořák different."[6]

No one, however, agreed when trying to describe their sound. Was it Russian? Was it German? Jewish? Joe thought of their tone as "fat and softig, but never 'schmalz.'"[7] Critic Harold Schonberg believed their sound was Russian—warm, generous, soaring, and emotional. But another critic, Paul Hume, called their playing "immaculately clean." He and many others—critics and musicians alike—invoke Toscanini's name and influence to describe the Budapest's sound, using adjectives like "clear," "crisp," and "precise," too. They cleared away "the underbrush," critic and writer Allan Kriegsman said.[8]

On the other hand, Arnold Steinhardt of the modern Guarneri Quartet thought the Quartet's style was urbane, an amalgam of German and Russian. Record reviewer Robert C. Marsh likened their "rich colorations" to "the robust browns of a Rembrandt."[9] R. Peter Munves, who grew up in an orthodox home, recognized in their playing the same inflections he heard as a young boy when his parents spoke Yiddish. To Michael Tree, also of the Guarneri Quartet, the Budapest played with what he called "expressive intonation." They "leaned" in the direction that a note was headed: "If it happened to be the key of D major and it was the leading tone, they played C sharp. If it was in the key of C minor then the D flat would be a tiny bit on the flat side. In other words, they used intonation as an expressive device and did not just play mechanically." Whatever it was, the sound was unique. Violinist Jaime Laredo said he could tell when a Budapest record was being played on the radio by hearing only one bar.[10]

In retrospect, it was a combination of factors that led to the Quartet's success—their willingness to be on tour for long stretches of time; their playing, to be sure; and, of course, the favorable reviews (plural) that they received. Then, too, there was an American public whose appetite had been whetted by a host of European artists and which was thirsting for more; the refugees who crowded their concerts were among their earliest supporters; radio broadcasts that publicized their name and their music produced new fans; and finally, but by no means least, there was their personalities, habits, looks, *joie de vivre*—an almost natural ability to attract the attention of newspaper and magazine writers.

Coming out on the concert stage, dressed in tux, tails, or striped pants and cutaways, the Quartet members looked the epitome of the classical musician—serious, dedicated, and in Joe's case in particular, regal. They seemed to fit the stereotype even, in the case of the Schneider brothers and Boris, when it came to their long hair, which one expected to fly wildly at feverish climaxes in the music. Off stage, greeting admirers in the green room after a concert, at a reception later, or with their friends, they exuded warmth and conviviality the way bear-hugging Russians can. Like most musicians, they loved jokes; Sasha wrote down the ones he heard in a little notebook. And when they told jokes, their accents produced smiles even before the punchline—this" was "dis," "that" was "dat," "what" was "vat." Mischa had trouble saying "thirteenth"; it came out "sirteent." When the others kidded him about the trouble he encountered in making appointments, Mischa told a reporter, "I am fooling them, however. I am telling people to meet at the elevator on the floor between twelve and fourteen."[11] Boris especially mangled the English language. Once, at a campus concert, the school officials suggested that one of the quartet members talk about the music beforehand to the students, to explain what they would be hearing. Boris volunteered. No one understood a word he said.[12] For Boris, "wrapping paper" turned into "raping paper," a "plan" was a "plane," and if he spoke of another musician as being "talentless," somehow it came out sounding like "relentless"—"ta-lentless." Boris, Mischa, and Sasha were fun to be with.

The Quartet never had a press agent; nor did Annie Friedberg do more than schedule performances, arrange travel accommodations, and mail out a few advance press releases. Yet their name soon became widely known, and as it did, the demand for them increased proportionally. There were new audiences clamoring for them to perform all across the country. In the spring of 1938, the Budapest performed its first Beethoven cycle at the 92nd Street Y in New York City. It was part of a commemoration of the 110th anniversary of Beethoven's death and was the first time that all his quartets were played in New York. "If you are a musician you will appreciate the importance of this announcement," read a subscription circular from the Y announcing the cycle, "if not, just ask any real musician, and you will be convinced."[13]

Boris noted gratifyingly that the Quartet earned $6,350 in concert fees in the United States alone during that spring and $10,550 more in America that fall—at a time when the country was still in the Great Depression and one could buy a good cigar for a nickel.[14] If he still had any doubts about remaining with the Budapest, he did not voice them. The Arts Society of Batavia Center now opened negotiations for the Quartet to return for another tour of the Dutch East Indies—twenty concerts for ten thousand guilders (about five thousand dollars), plus two hundred fifty guilders for every extra performance.[15] And a concert manager in Mexico City sounded them out about a series of recitals in the Mexican capital.[16]

The Quartet was in the midst of enjoying what was the first of two high points in its long career. The first peak began when Kroyt joined the ensemble in 1936. It would last for almost eight years. But for all the achievements during that time, these were years of struggle: of a daily routine of six hours of rehearsals, loud and seemingly bitter bickerings over musical matters, an ever-expanding and demanding concert schedule, always tedious record sessions, constant traveling. Measured in personal costs, success took a heavy toll on the Quartet members' private lives. Sasha's marriage to Gerte lasted all of one year. That is not surprising, considering the compulsiveness with which they both entered into it. But Mischa's second marriage also failed; Dorte did not want to put up with the endless packing and unpacking, particularly with their daughter in tow.

Only Joe and Boris adjusted well. Pola sometimes traveled with Joe; and both Sonya and daughter Yanna frequently accompanied Boris. Yanna was the only child of any member who ever went with the Quartet on its tours; at one point, she went regularly to six different schools every year as the Quartet moved from Washington to New York to the West Coast and then back to New York before returning to Washington. Yanna was the center of attention of feature writers when the Budapest toured Australia and then went on to Indonesia in 1937. Though only four years old, she could already speak German and French, and she quickly picked up both English and Indonesian. Her father, one reporter noted, "knows no English to speak of,"[17] so "Uncle Mischa" read to her.[18] She was the Quartet mascot and, for one brief moment, was thought a musical genius. Boris had to baby-sit for her one day when his wife was busy. He had a rehearsal, so he took her with him. She sat on a piano stool and did not move for three hours. The others were amazed at her attention span; surely, it indicated she was a prodigy. Then Boris went to pick her up. She had peed in her pants and was afraid to move.

No one raises an eyebrow nowadays when Winton Marsalis starts blowing riffs on his trumpet or Richard Stoltzman plays his clarinet with a jazz combo. But in the thirties, long hair mixing with short hair, high brow with low brow, was unheard of—that is, until an unusual combination was formed: the Budapest String Quartet and probably the most popular, if not best known, band leader in America, Benny Goodman. While the Quartet was in New York in the fall of 1937, Sasha went to hear Goodman's combo play in a nightclub. He was taken there by John Hammond, who was both a jazz and classical-music aficionado. Hammond was an amateur violist. Goodman was a friend of his; in fact, he later married Hammond's sister. Goodman enjoyed playing classical music for fun with Hammond and a group of amateurs, particularly Mozart's Clarinet Quintet in A.

Sasha was immediately taken with Goodman's clarinet playing; it was "extraordinary," he said.[19] When they met afterwards, Goodman said that he would like to play the Mozart quintet with the Budapest Quartet, and he even offered to audition for them. (What he did not tell Sasha was that he had been scheduled to record the same work with the Pro Arte Quartet a year earlier. Goodman had showed up at a Chicago studio after an overnight bus trip from Wisconsin, blew a few bars on the same reed he used at the previous night's dance date, and was so embarrassed by what he sounded like that he got up and walked out without saying a word to the astounded Pro Arte players.[20] Goodman did not realize until then that most clarinetists who play classical music and are concerned about a consistent, clean tone prefer a heavy reed with a small opening between the reed and the instrument's mouthpiece. Jazz musicians prefer a soft reed and a wider opening that permits them to bend notes more easily.)

The next day, Sasha conveyed Goodman's offer to Joe, Mischa, and Boris. They looked at him peculiarly. None of them had ever heard of the "King of Swing," but they agreed to grant him an audition. One morning soon afterward, Goodman appeared at the Great Northern Hotel with his clarinet case under his arm and an entourage in tow. He had spent the previous day recording and the previous night performing until the early hours of the morning. Everyone crowded into one of the Quartet member's rooms—Goodman's entourage hugging the walls of the small room while the musicians sat before five music stands that girded the bed. They started the Mozart. Goodman, said Sasha, played "very beautifully."[21] Right then and there they decided to record the piece for RCA Victor, the American subsidiary of His Master's Voice.

Goodman always regretted that they did not perform the Mozart in public before recording it. That would have allowed for more rehearsal time. "I thought," he said, "that chamber music could be tossed off pretty nearly as easily as a good jam session." He did not realize "that the astonishingly high standards of the Budapest Quartet came from everlasting, painstaking attention to detail through every rehearsal and performance of every work in their repertoire."[22]

The Mozart quintet was recorded at a single session in RCA Victor's Studio 2 on April 25, 1938. Neither Goodman nor members of the Quartet felt completely at ease. Because of the four-minute limit that 78-rpm disks had, each movement was recorded in two parts. The first part of the first movement had to be repeated.[23] Only one microphone was used. The Quartet sat in a semicircle, with Goodman on the outside next to Boris, but the balance was perfect.[24] Goodman, however, determined that he could never again "record classical music without the most meticulous preparation, and preferably after a public performance of the work."[25]

Despite his misgivings, the recording sold well. Goodman earned the cachet of being not only an expert jazz clarinetist but a serious musician as well, while, at the same time, the hitherto little-known Budapest Quartet was suddenly recognizable by name all over the country. For his part, Goodman went on to commission pieces for clarinet by Bartók, Copland, and Hindemith and went on to record with Joseph Szigeti and symphony orchestras.

Goodman joined the Budapest Quartet three more times to perform the Mozart quintet in public. The first time—when the Quartet returned to America in the fall of 1938—was a try-out of sorts for a more important appearance with them in Town Hall. The "try-out" was performed at the Hotchkiss School, an all-boys prep school in Lakeville, Connecticut, on October 30. It was the second time that Goodman ever wore full dress for a concert; he had donned the formal garb for his historic jazz concert in Carnegie Hall earlier that year, on January 16.

The Town Hall concert, six days later at 5:30 P.M. on Saturday, November 5, was advertised as the "concert of the year!—The King of Swing's classical music concert debut with the great Budapest String Quartet."[26] All but a few of the seats were gobbled up by a "large and cordial" audience. However, it was a critical disappointment. Goodman and his band were appearing at the time in the

Empire Room of the Waldorf-Astoria for dinner and supper dancing. Whether it was tiredness or nervousness, again he did not relax—and the Budapest players picked up his edginess. Harold Schonberg, who would later be the *New York Times* music critic but was then a young reviewer of records for *American Music Lover,* was one of the nearly fifteen hundred persons who attended the concert. "For the first time," he recalled, "the Budapest Quartet sounded very careful." So, too, was Goodman, who had "none of the freedom that apparently I'm told he had in his jazz playing. I mean it was metronomic. It was like a book. Every note was there. There was a beautiful sound—after all, he had a marvelous embouchure. But there was no imagination there. There was no fluctuation of tempo. There was no Romanticism, no feeling of joy in this incredibly beautiful piece of music."[27] Olin Downes, who was then the *Times* critic, thought the clarinetist was "overcautious," though he went to some length to praise the performance. "In some classic breasts," he wrote, Goodman's appearance "roused apprehension, but the alligators and the Jitterbugs said that Benny would show them! And he did, in the most legitimate matter." Goodman "sang with a beautiful legato and fine feeling" in the slow movement, but "there were places where the capacities of Mr. Goodman's instrument would have permitted a greater variety of volume and color than he attempted. In the first movement he was a little stiff. But always he showed his sincerity, his proficiency and his earnest regard for the music."[28]

Goodman and the Quartet played together once more, on Sunday afternoon, August 17, 1941, at the Ravinia Festival outside Chicago before an astonishingly huge crowd of 2, 853 persons, undoubtedly the largest audience up to that time ever to attend a chamber-music concert. The *Daily Tribune* critic said that Goodman "made an honest job of his share in the Mozart quintet," displaying "a reasonable mastery of his instrument and a great desire to cooperate with the other members of the ensemble, but the actual result, when all is said and done, was pallid."[29] On the other hand, the reviewer for the *Daily Times* said that Goodman played "as if he had written the music." It was not "the Budapest String Quartet and Benny Goodman. No, there were five artists, and they were, as Benny would put it, going to town."[30]

There had been talk of Goodman's joining the Quartet in recording Brahms's Clarinet Quintet in B Minor, but a snag developed with RCA Victor, one that had far-reaching implications for the Budapest's recording future.

10

For the Record

The Quartet never did record the Brahms clarinet quintet with Benny Goodman. For some time, before the idea was broached, the Quartet members had been unhappy with the Gramophone Company, which held their recording contract.

Nearly every year since first signing with His Master's Voice in 1925, the Budapest recorded some works, either in total or in part, first at the Beethoven Saal in Berlin, then at HMV's Abbey Road Studio in London, and from 1938 on in Camden, New Jersey, where HMV's American subsidiary, RCA Victor, had a studio. In all, close to fifty quartets and one quintet were on 78-rpm masters, but not all had been released. Moreover, the Quartet was eager to record all the Beethoven quartets, but Victor was loathe to do so because it had a number of pressings made by both the Coolidge and Busch quartets and was contemplating issuing a complete low-price set.

Gramophone's backlog was so extensive that it was reluctant to record any more. It already had in its vaults seven works the Budapest had recorded—including two Beethoven quartets, two Brahms works, a Bartók, a Dvořák, and a Grieg. "On looking through our list of records in reserve by your Quartet," one of its executives wrote in the fall of 1938, "I find that we have sufficient to last us for at least twelve months. In this case, there will be no necessity to record during your next visit to London, as there is no object in accumulating too large a reserve."[1] Four days later, when the question arose about recording again with Benny Goodman, the same executive warned that "we cannot promise that the work will be issued in England, since we have quite recently issued the same work by another organization."[2] When the Quartet protested Gramophone's restrictions, the same executive simply repeated the company's policy: "Owing to trading conditions existing to-day, this will be sufficient to last us for some considerable time."[3]

The Budapest's contract was due to expire in June 1940, and with the Quartet now based in America and the political situation in Europe uncertain, Gramophone asked its "associates with the Victor Company" to take over the negotiations for a new contract, usually a routine matter. For some inexplicable reason, the executive responsible for dealing with the Quartet dawdled. He never comprehended the Budapest's dissatisfaction, nor seemed to recognize the significance of its increasing popularity. In addition to their wanting to record the Beethovens and other works, the Quartet members felt they were now worth a yearly minimum royalty guarantee. A meeting at the Great Northern Hotel produced nothing more than a gratuitous thanks for an "an interesting list of selections to be considered for recording" but no commitment unless a study of previous sales "will justify it."[4] Sales, the Victor official wrote nine days later, did not justify either doing the entire list or "an annual guarantee which in all probability will mean some loss to us."[5] Further discussions through the mail brought additional reservations—the Victor official did not want to record Smetana, "Beethoven, I would like to postpone entirely for this year. . . . Schubert I would like to postpone also. . . . The Debussy Opus 10 should be done later." He offered a number of alternative selections, but Mischa responded that the list was "alright only we are disappointed about Beethoven as the demand is great."[6] Finally, after much dickering, the executive offered the Quartet an advance of two thousand dollars.[7]

It was too late. The Quartet members were already put off, first by Gramophone's refusal to release them from their contract even though it was not interested in doing any further recordings, then by RCA Victor's almost lackadaisical attitude about renewing the contract once it expired. So they decided to approach the fast-growing Columbia Recording Corporation through Sasha's friend John Hammond, the jazz and classical music lover who had brought them together with Benny Goodman and was now with Columbia. Columbia was then in the midst of a major raid on Victor's recording artists, drawing them away with more favorable contracts and an aggressive, optimistic sales philosophy.

Columbia was willing to sign a two-year contract and guarantee twenty-five hundred dollars in royalties. The company was "sure," Hammond said, "you will earn far more than this from royalties."[8]

As for what would be recorded, another Columbia official, Moses Smith, insisted, "I want you to have as much of a choice of repertoire as possible." In fact, said Smith, after looking over the list of what the Budapest had recorded for both HMV and Victor, "I can readily see that we are going to have no difficulty in assigning your repertoire. Our catalog, as you realize, I suppose, is wide open." He added, much to the Quartet's pleasure, "You will understand that it is to our interest, as well as to yours, to assign big-selling repertoire to you."[9] On April 25, 1940, Smith sent Mischa the agreement finally worked out—the Budapest to be guaranteed twenty-five hundred dollars and to get 10 percent on all recordings, 8 percent if a guest artist participated. There was even talk of getting Goodman to record again with the Quartet, and Goodman suggested Oscar Levant as a possible guest artist. "The combination of Levant, Goodman and the Budapest Quartet, especially in Prokofiev's racy music," an enthusiastic Smith said, "would almost guarantee a large sale."[10] The first recording dates were set for immediately after the HMV contract expired, in the first two weeks in July in Columbia's recording studio in Liederkranz Hall on East 58th Street in New York City. In the meantime, however, Smith sent the Quartet a form letter being mailed to all Columbia artists, requesting that recording sessions, repertoire, and contract details be kept confidential and not be disclosed "prematurely."[11]

When the news about the Budapest's signing with Columbia did become public, RCA Victor was stunned. "We are astonished," said the executive they had dealt with, suddenly jolted awake. "I am taken by surprise." Moreover, he wrote Mischa, "You will forgive me, I trust, if I regard your action as perilously close to a definite breach of faith."[12]

The path to subsequent success that the Budapest enjoyed with the Columbia Recording Corporation—and later with its metamorphoses into CBS Records and Sony Classical—was fraught with difficulties at first. The problem Mischa and Sasha had with the musicians' union—which Victor had handled without a ripple of nuisance—threatened to stymy the very first recording sessions.

The union insisted that unless and until the Schneiders joined the union the Quartet could not make any recordings. The problem so unnerved Columbia that it asked the Budapest to sign an agreement allowing Columbia to terminate its contract with them if the union blocked any recordings. Under pressure from both the Quartet and Columbia, the AFM relented somewhat. Once the Schneiders paid their initiation fees and dues, as they did in order to perform in public, the Quartet also could record if two union standbys were hired at prevailing union rates—thirty dollars per man for each three-hour session—and if more than three 12-inch masters were made, ten dollars for each master after that.

At first, Columbia balked at the union's demand, figuring that it would cost the company twenty dollars more a master at a time when it had just announced an almost 50-percent reduction in record prices. It was now charging a dollar for its 12-inch classical records and seventy-five cents for its 10-inch ones. The reason for the reduction, Columbia's president wrote to its recording artists, was that "during the past few years there has been increasing evidence that interest in good music in this country has become something no longer limited to a small class of people." The improvement in the quality of records and "the tremendous impetus given" by broadcasting companies playing classical music, he said, "has resulted in love of good music in this country becoming a thing of the masses." He was certain the lower prices would therefore result in "a substantial increase in royalties."[13]

The Quartet members were reluctant to shoulder the cost of the standbys—they were livid, in fact, at the thought of paying someone to do nothing—so an impasse developed. It was eventually settled by Columbia's agreeing to share the costs with the Quartet, though the four were still annoyed that they could not choose the standbys themselves.

Between October 21, 1940, and December 5, 1941—on the eve of America's entry into World War II—the Budapest held nine recording sessions in Leiderkranz Hall, sandwiching them in between concert engagements whenever their hectic schedule brought them to New York.[14] Columbia was disappointed. Hoping for a much greater share of the Quartet's time, Moses Smith said he was "disturbed" that the Budapest was so busy concertizing and wondered "how soon we are going to get you people into a recording session."[15] However, his unhappiness soon became academic, because the war precluded additional sessions—the materials for making records were severely limited, and production, as a result, was cut back dramatically. A federal order restricting the production of phonograph records for the duration of the war affected Columbia so "severely," Smith conceded, that the company could only provide the four members of the Quartet with one copy of each release instead of the usual four. "It seems as though sugar will be easier to get from now on than a gratis record."[16]

On top of that, the AFM struck Columbia in the fall of 1942, effectively stopping all Columbia artists from cutting masters. More than eighteen months went by before the War Labor Board entered the stalled strike talks and forced a settlement. The Budapest was not able to resume recording sessions until just before the end of the war, in early February 1945.

Despite the war shortages and restrictions, though, the Budapest earned $56,670 in royalties between 1941 and 1946 from Columbia alone.[17] They received at least $16,500 more from Victor, which was still selling its Budapest recordings.[18] Goddard Lieberson, president of Columbia Records, was sanguine about the future, too. "As a token of good faith," he said, Columbia was prepared to guarantee the Quartet "that their earnings will never be less than $6,000 a year for any year of the contract."[19]

A recording session of the Budapest—as Lieberson discovered—was a study in controlled chaos. To those who were not accustomed to Russian flamboyance, the eruption of raucous, boisterous, bitter arguing, at an emotional level created by four voluble and volatile egos (yes, even Roisman got his dander up at times), made it seem as though the Quartet members would end at arm's length rather than knee-to-knee at their stands. In that sense, they played music the way they played bridge, which was always a catalyst for volcanic-like flare-ups. "There were the most violent outbursts in Russian," said a friend who played cards with them. "They would never play with each other again, they said. And then they would start right out again, dealing."[20] The outbursts were a catharsis. "I'd be thinking that they would never speak to each other again," said Lieberson, who became their recording director, "and then they'd sit down and play heavenly music."[21]

The truth is that they did not like to record. They knew it was for "the future"; the royalties were a pension for their old age—which the Library of Congress did not provide—and, in Mischa and Boris's case, something tangible to pass along to their children. Joe complained of having to record in the morning and early afternoon. "It was far from normal playing," he said. "The best you could do was not too good. I was used to wearing evening tails—that's when you play."[22] Mischa groaned about what seemed interminable repeats until they were all happy with the result—this at a time before tape, when there was no such thing as splicing possible. The 78-rpm recordings they made in the 1930s and 1940s required four minutes of perfect playing, and sometimes at tempos swifter than usual in order to fit a movement on one side. The Quartet once asked Sibelius whether it could drop a repeat in his Quartet in D Minor ("Voces

Intimae") so that they could fit a section on one side of the disc, but the composer refused to allow them to do so.[23]

And who, by the way, was to say what was perfect? At the playback in the studio, it was not unusual for Mischa, for example, to say, "very good," but for Boris to qualify that with, it was "almost all right." Joe would shake his head, "I don't like it"; while Sasha, more forcefully, exclaimed, "Terrible! There's no life in it."[24] Howard Scott, who later became their recording director, said, "They never agree on anything, but when you hear the recording, they seem to agree completely."[25]

In all, Columbia released seventy-seven different works that the Budapest recorded for it. Seventeen of them were the Beethoven quartets, which they recorded anew each time recording technology advanced, and for good reason. The Quartet was identified with the Beethoven quartets and *Grosse Fuge* more than with any other works. They were, as Mischa used to say, their "bread and butter."[26] Boris likened them to "the tragedies of Shakespeare, the novels of Dostoeivsky [sic], the shadow paintings of Rembrandt."

In the only article he ever authored, Boris described the Beethoven quartets as

> without a rival as disclosing the innermost musical thoughts of their composer. They are the reflection of a man and a spirit which, for some thirty years of activity, lived and struggled and was tormented to an extent rarely known in human life. They are the incomparable utterances of a fine soul impulsively eager to pour itself forth, to communicate its message, to become *en rapport* with fellow-men and lessen the burden which life imposes on so many individuals. They *may* mean something different to each person, but, again uniquely, they *can* mean something vital to every person.

Kroyt believed the Budapest's familiarity with the quartets made them "elusive." The more they played them, "the more they must be practised, for with every rehearsal comes a new revelation of beauty not previously perceived. It is in this sense that they are inexhaustible, a well-spring of aesthetic and emotional enjoyment of endless variety and satisfaction." Boris felt that "the greatest responsibility a chamber music group can undertake" is to play the Beethoven quartets. "There is no music more thrilling to the performer."[27]

The Budapest recorded on 78-rpm the Beethoven quartets they had not done for Victor, the entire cycle on long-playing discs when LPs were introduced in the 1950s and the cycle again in stereo in the 1960s. The Beethoven cycle recorded in the 1950s was made at the

Library of Congress using the Strads. The Quartet had broached
the idea for doing so in 1940, and the Library was agreeable, but
Columbia officials at the time felt that it might be too expensive to
lug the necessary recording equipment to Washington.[28] The Library
had its own facilities from 1941 on and began recording Budapest
concerts and other recitals held in Coolidge Auditorium on acetate
transcription discs, but its operations were solely for archival purposes.

Taking into account the works the Quartet recorded over a period of more than thirty-five years for HMV, Victor, and Columbia—
and not counting any that were done in more than one version—the
Budapest recorded and released eighty-nine different pieces; among
them, string quartets, piano quartets, cello quintets, clarinet quintets, and piano quintets with such guest artists as pianists Clifford
Curzon, Mieczysław Horszowski, Jesús Mariá Sanromá, and Rudolf
Serkin; violists Milton Katims and Walter Trampler; clarinetist
David Oppenheim; and cellist Benar Heifetz. The Quartet was for
many years Columbia's leading classical-music seller, and its records won a number of awards.

It was their growing success that prompted the members of the
Quartet to think that they might do better with an agent other than
Annie Friedberg. They had been with her eleven years when, in the
fall of 1941, they asked Arthur Judson, president of Columbia Concerts, whether he would take them on. Judson studied their booking
schedule and fee structure. "Your business," he informed them,
"shows a constant increase" with "an average price of better than
$400." He thought that "Miss Friedberg has done a first class job for
you. I do not know of any Quartet in the United States enjoying the
amount of business you now have and at the prices you get." Judson
said that he did not think he could do much better. "My advice is for
you to remain under her management and give her all possible support in booking more concerts for you and increasing your fees."[29]

With Judson's comments in mind, the Quartet signed a two-year
contract with Friedberg in the spring of 1942 that was the model for
their relations with her for the next twenty-five years. It stipulated
that she would not contract for any concerts for less than four hundred dollars a performance, or three hundred dollars in or near New
York City. She was to get 20 percent if the fee was above four hundred dollars, 10 percent if below that, only 5 percent for the Library
concerts, and nothing for the recitals for Mills College, which the
members arranged themselves. On the other hand, the Quartet
agreed to pay half the cost of advertisements, posters, circulars, and

publicity photographs, which Friedberg promised to circulate at her cost to at least a thousand concert managers and concert groups around the country.[30]

With the recording situation settled and their concern over Friedberg put to rest, the members should have been able to go about their concertizing and recording with no further worries. But that was not the case. They now faced the most serious crisis in their career together. Sasha wanted to quit.

11

Exit Sasha

The others—Joe, Boris, his own brother Mischa—were sure that Mrs. Coolidge was to blame. They all believed that she was trying to break up the Quartet, that she was jealous over its success, particularly because the quartets she sponsored—the Coolidge and the Berkshire—never did as well.

The truth is more complex than that. Mrs. Coolidge evidently heard the Budapest perform in the early 1930s, when Hauser was first violinist, and dismissed them out of hand at that time. She may, indeed, have envied the Quartet's meteoric rise in popularity after 1938, but she also appreciated their talents once they began playing at the Library of Congress and even tried to engage them to perform in Massachusetts. Writing to Roisman after hearing them play both at the 92nd Street Y in New York City and later at Ravinia in 1941, she said she "should love dearly" to have them repeat a series of Mozart concerts "for me some time." She realized, she said, that the Quartet was already signed for concerts "in my auditorium in Washington" and that Luther Marchant at Mills College did not like his summer artists appearing within a two-hundred-mile radius of the campus. But perhaps the Quartet could arrange to play a New England series that she would underwrite and offer free to the public.[1] The idea never worked out, though not for want of trying. Mrs. Coolidge contacted concert managers in a number of New England towns, but they were afraid free concerts by the Budapest would erode paying audiences for performances by other artists. None was interested in pursuing Mrs. Coolidge's idea—"which," she said, "I suppose, is natural, for fear of diminishing their sale of tickets."[2]

Joe, Boris, and Mischa correctly sensed a growing rapport between Mrs. Coolidge and Sasha. He was "my dear boy" to her.[3] She was his "goddess of chamber music"—"a friend, adviser and guide of my life."[4] He later would spend three weeks at her home in Pittsfield and got so accustomed, he wrote her, to going for drives with her and afterwards talking at length over dinner "that it was quite strange for me for the first few days in New York."[5] His letters to her, telling in detail about his plans, were signed "Your devoted, Alexander Schneider" and "I give you the heartiest kiss, yours always devoted."[6] The two most important influences who helped "to shape all my decisions as a human being and a musician," he told her, were "you and Pablo Casals."[7]

Sasha wanted to do so many things—all of them outside the Quartet's life. In the fall of 1941, harpsichordist Ralph Kirkpatrick performed a Bach concerto with the Budapest during a festival in Williamsburg, Virginia. Sasha and he struck up an immediate friendship. They played through almost all of the violin music in Thomas Jefferson's collection, enjoying the experience so much that they spent several weeks the next summer playing together at the home of a mutual friend. Mrs. Coolidge heard the two perform some Mozart sonatas and engaged them to play a concert at Harvard. It was Sasha's only public appearance outside the Quartet, and though he did not repeat it, he and Kirkpatrick continued to make music together for themselves and for friends. In the back of their minds was the thought of concertizing in public on a regular basis.

One of Sasha's other ambitions was to perform all of Bach's tremendously taxing unaccompanied violin sonatas. "I wanted very much . . . to do some different work other than just playing string quartets." He "didn't think the Budapest boys were quite right—you could play quartets and do other things at the same time." He was never "a 100 percent quartet player," Sasha declared, "but no one knew this, not even my brother."[8] But Mrs. Coolidge did. Recognizing Sasha's ambition and talent, Mrs. Coolidge counseled him to go off on his own, to be independent, to make all the music he wanted to make. "I don't think I have to tell you again," a grateful Sasha later wrote her, "how much you helped to shape my future and my career in helping me to make the decision, and giving me enough confidence, to leave the Budapest Quartet."[9]

There was another factor as well in Sasha's decision to leave the Quartet, one he did not admit to but was apparent to others. "Hello," he liked to answer the telephone, "this is the world's greatest second violinist."[10] It was meant as a joke, but it was a bittersweet one that hid the truth about the way he felt about himself.

Being second violinist—the second fiddle—has always carried with it a certain stigma. Historically, the second fiddler is often second-rate, not good enough to be first, the least competent player of the four members of a quartet, so weak a musician that he, or she, could not play first violin. And if he is a good musician, he is still usually considered to be what Boris called "a stepbrother who seldom has opportunity to show himself."[11] Who would want to be known as a second fiddle?

Sasha, moreover, felt stifled within the Quartet. The Budapest's rule against outside performances prevented him from exploring and experimenting with different musical experiences. And he also felt blocked by Roisman, who would not relinquish his seat when the Quartet played trios or piano quartets, which require only one violin. Joe would not switch chairs with him even at rehearsals, as the first and second violinists of the Flonzaley Quartet had.

Many years later, Sasha advised the members of the newly formed Guarneri Quartet, "Whenever you play string trios and piano quartets, make it a rule that the second violinist plays it and not the first violinist." Sasha's rationale was that if the second violinist did not get the opportunity to perform the first violin's part in a quartet, "he deteriorates in his playing."[12] It was "something very strange— if you play only second violin in a quartet and don't do anything else, you get stale for other things. Even first violin, when you play quartets you also get stale. It's very important to do some other things. . . . You can't play all the time the same thing. It's no good, it's not good for the music. It gets stale, it gets square."[13] He said it took him three years after leaving the Budapest Quartet "to get back to good playing condition."[14]

Ironically, Sasha really was the world's greatest second violinist; probably the greatest in the history of chamber music. He revolutionized the role that the second violin serves in chamber music, making it pivotal. Together with Kroyt, he made the middle voices of a quartet stand out as never before. He recognized that the Budapest was not, as virtually every other quartet before them, "just a star violinist combined with a frustrated second fiddle, a disappointed violist and an indifferent cellist."[15] The "most important voices" in a quartet, he wrote, "are the middle voices, which fill out and bring out the sound of a quartet to perfection, and if both of them are just as good musicians, then you have a first class quartet."[16]

Sasha never took credit for what he achieved, but colleagues were quick to praise him. Felix Galimir said he made "the stupidest" decision in his life when he was asked by Annie Friedberg whether he was interested in replacing Sasha. Galimir, then in the NBC orchestra, rejected the idea because he was "young." He had no idea then, he said, of the importance of the second violin in a quartet, even though he had a quartet of his own. "The first violin is the President of the United States, you know, he's the head, but the second violin is the general, he makes things happen. He has an enormous job." For Galimir, the Budapest was the "first 100 percent professional quartet, the landmark" for others, that underscored the importance of the middle voices as the mark of a great quartet. Sasha and Boris were

> aggressive, in a good sense, because the second violin is always in the worst register in order to match up with the brilliant register of the first violin. You have to overplay in a certain sense. If you don't do that, there is a hole in the middle voices. And so is the viola player—he's being overshadowed by the cellist. In my mind, the necessity in a really great quartet is the middle voices with a very firm sound, a little aggressive sound.[17]

Sasha wrestled with the idea of resigning from the Quartet for more than a year, but his actual decision when he made it was abrupt. The Quartet now faced the hurdle of informing the Music Division of the Library of Congress and Mrs. Whittall. The Library's concert season revolved around the Budapest's appearances and its use of the Strads she had donated.

"My brother informed today the Quartet that he wishes to be relieved of his duties as second violinist," Mischa wrote Harold Spivacke on November 26, 1943, while the Budapest was on tour in Omaha. "He feels that he wants to be independent. We have accepted his resignation."[18]

Spivacke was surprised, although earlier that year, Sasha's desire to quit had surfaced. Spivacke had taken him aside and had advised him against it. Sasha was thankful at the time. "I decided to stay with the Quartet and not to make any 'trouble' as you would say!" he informed Spivacke back in January 1943.[19] But the ever restless young Russian—he was only thirty-five years old—wanted "to be independent." After eleven years in the Budapest, he felt shackled. Encouraged by Mrs. Coolidge, he gave his Quartet colleagues several months to find a replacement. "I am sure you will understand my decision," Sasha explained to Spivacke; "as a matter of fact," alluding apparently to Mrs. Coolidge's support, "I have the feeling you know more about it than I do."[20]

Spivacke did not. Neither he nor anyone else at the Library had any idea that Sasha was still contemplating leaving. They were shaken. "The news," Spivacke's assistant, Ed Waters, wrote Mischa, "was tragic. Harold wants to know how soon you can run down to Washington so we can talk things over and discuss the situation from all angles. It's terribly important. . . . I don't suppose you like this turn of events any better than we do. Of course we are maintaining complete silence about it for the time being, and I am of the opinion that we shall all be better off if you can talk with us here before you begin looking for a substitute for Alex."[21]

The Quartet members, however, had no intention of bringing the Library into its selection of a new second violinist. "The concerts beginning in March and ending first of June 1944," Mischa informed Spivacke, "we shall play with a new second violinist. We do not know of course yet who the violinist will be but we can assure you that the artist will be one worthy of the name of the Budapest Quartet." Mischa said they had "several violinists in mind" whom they planned to contact when in New York, "and we hope by the time we arrive in Washington, in December, to know who will be our next colleague."[22]

On January 1, 1944, Mischa was happy to announce, "The birth has happened yesterday and we have a new violinist."[23]

Sasha never questioned the Budapest's wisdom in not allowing him to perform outside the Quartet. "I am the kind of man who couldn't stay," he told a reporter, "but the Budapest Quartet would have been something less than it is if I had stayed with it and even drawn a bow elsewhere."[24]

He was wrong about that. It was something less.

12

Second Fiddle Number One

The second violinist the Quartet members selected to replace Sasha seemed like a logical choice. He was the same musician Joe approached in 1936 about taking over the viola position, Edgar Ortenberg. It is interesting to speculate what might have happened to the Quartet had he become the violist, considering what did happen when he became the second violinist.

Ortenberg—thin, debonair, handsome, personable—was in his early forties, five weeks younger than Roisman and a product of the same early musical background. Like Joe, he had studied violin with Pyotr Stoliarsky, though he had trouble adjusting to the instrument because he could not stand "the scratching."[1] Unlike his fellow Odessans Joe and Boris, Ortenberg came from a well-to-do family; his father had been a director of a bank. That made the war years, the Russian Revolution, and the aftermath of those upheavals seem more of a hardship to a young man accustomed to comfort and ease. To keep warm, his father had burned books in a stove in the living room, and the family had slept with their coats on. One day, the floor had turned to ice after being washed with soap and water. Perhaps as a result of the stress of years of deprivation and anxiety, Ortenberg began to go bald at the age of nineteen.

Upon graduation from the Odessa Conservatory in 1921—winning the gold medal after studying with Naoum Blinder—Ortenberg was immediately hired to teach there. He became a member of a faculty quartet and replaced Roisman as concertmaster of the

Odessa Opera Orchestra when Roisman left to tour Russia. To make ends meet, he also taught in Moscow and for an annex of the Moscow Conservatory in Odessa. Finally, "after seven years of starvation," Ortenberg decided in 1924 to go to Berlin to improve himself as a musician—a decision that led fatefully to the same peregrinations Joe, the Schneiders, and Boris experienced, with some variations.

After three sleepless nights on a train, Ortenberg arrived in Berlin, his violin in one hand, a suitcase in the other, and one dollar in his pocket. He knew no one there and could not speak German. By happenstance, the train station was two blocks away from the Hochshule für Musik. As he walked by it, he heard music coming from an open window. Ortenberg went in and was able, with the help of a student who spoke Russian, to arrange an audition with its director, Willi Hess. He was accepted on the spot as a scholarship student and taken into Hess's home as well.

As was the case with the Schneiders and so many other Jewish musicians, Ortenberg changed his name. Not Ortenberg—that "was good German." Rather, his first name, which was Eleazer and decidedly Hebraic. Eleazar Ortenberg was now Edgar Ortenberg. He then started his own quartet, which was called, with the mayor's official approval, the Berliner Streichquartett (the Berlin String Quartet), though only one of its players was German. The ensemble toured throughout Europe until 1933, when Hitler came to power. Soon afterward, Ortenberg was listening to the radio when a concert of his ensemble was advertised. He listened in stunned silence as the players' names were announced. They were four musicians he had never heard of. Ortenberg sought out the local minister of culture, an old friend, who told him, "Forget we are friends. I am Professor Havemann and you are the Jew from the East. I give you good advice: Leave."

Edgar took the advice. In July 1933 he and his wife of four years, Tamara, a cellist whose family had escaped from the Soviet oil city of Baku, moved to Paris. Ortenberg was no stranger to the city. He had gone there in 1927 to study with Jacques Thibaud. He soon was hired by the Russian Conservatory in Paris and formed what was called, through a phonetic interpretation of his name, the Quator Ortambert. After two summers spent rehearsing, the ensemble toured France, Italy, Belgium, and Holland with some measure of success. He was, in fact, performing with it when Joe Roisman first contacted him about joining the Budapest Quartet as its violist.

For all intents and purposes, Ortenberg started to consider himself French. In 1937, he became a naturalized French citizen, and so, of course, when war threatened two years later, he was drafted into the French army. He was assigned to the intelligence service because he spoke both German and Russian, but he still had to carry a rifle in training. Afraid that he might injure his hands, he wore gloves in the field. When an officer questioned him about them, he explained that he was a violinist. The officer arranged for Ortenberg to play for other officers and their wives and for another soldier to carry his gun.

Ortenberg was discharged in April 1940 because of illness. He returned to Tamara in Paris, but with the German army advancing upon it, they decided to flee. They left just in time, barely twelve hours before the Germans entered the city. The Ortenbergs walked all the way to Marseilles and eventually were able to get to Portugal. There they had to share a room with other families while they waited for a Jewish agency to arrange their transportation to America. They finally left for the United States on what turned out to be the last Spanish ship to leave Portugal.

New York was a safe haven but no paradise. Ortenberg struggled to make a living. He taught violin to the children of French Jewish émigrés and tried to form a quartet but could not find anyone willing to spend the necessary six months of daily practice before performing in public. Fortunately, he was able to get a union card with the help of a friend, Vladimir Golschmann, conductor of the St. Louis Symphony, and was subsequently hired to play with the WQXR radio orchestra. When Joe Roisman contacted him—for the second time—about joining the Budapest, he seized the opportunity without thinking through the decision's consequences.

Edgar auditioned for the Quartet in December 1943, playing with Joe, Mischa, and Boris for two days and almost two nights in a room at the Great Northern Hotel in New York. On New Year's Eve, Joe phoned him from Washington. "Is this the second violinist of the Budapest String Quartet?" Joe asked. "Not like the first time, switching to the viola," Joe made a point of adding. Edgar—with Tamara's approval this time—eagerly accepted.

Edgar was not scheduled to join the Quartet on stage until the 1944 spring round of concerts at the Library of Congress. Meanwhile, the Budapest, with Sasha still in the second-violin chair, was on tour in the Midwest. During a break in their traveling, they returned to New York, where Joe, Mischa, and Boris sat down with Edgar and began to go over their repertoire. "We just finished our two first rehearsals of the Op. 18.3," Mischa hastened to assure Spivacke at the Library of Congress. "I just can tell you that we are going to have a very good violinist in our Quartet."[2] Even Sasha found it necessary to allay Spivacke's concerns. Ortenberg, he wrote, was "a very good violinist *really*."[3]

By late February, when the Quartet was back on tour, Edgar was in Washington, practicing on the Betts Strad at the Library. It took him three weeks to get accustomed to it. "It wasn't used to sleeping with me. It took a week or two till it started to kiss you."[4] By the time the others got to Washington in early March, there was not much time left to prepare for the first three quartets of the Beethoven cycle that was planned for six repeat-night concerts between that month and May. Spivacke had not been eager to do the cycle, but Mischa persuaded him that it was important to the Quartet that Edgar learn to perform all seventeen works with them.

Ortenberg was beside himself. He had never played second violin before. For another thing, like many other quartet players, he had never performed the difficult late Beethovens. It was the Budapest that had resurrected them from almost total ignominy and made them part of their standard fare. "Late Beethoven came into my life with the Budapest. I knew them from listening, but now I had to study scores." There were rehearsals on Monday, Tuesday, and Wednesday before Edgar's debut on Thursday, March 9, 1944. "I was scared and I told them my behind, its nerves are naked. Whereas they know ahead of time whomever will do whatever. I was very nervous."

Despite Edgar's worrying, the first concert—of Beethoven's Quartet in D, Opus 18, No. 3; the Quartet in F Minor, Opus 95; and the E-flat, Opus 127—was a resounding success. The critic for the Washington *Post* said it would "take time to become accustomed to the altered personnel," but Sasha's successor "fits so adaptably into the ensemble, however, that the fused tone sounded the same."[5] Alice Eversman noted in the *Evening Star* that the Budapest had "adjusted the volume and spirit of their performance somewhat" to account for "the lyric quality" of Edgar's tone. "The result was polished and interpretively understanding." The second concert in the cycle brought kudos, too. Eversman thought it was "one of the finest this famous group of musicians has presented."[6] Glenn Dillard Gunn in the *Times-Herald* said the Budapest members "play the music of Beethoven with far greater authority today than when they first came to us."[7] Everyone forgave an error in the third concert, when the Budapest began the popular Quartet in E Minor, Opus 59, No. 2. Edgar, used to playing first violin in his own quartet, came in on the first-violin part, much to his embarrassment. But Joe laughed, and so did the audience, and the Quartet simply started the piece again.[8] After the final concerts in the cycle, Gunn declared that "technically it has been an achievement of the greatest brilliance."[9]

Reviewers in other cities felt the same way—at first. A San Francisco critic called Edgar "clearly a violinist of exceptional authority and musicianship."[10] An Oakland reviewer quoted a sailor in the audience as saying the Quartet was "right in the groove." Its playing, the reviewer agreed, "is unexcelled for smooth blending and sympathetic interpretation."[11] "What has not changed," said a Chicago critic, "is the perfection which distinguishes the playing."[12] A reviewer on a rival newspaper in that city said that "fortunately" Ortenberg "fits without audible wrinkles into an ensemble America wisely has learned to cherish."[13]

Only one critic was less than enthusiastic. "If any criticism is to be made of him, it is that his playing is a bit too modest. . . . He is supposed to speak up . . . sometimes as the equal of his fellows, sometimes as their momentary soloist."[14]

Edgar's colleagues agreed. "They wanted me to play louder. I said, 'I am sorry. I play violin.'" His sound was "softer," he admitted, "more, should I use the word, 'delicate'?" Edgar felt the others "had to adjust not to be so rough."[15]

As far as the public knew, the Quartet was performing without hitches. "The story is told—and it may or may not be apocryphal," said an Indianapolis critic,

> that Bernard Shaw, after hearing Heifetz, told the violinist that the perfection of his playing bordered on the "unhuman," and that, to correct a perfection that well-nigh amounted to a flaw, Heifetz should go home and play at least one wrong note every night before retiring. One might almost wish that the Budapest String Quartet . . . might likewise go home and play a few phrases badly each night. . . . Haydn, Schubert and Beethoven were supreme geniuses, and they need comparable Titans to interpret them. The Titans are to be found in the Budapesters.[16]

Even those who had reservations about Edgar could say, as a Chicago reviewer had, that "incidentally, [he] has now improved over previous appearances so that he is an integral part of the ensemble."[17]

Edgar, though, was complaining that the Quartet did not rehearse enough. "I wanted to rehearse more and play more and to know them more and more." The situation got worse as one concert season blended into the next. "Boris would always put sticks in the wheels—to stop the motion of the cart. He didn't want to rehearse. He was too lazy to get up and rehearse."[18]

Mischa, meanwhile, was distracted. After fourteen years as a bachelor, he was getting married, for the third time. While the Quartet was in residence at Mills College in the summer of 1947, he met June Holden, a student who was working as a lifeguard, and married her there; he was forty-two at the time; she, twenty-four. It was an awkward situation. In attendance at the wedding was Mischa's daughter Natasha, who was married at the time to the son of composer Vittorio Rieti. Natasha, only five years younger than June, was visibly pregnant with Mischa's first grandson.[19]

It took Edgar two years before he said he felt somewhat comfortable playing with the other members of the Quartet, before he "knew exactly before, a few minutes before, some particular place would come, I would know—would feel—how they would phrase."[20]

By then, however, the others were having serious misgivings. They complained that Edgar was not practicing enough on his own. Boris said Edgar's hand would shake or tremble while playing. "Every performance," said Boris, "was just a collapse."[21] They urged Edgar to practice scales. He was so nervous, Mischa said, that "with him, you could hear it. It was a shame. People used to come to us and tell us, 'What are you doing? Why are you playing with him? Look for someone else.' It was no secret about it."[22]

Even the critics eventually picked up the signs. "The violin side of the ensemble was decidedly uncertain," Irving Kolodin wrote in the New York *Sun* after a Town Hall concert in November 1945.[23] B. H. Haggin in the *Nation*, said that there "can be no doubt of the loss to the quartet through Alexander Schneider's departure. One hears it in the altered sound of the entire group, in which the robust and dark-toned viola and cello are less well balanced by the two delicate and light-toned violins than they used to be. . . . And one hears it in Ortenberg's own playing, which lacks the vitality and style Schneider's had." And yet, Haggin acknowledged,

> the performances are unique, unapproached by others. One must, in fact, say of them what one says of Toscanini's—that they are not just great performances, or the greatest one has heard, but that in their province they are something on a different level of functioning from the best of other good performers and musicians, a product of a different order of powers of musical insight and execution. One must say this even though the performances are uneven these days—possibly as a result of fatigue and staleness from too much playing the last few years.[24]

For Ortenberg, fatigue was the culprit. He complained not only about the lack of rehearsal time but also that their concert schedule was too crowded and exhausting. He counted only twenty-three times that he had slept in his own bed at home during one twelve-month period.[25] The demand for the Quartet had, in fact, become so great that they upped their fee to eight hundred dollars a concert in 1946 and, at the same time, cut the agent's fee they paid Annie Friedberg from 20 percent to 10 percent. And Friedberg, without flinching or bothering to consult the members of the Quartet, rejected an offer that year from a Hollywood producer for the Quartet to appear in the movie *Carnegie Hall*. The offer was for three days' work—one day's recording, and two days' shooting—twenty-five hundred dollars. "I simply laughed when I got this letter!" she wrote Mischa. "I told him that I thought that this was a mistake, that perhaps he meant $25,000."[26]

The Quartet was so busy that Edgar claimed it was performing two hundred concerts a year, appeared in as many as twenty-three concerts in sixteen days, and had on three consecutive Sundays played four recitals in one day. Those figures are exaggerations, though there is some foundation for them. No complete schedule or set of programmes exists, but evidently the Budapest Quartet was performing close to a hundred twenty-five concerts a year. Travel in the 1940s was still a hectic mix of slow train and car trips—constant shuffling from one city to the next, from the East Coast to the West Coast and back, and at Mills (in Oakland) and Ravinia (outside Chicago) in the summer—so the four musicians always seemed to be on the road when they were not actually performing. At one point, Roisman estimated that the Quartet had played in six hundred cities, but that may have been an exaggeration, too, unless their travels abroad are counted. On at least one Sunday the Quartet did perform three times in the New York area—in the morning in Westchester County, in the afternoon at the Frick Collection, and in the evening at Town Hall.[27] There was talk sometime in 1946 or 1947 of cutting back the number of concerts they played to one hundred a year, but Boris and Mischa were against doing so. Carnegie Tech wanted them to be quartet-in-residence, to teach and play at the school, but they rejected that, too.[28]

The situation came to a head in the late fall of 1948. Roisman was so upset at Edgar's playing that he thought—despite what the critics wrote—that the Quartet was playing "like pigs."[29] While the Budapest was on tour in the South, Boris and Mischa took Edgar aside and told him the Quartet had begun looking for a new second violinist. His reaction, said Mischa, was "terrible."[30]

Edgar remembers it otherwise. "Joe had told me several times that the Budapest had not played as well as it had with me." Even Mischa and Boris, he said, always praised him. Edgar could not figure out what had gone wrong. He said he was offered no reason for the change of heart, nor did he ask for one: "When you're divorced, you're divorced. I felt I was not desired any more."[31]

Officially, it was given out that Ortenberg was leaving the Quartet because of exhaustion due to the heavy tour schedule. He was immediately swamped with offers from universities and was attached for thirty-five years to the Settlement Music School in Philadelphia before his retirement as head of the chamber-music department in 1984. He also taught at Temple University between 1953 and 1978 and was chairman of both its string and chamber-music departments.

Someone, meanwhile, had to inform Spivacke of the intended change. Joe, Mischa, and Boris hesitated. Better to tell him after they had found someone to replace Edgar. There was a young violinist whom they had thought of back in 1943 but had not approached because he was then in another quartet and they had not wanted to break it up by luring him away.

"What I am going to tell you may and may not be a surprise to you," Joe wrote Spivacke finally in mid-January 1949:

> I am sure you must have known that we had our difficulties with Edgar. For five years we have given him every chance to improve. We warned him year after year that if he is not going to start practicing in earnest some day there will be an end to it. Unfortunately, he did not take that advice seriously and we felt now that we can not go on playing with him any longer. It was imperative to the three of us and for the life of the Quartet to have a new second violinist.[32]

Edgar would remain with the Budapest through March 10, 1949, when the Quartet was to perform at Cornell. After that, Joe said, the new second violinist would be "exactly what we wanted." His name was Jac Gorodetzky. Would Spivacke mind scheduling the Beethoven cycle again at the Library that spring "because we are working on them right now and because we are going to play them also at Mills later in the summer"?[33]

The choice of Gorodetzky was a tragic one—for Gorodetzky.

13

Second Fiddle Number Two

Mischa should have suspected something when he met Daniel Guilet on a street in Manhattan one day shortly after Gorodetzky joined the Quartet. Jac had played for several years as second violinist in Guilet's string quartet. "I hope," the French violinist told Mischa, "you are not going to have any trouble with him." Mischa thought Guilet's reference to "trouble" might have been an allusion to the Quartet's previous difficulties with Ortenberg. He did not understand Guilet's remark at first but "slowly found out."[1]

Technically speaking, Gorodetzky was yet another Russian from Odessa. He was, after all, born there, just before World War I. But there any resemblance in background ended. He could not even speak Russian, nor was he at all demonstrative, as Russians can be. He was, first and foremost, American by upbringing and French in musical schooling.[2] He exuded what was mistaken for almost-youthful awe by his famed new colleagues in the Budapest String Quartet. The awe masked a fragile personality.

He was a middle-sized man, the most Semitic looking of the Quartet members, with a slightly larger than ordinary nose, and a face, otherwise, that bordered on the cherubic, especially behind the glasses he wore. He was a friendly man, the father of two daughters, and liked to swim and play tennis. Jac was in his mid-thirties when he joined the Quartet, some ten years younger than Mischa, fourteen years Joe's junior, seventeen years younger than Boris. The three of them had been playing together for almost two decades; he had performed in quartets with other string players for barely half that time. Somehow he seemed a generation and a world of experience apart. But why he doubted himself as a musician is unclear. No member of the Quartet ever questioned his talent or ability. Boris thought Jac was a much better violinist than Ortenberg "and sometimes even played better than Roisman."[3] What is certain is that Boris and Mischa and Joe never fully comprehended how profound his insecurity was.

Jac was the middle of five children of his parents—the father was a scholar; the mother, an innkeeper. Pogroms prompted the family to flee Russia when he was one year old. They went to London, where the oldest of the children, Aaron, a violinist who was more than fifteen years older than Jac, supported the family. The Gorodetzkys were able to emigrate before America entered the war and settled in Philadelphia, were Aaron got a position with the Philadelphia Symphony. Jac began to study music at about the age of eight, when Aaron purchased an instrument for him. The young boy studied at the Settlement Music School, and while in high school he became concertmaster of the City Symphony Orchestra.

The Settlement School's founder, Blanche Kohn, took a personal interest in Jac, underwriting his studies with André Tourret at the National Conservatory in Paris, where Jac won top prizes for his playing in 1935 and 1936—at the very time that Boris Kroyt first joined the Budapest Quartet in Paris.

Jac returned home to become a member of the Philadelphia String Art Quartet, and on a Wednesday afternoon in mid-April 1937 he debuted as a soloist in Town Hall in New York City. "Either by the dictates of temperament, his recent French schooling, or both, Mr. Gorodetzky's style tends toward the small scaled and over-refined," the review in the *New York Times* read the next day. Jac was lauded for his "sensitive and conscientious musicianship," but the reviewer said that he "is still a young man whose definite style has surely not been reached." His qualities, it was apparent, "fit him admirably for a chamber musician."[4] Reading between the lines of those remarks, it is clear that the reviewer thought that Jac's French sound—of the same "delicate" genre Ortenberg displayed—was not robust enough for a soloist's career but would adapt well in small ensembles.

The review was evidently a major factor in Jac's deciding not to pursue a solo career. He started looking for work in New York and elsewhere. Hearing that the Cleveland Symphony Orchestra was auditioning, he went there and won a position with it. He settled in the city and there married a young violist named Harriet, who was nicknamed Honey.

When America entered World War II, Jac was drafted into a unit based in Boca Raton, Florida, where B-17 bombers were assembled and outfitted with secret Norden bombsights. By happenstance, his unit's captain was an amateur trumpet player and a frustrated conductor. He went around the country recruiting musicians for his unit from dance bands and symphony orchestras; they signed on as bakers, cooks, and what-have-yous. Thus, he was able to assemble a full symphony orchestra. The captain conducted it in concerts at the base all during the war, evidently without anyone the wiser or any complaints.

After Jac's discharge from the army, he joined the Guilet Quartet and played with them for about three years and also for the CBS Symphony Orchestra.

There was no indication, apart from Guilet's misunderstood remark to Mischa, that there was anything amiss. He auditioned well for the Budapest, and Joe reportedly felt right off that he fit in to the Quartet like he had played with them all along.

The critics agreed. "The combined tone," said Paul Hume in the Washington *Post* after Jac joined the Budapest at the Library for the first time in March 1949, "is velvety where past months have found it a bit brittle. Their intonation is again immaculate, where last year it was hazardous. . . . Beyond that, it is something like reviewing Heifetz: what is there to say? . . . The music could hardly have been played more perfectly."[5]

Mischa agreed that all was going well—in fact, he was ecstatic, writing Spivacke that a series of concerts at the 92nd Street Y in the fall of 1949 were "a great success, everybody says that since Alex' departure the Quartet never sounded like that and the series are packed. We are very happy with Jac."[6] Encouraged by the reviews the Quartet was getting and responding to the note of confidence in Mischa's report, Spivacke offered the Quartet a three-year contract for sixty concerts at the Library.[7]

The Quartet's reception around the country seemed like a case of *déjà vu*, bringing to mind the reviews it received when Edgar Ortenberg initially joined the Quartet. "The Budapest ensemble was in top form, magnificently integrated," wrote the critic in the Miami *Herald*.[8] "Over the years," a Pittsburgh reviewer said. "I can think of no other ensemble that so consistently gives performances of chamber music of such high caliber."[9] Another in Buffalo called Jac "a sympathetic addition to the ensemble."[10] His "alto quality," said a

Louisville critic, "provides better balance to Mr. Roisman's soprano than did the tone of the last incumbent."[11] A year later, another Louisville critic congratulated the Quartet on finding "in Jac Gorodetzky a second violinist remarkably equipped to join their ranks. This is his second year with the group, and his violin is now completely integrated with the other strings."[12] The critic of the Ithaca *Journal* waxed, "A string quartet, unlike Gertrude Stein's rose, is not necessarily merely a string quartet. When, for example, it happens to be the Budapest String Quartet, it is something like poetry, for which no words are quite enough. . . ."[13]

"Chamber music used to be strictly high-brow country," *Time* magazine reported in August 1951, after the Budapest Quartet appeared at Ravinia, "nowadays it is close to becoming a U.S. fad. One of the best examples of the current trend: the steadily increasing popularity of the Budapest String Quartet."[14] The Budapest that summer had played four concerts at Ravinia with pianist William Kapell, attracting fifteen thousand people. In the concert season that followed in the fall, two series by the Quartet outstripped in attendance every other series at the 92nd Street Y by a margin of at least five to one. Their ten concerts drew more than six thousand people, an average of more than six hundred per concert. The New Music Quartet drew an average of a hundred twenty persons for its five concerts, and a quartet that Sasha Schneider had formed attracted only 146 persons for each of sixteen performances in a Haydn series.[15] The Budapest subscriptions cost $10, or $2.40 to $3 per recital, twice as much as the Y was charging for the other groups.[16]

When the war had ended, Europe and Japan had beckoned. The Quartet members had been unanimous about refusing to consider returning to Germany to play. The Schneiders had found out that their mother and sister had died in Auschwitz in November 1944. Until then, said Mischa, "I did not believe in the atrocities the Germans have committed. It is incredible that human beings can come down to such barbarism."[17] Sasha had been appalled that anyone would even consider returning to Germany, or Austria for that matter. "I have never been able to understand how European Jews, who were thrown out of Europe by the Nazis and who, in many cases, lost friends and relatives in the Holocaust, could go back to Germany to play or to conduct as soon as the war was over."[18] Afraid of bringing up a child in Germany, Pola Roisman had had several abortions when the Quartet had been based in Berlin in the early 1930s and, as a result, could not afterwards conceive; so both she and Joe had had their own reason for resenting the country.[19]

So the 1950 Budapest tour, its first on the Continent and in England in eleven years, focused on Switzerland, Italy, France, Holland, Scotland, and London. There were twenty-eight concerts in Europe and England, a score more in South America—all crammed into their already-heavy U.S. round of tours. It is no wonder that Joe, Mischa, and Boris were too busy to pay attention to the danger signals arising.

It is easy to call Jac's problem a simple case of stage fright. But every performer has that to some degree; without it, a musician will tell you, a performance has no edge. "There is no one who goes out on the stage in cold blood," according to Mischa. "You have to have a little of this excitement in order to perform."[20] Boris felt the same way. "All musicians have to be somehow temperamental if they are good musicians. How can you be neutral when you perform? It never hurts to have a little bit stage fright always."[21]

But Jac's nervousness went beyond normal. It manifested itself dramatically by his refusal to step out on stage. Mischa said they almost had to drag him out. Jac got "uptight, more than he should have been," recalled an aide at the Library of Congress who worked backstage on concert nights.[22] "It got worse and worse," said Mischa. "He had anxiety—nerve anxieties." Once, on tour, Jac telephoned Mischa in his hotel room on the afternoon of a concert in which they were to play a Brahms quartet that they had performed with Jac "innumerable times" and which Jac had performed with the Guilet Quartet. "You know, we would travel, arrive somewhere, lie down on the bed to have a rest," Mischa said. "He would call up, 'I have to have a rehearsal to play the Brahms.' 'But Jac, we played it so many times.' He said, 'We don't rehearse, I can't go out on the stage. I can't remember how to do this or do that.' And we had to do it."

"We played with Jac the first concert of the Beethoven cycle in New York," Mischa continued. "Afterwards I came to the hotel and I found the message. Jac said, 'Mischa, I'm not going to play the concert tonight and don't try to get me, don't try to talk to me that I should go out because when you are going to be in the hotel I will be already on my way to Washington, to be with my family.' And we had to cancel the concert."[23]

In hindsight, Boris thought Jac was confused and not strong enough to express his own opinion—to "expose himself," as he put it. The difficulty began with a problem all quartets have in breaking in a new member.

You know, when a new member comes he has to adjust himself. See, our quartet, I must admit, it's not a very flexible quartet. What they know, what they learn, they never changed. Or it took them a long time until they changed something. So, it was always a big problem if a new member came to the Quartet. He had to adjust himself. Now, the characteristic of each player is different, as you can imagine. The technique is different and all that, so there is a problem.

Roisman, said Boris, was chiefly to blame. "He's the worst teacher in the whole world. He doesn't know how to explain something or how to tell you something, how to execute these things." Roisman, Boris said, would tell Jac "'You have to play this way so.' Mischa said to him, 'You have to play—.' Now he was sitting there like a nebbish and didn't know what to do, you know. So when it came to performance he was so nervous he couldn't play. He never could perform anything properly." Boris said, Jac "thought that what we are doing is right and what everything he is doing is wrong. But this wrongness comes only because he was unsure of himself. Was so unsure of himself that every performance he was insecure."[24]

Howard Scott, who was supervising the Budapest's recording of the Beethoven cycle on the Strads at the Library, thought the problem was one of background. Jac "was not of the same piece of cloth." Scott said the others did take the time to explain such musical matters as phrasing and tempo variations to Jac. "They were nice—said, 'Here's the way we play this.' They explained, discussed, were not overbearing."[25]

Mischa thought that once Jac was on stage—once he was sitting—his doubts were disspelled. "Then he played. But it was the preliminaries. Can you imagine to be with a colleague for years and always not knowing is he going or is he not going to play?"[26]

Jac, like Ortenberg before him, complained that the Quartet members would not rehearse enough with him, especially on the Beethoven cycle. "He was scared to death," according to a friend who knew him when he was in the CBS Symphony Orchestra.[27] Honey Gorodetzky approached Joe, Mischa, and Boris separately to plead with them to rehearse more with her husband. "He doesn't need the rehearsal," she was told by each of them. "He doesn't need to go through it. Look how he plays!" Jac, she said, eventually "hated to go out on stage."[28]

If the others—Joe, Mischa, Boris—were not as alert or responsive as they should have been to Jac's increasing desperation, one answer might be that the Quartet faced what appeared to be a more pressing crisis while on a tour of Japan in 1952—what was afterwards called "The Night We Lost Roisman."[29]

The Quartet arrived in Tokyo on August 31. The "misgivings" they had about how they would be received—they were the first quartet to tour Japan since the end of World War II—were quickly disspelled. To their astonishment they were greeted by a banner, "Welcome, Budapest Quartet," at the airport, and as they deplaned, four Japanese girls bearing flowers presented bouquets to each member, a ritual that was repeated in every city they went to. Although there were only two or three chamber-music societies in the country, tickets for their thirteen concerts and two nationwide broadcasts had been gobbled up within two hours of going on sale. The opening concert in Hibiya Public Hall in Tokyo drew nearly three thousand "cheering" people, including Prince and Princess Takamatsu. Students, in particular, flocked to their performances, music scores in hand. Of the five program choices the Quartet offered, the most propular included Mozart's "Hunt" Quartet, Schubert's "Death and the Maiden" and Beethoven's Opus 59, No. 3. But there were requests, too, for Bartók's Quartet No. 2, which surprised the Quartet. The Japanese were "music hungry," said Mischa.[30] A fan wrote his thanks for their giving him what he called a "deep impression of music."[31] Another, an excitable student, said, "You made me like a mad girl."[32] It was heady stuff, an experience none of them ever forgot. "We felt like prima donnas," Mischa recalled. "After each concert we returned with our arms filled with flowers."[33]

The tour was sponsored by the Broadcasting Corporation of Japan (NHK), which assigned four men to accompany the Quartet members. One attended to their luggage, a second handled their hotel and travel arrangements, a third took care of money matters, and a fourth, American Marcel Grilli, acted as their interpreter. Wherever they went—Nagoya, Osaka, Kyoto—they were chaffeured from hotel to concert hall to restaurant to hotel. They felt cramped, so one night in the second week of September—"a beautiful, cool" evening—after playing a concert in Okayama, "we said," Mischa recalled, "'Let us go once, walk.'"[34] They started walking back to their hotel. It was dark out, and soon Mischa and Jac had gotten well ahead of Boris and Joe. The latter two were walking along the narrow road when the headlights of an oncoming car came into view. As it drew closer, Boris stepped slightly aside onto the shoulder of the road and continued walking and talking. Just behind him, Joe stepped too far to the left and fell into the black hole of a nine-foot irrigation ditch. Boris did not even realize what had happened until he was several yards away. He called, "Joe? Joe?" then cautiously started back along the road. Joe was crumpled at the bottom of the ditch. His left wrist—his fingering hand—was broken.

The Japanese wanted to take Roisman to a local hospital, but the Budapest members insisted on rushing him to the American military hospital in Tokyo, where his wrist was set.

Mischa wrote Spivacke, to alert him of the possibility that the Quartet might not be able to meet its initial 1952 commitments at the Library. Not realizing the extent of the injury, Mischa described the wrist as "bruised." The doctor, he said, told him that "Joe would not be able to play for at least one month." He asked Spivacke not to tell Pola Roisman "about it, if you can avoid, because Joe is very worried about Paula's knowing about it until he arrives."[35]

Pola was shocked when the four Quartet members stepped from the plane in Washington. Joe's arm was in a sling. Moreover, when they went to his doctor to check on the cast, they learned that the wrist had not been set properly. Three weeks after the accident, the wrist had to be broken again and reset. Now it was not a question of whether it would be a month, or maybe two, before Joe returned to the Quartet but rather whether he would ever be able to play the violin again.

In his quiet way, however, Joe was undaunted. While Mischa, Boris, and Jac hastily switched the Quartet's scheduled programs to trios and piano quartets, Joe began a painful effort to regain mobility in his fingers. The cast came off in late September, but Joe was unable to lift the violin, so Pola put it under his chin and held it up for him so he could try to play. At first the fingers of his left hand pointed upwards stiffly. "It was terrible," said Joe. "I had to start from scratch."[36]

Meanwhile, worried about the implications to their concert bookings, none of the Quartet members talked about the seriousness of Joe's injury. "'Twas a well-kept dark secret!" reported the magazine *String Player*.[37] That is hard to believe. The Budapest had to cancel a Beethoven cycle at the 92nd Street Y that fall, and the Quartet broke previous practice and played trios and piano quartets. It had never before switched its programs to such works, even when one of the members had suddenly became ill. Artur Balsam and Mieczysław Horszowski were repeatedly joining Mischa, Boris, and Jac in recitals. But no one suspected how critical the problem was.

By rearranging their programs, the others were able to salvage most of their scheduled recitals. Writing for the Washington *Evening Star*, Elena de Sayn, herself a violinist, expressed gratitude for hearing a Reger trio, which offers, she said, "often-needed variety in program building. It is too bad that only an accident should be responsible for its performance."[38] Paul Hume in the *Post* said that Gorodetzky "moved into the first chair with an ease that reminded us of the fact that any violinist playing second violin in the Budapest Quartet must be an all-around first-class player."[39] But Alice Eversman of the *Evening Star* was not as generous in her review of a subsequent concert at the Library: "His tone has not the lyric quality of Mr. Roisman's to offset the darker hued instruments," though she conceded that "some slips from accurate intonation and occasional blurring of rapid passages . . . may have been due to the tension of the occasion."[40] Joe was in the audience that night.

It took four months of hard work and an iron will, practicing scales and études, until "finally," Joe said, "my hand was all right."[41] Miraculously, he was back in the first chair for the start of a Beethoven cycle in Portland, Oregon, on January 12, 1953, without any indication that his injury had marred his playing. "For all their time together," the *Oregonian* critic said, "there is no hint of aging in the Budapest ensemble. They are as alive, as intent, as assertive and free as youngsters."[42] Mischa's assessment to Spivacke was that the concert was "alright. Joe has the most terrific determination. He played very well and one would not know that he had the accident." Mischa said that "nobody except the manager knows of his accident." However, Mischa asked if the Budapest could switch a piece in an upcoming Library program from a Křenek quartet to a Rieti, because "Joe feels it will be too much studying for him with the Schönberg and Martinů. The Rieti is much easier than the Křenek."[43]

By the next month, February, Mischa was exuberant about Joe's recovery. "Joe is his old self, quiet, composed and not a trace of his accident," he wrote from Chicago to the Library of Congress.[44] And in March, in Huntington, West Virginia, the cellist was positively jovial:

> The Opera is in full swing. Yesterday they played "The Naked Spur" with the famous basso Jimmy Stewart in the "role," on the other side of the street the Philharmonic Symphony Society performed with Marilyn Monroe as conductor. . . . To-night our band is performing the new hits: Beethoven, Mozart and Ravel. . . . Speaking of hits—I want to remind you (I know how excited you will be!) that our band will soon invade the Music Division.[45]

That May, the Quartet signed another three-year contract with the Library.

Obviously, the crisis with Joe kept Jac's difficulty under temporary control. But as soon as Joe returned and all seemed back to normal, Jac's condition began to worsen. By the time the Quartet returned to Japan—in January 1954—he was almost in a state of paralysis, and the tension was spreading to the others. They all got lost in the last movement of Bartók's Quartet No. 5 when performing at a college outside Boston. "We were sort of swimming," said Mischa. The audience was unaware of the problem and eventually "we came together, we found ourselves. But after that, we never played that quartet again. It was really just that something like this should not happen to a quartet."[46]

Maybe people in the audience were not aware of the difficulties Jac was causing, but newspaper critics had already been picking up the fact that something was wrong. "Budapest Would Not Be Proud / Quartet Not at Best Here" was the headline in a Pittsburgh paper.[47] "Budapest Group Uninspired in Mozart Offering" ran a headline in the Washington *Times-Herald*.[48] A Chicago reviewer thought their Mendelssohn "was rather a solemn performance, coarse grained to suggest that the hall's acoustics had overblown the sound."[49]

The second Japanese tour in 1954 was more extensive than their first visit sixteen months earlier. It included five concerts they had missed because of Joe's accident and twenty-two others as well, not to mention a command performance for the Empress in the Imperial Palace. They were to visit twenty-one cities in all. Seven concerts were scheduled in Tokyo alone. The enthusiasm of their first tour in 1952 was echoed multifold. "String quartet music had been regarded as recondite art in Japan," Marcel Grilli wrote in the *Nippon Times*. "Suffice it to say, that in their wake the Budapest String Quartet stimulated a striking upsurge of activities on the local scene in this medium of music expression." Grilli singled out for praise the Quartet's choice to play quartets by Samuel Barber, Darius Milhaud, as well as Bartók. "Anywhere in the world, but especially in Japan which is still in its chyrsalis state of classicism, such a program would serve as an eye-opener to the richness and fecundity of contemporary music. . . . In retrospect, it becomes especially commendable that a group like the Budapest String Quartet should devote so much attention to modern music."[50] Klaus Pringsheim in the *Mainichi* said that "thousands of Japanese music lovers" were "waiting for an opportunity to get some of the great masterpieces of chamber music performed in a model fashion." He noted that a "mounting interest in chamber musical events (and of *ad hoc*–organized groups of instrumentalists) has of late been noticeable."[51]

Mischa, for one, could not get over how "attentive and appreciative" the audiences were; more so than any others in the world. Every seat but one was taken for one concert. On the lone empty seat was an urn; in it were the ashes of a man who had hoped to hear the Quartet in 1952 but had missed doing so because of Joe's accident. The man's brother, knowing how he wanted to hear the Budapest perform, purchased the extra seat and brought the urn. (No one told Joe about the touching incident, though, because of his being superstitious about his father's death when he was a youngster.) "You would see a hall of white shirts and black hair," said Mischa. "And no higher people, and no lower. All in the same size. And just like hypnotized, sitting and listening to music. And there you really felt you give something to the people. That was very, very great satisfaction, and we felt that we played well."[52]

But the "we" did not include Jac. He never felt that he played well. He was suffering from severe depression and was now under the care of a Washington psychiatrist who evidently also misread some of the signals Jac was sending out.[53] Jac did not want to go to Japan at all. At the airport in Seattle, he told Boris, "When I go out on the stage, my hands are frozen."[54] That Jac did go may have been due, in large part, to the fact that Honey accompanied him. She, Pola, and Sonya joined their husbands for the tour. Only Mischa's wife, June, stayed at home, to take care of their two young sons, Greg and Mark.

It was bizarre. Day Thorpe was writing in the Washington *Sunday Star* that "We have no Rolls Royce, no Paetek Phillipe, no longer a Walter Johnson, no Chez Point Restaurant, no Steinway, no Thornton Wilder, no Picasso. We do have the Budapest Quartet. . . . That the Budapest Quartet is the standard of the world it is futile to deny."[55] And yet at the very same time, Jac Gorodetzky was contemplating suicide. He had told Boris in Seattle that he wanted to jump out the window. He spoke of suicide to Mischa, too. But still none of the Quartet members took him as seriously as they might have. It was not so much callousness as a lack of sensitivity to the psychological overtones inherent in Jac's words. They were used to making exaggerated statements; it was part of the colorful way that they expressed themselves.

Jac, a friend recalled, began having "jitters."[56] He "seemed to be on a hot wire," another said.[57] His bow hand trembled. He began missing more and more concerts. Hurried telephone calls were put to Sasha to fill in for him. "Alexander Schneider is substituting for Mr. Gorodetzky who, because of illness, in unable to appear" became a typical announcement in newspapers around the country. Sasha took his chair also when Jac did not want to go on a South American tour. "He was such a tortured man," said Honey, especially the last year, which was "traumatic." After performing a concert with the Quartet in New York, he announced to her, "I can't take it any more."[58]

In late February 1954, Jac told Spivacke at a Saturday night conference that he was going to leave the Quartet. The others in the Quartet hoped it was only temporary, a leave of absence until he felt better. "If they are not giving up hope," Jac said, "I am not either and perhaps there is some more thrashing to do when they return" to Washington.[59] But the situation did not change. Jac talked about teaching violin and chamber music now that he was no longer in the Quartet. He took long walks with his psychiatrist, who still did not grasp the severity of Jac's despondency. But a family friend did. That summer, she asked Jac to accompany her to help open up a children's camp she operated. She wanted to get Jac out of Washington and into the countryside where, perhaps, he might relax. But she knew enough about his mental state of mind to be worried. She asked the camp nurse to join them and to keep an eye on Jac, who was given a bedroom in the infirmary. "I knew," she said, "that I had to watch Jac all the time for fear that he would do something to himself."[60]

In early November 1955, Jac evidently told his wife he was going to get a haircut. He went to a small hotel near Union Station in Washington and took a room under an assumed name. He hung a "Do Not Disturb" sign on the doorknob. The next afternoon, after repeated efforts by the chambermaid to awaken him so she could clean the room, the maid unlocked the door and went in. Jac was dead, apparently from an overdose of barbiturates, though no mention of suicide was ever made in the newspapers.[61] He was forty-two years old.

Joe, Mischa, and Boris were shaken, numbed. They felt guilty and contrite and tried to make up for what now seemed a heedless disregard for a colleague's feelings. A little over a month after Jac's death, they played a benefit concert at the Settlement Music School in Philadelphia for a memorial scholarship fund in his name that was established by his early patron, Blanche Kohn. They returned to Philadelphia for a second benefit in December 1958, joined this time

by Mieczysław Horszowski and Edgar Ortenberg. (Ironically, Ortenberg, whose wife had not wanted him to be the Quartet's violist,
played the second viola part in a Mozart quintet.) Many years later,
Mischa donated all his cello music to the school, and Joe bequeathed
it his entire estate, worth nearly half a million dollars.

With Gorodetzky's resignation, Roisman had had enough with
second violinists. He told Mischa and Boris that he would quit rather
than train a new one. If Sasha did not return to the Quartet. . . .[62]

Mischa put in a call to his brother.

14

Twin Peak Number Two

Sasha's departure from the Budapest Quartet in 1944 had been like the lift-off of a rocket into space. On his own for the first time in America, he burst into the musical world full of energy and full of ideas. He was offered the job of conductor of the Metropolitan Opera; he turned it down. He was asked to take over the leadership of the Pro Arte and the Paganini quartets; he rejected both proposals. Harold Spivacke asked him to form a quartet; he dismissed the idea.

Relating all that Sasha did do in the decade he was away from the Quartet would make a book in itself. He was a veritable dynamo. He toured with harpsichordist Ralph Kirkpatrick. He played the unaccompanied Bach—all six works in one night alone in Toronto. He was the "Al" in the Albeneri Trio—the "ben" was cellist Benar Heifetz and the "eri" pianist Erich Itor Kahn.

He went to Prades, in French Catalonia, to study with Casals. He persuaded the great cellist, in his seventies, to come out of his self-imposed exile in 1949 to participate in a festival honoring the two hundredth anniversary of Bach's death. That led to subsequent festivals with Casals in Perpignan and Prades, to the start of the Festival Casals in Puerto Rico, and eventually to Casals's participation in a cello festival in Israel and at the Marlboro Music Festival in Vermont—all with Sasha at his elbow.

In 1949, Sasha formed a string quartet to perform and record all eighty-three of Haydn's quartets—a project that fell short of its goal when the sponsor, the Haydn Society, ran out of funds.

Perhaps more than anything else during those ten years, Sasha was a one-man promoter of chamber music and was especially interested in making it available to young people. What he wanted, he told Elizabeth Sprague Coolidge soon after leaving the Quartet in 1944, was to tour war-ravaged France, England, and Italy "without remuneration," if she would pay the expenses, because "the civilian populations of these countries are starving for good music."[1] That tour was not possible, but later he came up with the idea of having free chamber-music concerts during the summer in Washington Square Park in New York City's Greenwich Village (Mrs. Coolidge paid half the costs). They were the first free outdoor concerts in the city's history. Sasha then convinced the Circle in the Square theater nearby to hold chamber-music concerts also, for two dollars a ticket. On December 24, 1955, the first of his annual series of Christmas Eve concerts with young musicians from all over the country was held at Carnegie Hall.

Sasha's circle of friends included artists, photographers, writers, actors. He met *Life* photographer Margaret Bourke-White in 1948 and immediately fell in love with her. They lived together at his apartment in Beekman Place for three years. A year later, actress Uta Hagen introduced him to Geraldine Page, who became his second wife in 1954.

Despite his frenzied career, busy social life, the constant traveling, Sasha had never been very far away from the Quartet. When Ortenberg got sick and missed six concerts, Sasha filled in for him. If the Quartet played at New York City's 92nd Street Y, Sasha was there with Kirkpatrick or the Albeneri a couple of nights earlier or later. The same happened in Boston, Cleveland, and other cities, as a typical winter concert season for both the Quartet and his ensembles crisscrossed the country. As a result, he was usually nearby and available to play with the Budapest when Gorodetzky would not or could not go on stage.

When Sasha received the news from Mischa that Jac was resigning from the Quartet, he had no one to consult with. His mentor, Mrs. Coolidge, had died two years earlier. But Sasha had learned his lesson and valued his independence: "I knew I couldn't give up my activities which I had already established for so many years." Sasha was firm about the conditions under which he would return to the Budapest. He again refused to move to Washington, to comply with the Library of Congress's stipulation; but he would stay with Mischa and his family when he had to be there. More important, the old rule that prevented him from having a separate career would have to be waived. He would do his utmost to schedule his musical life around the Quartet's concert tours, but unless Joe, Mischa, and Boris were willing to let him do his own thing. . . .

Fortunately, the others—in particular, Joe and Boris, who were now both well into their mid-fifties—did not want to concertize so much. "They asked me," said Sasha, "if I would continue playing in the Quartet besides doing all my other activities. I must say, it was really the most beautiful time we spent together, since all four of us had realized in those years of separation that we not only respected each other but really enjoyed making music together. We had all grown up to be more understanding of human beings."[2]

It was like he had never been away. "He was like an old glove, even after eleven years," Mischa happily reported. As far as Mischa was concerned, the Budapest played its best after Sasha rejoined it. "We were just stagnant," he said. "At that time there was no interest any more. Then Sasha returned. We had our ensemble back again."[3] To Sasha, playing out the concert season in 1955 with them "was like a beautiful reunion of coming home."

"I felt great and I felt wonderful and at once I was saying to myself, 'My God, we, all four of us, at last, really enjoy making music and enjoy our lives.'"[4]

Needless to say, audiences everywhere welcomed him back. Everybody, even musicians, agreed with Mischa that the Budapest had not been the same quartet without Sasha. Violinist Jaime Laredo recalled attending a Quartet concert at which they played Debussy's familiar Quartet in G Minor. "It was like I heard it for the first time," he said. Cellist Leslie Parnas was introduced to the way they played while in the Navy during the 1950s. He said that his hair "would stand up on end" when they performed the late Beethovens. Howard Scott, their recording director, found them "more relaxed" once Sasha was back—"it was like putting on an old pair of slippers." Sasha, however, was anything but an old pair of slippers. He galvanized the others. He would not let them "sit on their duffs," Scott said. "He didn't shut up, and Roisman didn't want him to shut up," said violist Walter Trampler. There was "friendly competition" among the members, CBS Records executive R. Peter Munves remembered, but no one ever took "star turns." Musicologist Joseph Machlis compared them to "a couple who loves each other for years."[5]

And, suddenly, critics—the same ones who had heralded the debuts of Ortenberg and Gorodetzky—now spoke of how Sasha brought back the energy and fire so long missing from the Quartet. "Like the first robin of spring," wrote one, "the Budapest group is familiar but not the same this year. Among the remembered things one must count the rich tone that no other quartet can match, and the compelling ease of their playing which bespeaks long association. Refreshingly new is a vigor and drive that seemed not there before; everyone is a year older, but the quartet seems more than a few years younger."[6] A reviewer in Greensboro, North Carolina, said the Quartet's performance "aroused the audience to a degree of enthuisasm [sic] seldom encountered in local chamber music history."[7] Day Thorpe, writing in the Washington *Star*, thought a performance of piano quintets by Schumann and Dvořák and a Mozart piano quartet with Rudolf Serkin "was one of those concerts which relatively few organizations other than the Budapest can make come alive—a collection of old favorites." Thorpe added, "The Budapest Quartet has the happy genius of making the most familiar music sound fresh and new, because even decades of concerts have not dulled the beauty of the music in the ears of the players themselves."[8]

"Chamber music," *Newsweek* proclaimed, "is now a staple on the American musical bill of fare, and no one can cook it quite so well as the Budapest String Quartet."[9] The metaphor undoubtedly was appreciated by Sasha, a lover of good food and wine and a gourmet chef.

The Quartet, Sasha said, was having fun. Even Joe was happy, Mischa remarked. But how was it possible they could be, especially since it was bandied about—everyone knew, did they not?—that the members did not get along? That myth—which would ordinarily be considered a great publicity ploy because it drew so much attention to the group—was reinforced by a photograph that *Life* photographer Gjon Mili, a friend of Sasha's, took in an airport on the West Coast. Mili posed the four musicians sitting separately on wide couches, facing in a different direction, waiting for their plane to be announced, and looking as if the last thing in the world they wanted to do was to talk to each other. They can play together magnificently, the photograph seemed to say, but they cannot even sit with one another.[10]

It is easy to see how such a myth could grow. The Quartet members often spent as many as six hours a day together rehearsing, many times on the day of a concert—that is, if they were not on a train or a bus or a ship traveling somewhere together. It became important to keep some semblance of a personal life, what little there could be, apart from the Quartet. Way back at the turn of the century, each member of the Kneisel Quartet had learned not to intrude into the others' personal lives. They would tell a hotel reservation clerk, "Please reserve four single rooms, to be located on different floors of the hotel, or as far from each other as possible. Location as stated is IMPORTANT."[11]

As much as possible, Joe, Mischa, Boris, and Sasha tried to travel alone, requested rooms on separate floors of a hotel, dined separately, and ordinarily went their own separate ways after a concert. Each also had his own set of friends—bohemian types in Sasha's case; doctors, lawyers, professors, businessmen in the case of the others. "We were like a family in the concerts—in every concert we were like a family," said Joe, "but when we were on our own, usually, we went on our own way."[12] Once when invited to a dinner party in Cleveland, Joe asked whether the others were going to be there. When he was told they would not be, he accepted.[13] It was "necessary," Joe explained, "because we were so much together. We were together on the same boat, the same plane, or in the same hotels and I think that helped to prolong our life together. It's just like a marriage."[14]

Sasha, both of whose marriages failed, insisted, "It is much easier to be married to one person than to be married to a string quartet." The Budapest, he said, had a

> great arrangement never to get together socially after work or discuss any personal problems with each other because if you rehearse three hours and play concerts practically every day and then go to parties together after concerts, you are together at least eight hours every day. You not only get on each others's nerves because you know each other so well, as in the best of marriages, but you end up not talking to each other. Believe me, it's four times as hard in a string quartet as in a marriage. You really know not only the good but the bad parts of each other, and the worst is to have to listen to the same stories and jokes for days, weeks, months and years on end. So we tried very hard to travel separately and live separately when we were not making music.[15]

Both Joe and Sasha made it sound as though the Quartet members did their best to avoid one another, but they were exaggerating, as was their typical Russian manner. There were many times when they went to the same party after a concert. Boris customarily spent Christmas Day with Mischa's family, and both he and Mischa always went to New York to attend Sasha's birthday parties. Sasha liked to throw open his home to all of his friends, treat them to good food and wine, and maybe play a bit of music, too.

The Quartet members also realized how important it was to relieve the tensions of constant tours and travel. Once in a while at a rehearsal, just for the fun of it, they switched chairs—Boris playing

first violin; Mischa, second violin; Joe, the viola; and Sasha, the
cello. Sasha once discovered a bass drum and a set of cymbals, both
with foot pedals, in the corner of the studio during an exasperating
recording session in which they were disappointed with a variation
in a Beethoven movement. He lugged the drum to his chair, Boris got
the cymbals, and they played the problem passage, banging away
like crazed musicians. After hearing the playback of that organized
chaos, they felt inspired to run through a few Russian dances, and
then they recorded the troublesome variation without any difficulty.
The way they handled stress was exemplified one day at the Library
of Congress for a writer of *New Yorker* magazine who was doing a
profile on the Quartet and was allowed to sit in on a rehearsal with
the Stradivarius instruments in the Coolidge Auditorium. As they
played, the reporter recognized the opening movement of Beethoven's Opus 18, No. 4:

> When the Budapest played a sudden *forte-piano*, all four men reduced
> their bow pressure at the same instant. After Roisman had brought off a
> magnificent semiquaver passage, Mischa Schneider looked up at him
> approvingly, and Alexander shouted, "Bravo, Joe!"

As the rehearsal progressed, the Quartet reached a part in which
the second violin carries the theme. Sasha leaped from his chair and
with violin held aloft "played the passage with exaggerated schmalz
[sic], like a street fiddler in Naples":

> Kroyt, always the perfect partner, stopped playing and started singing a
> Russian song. . . . Mischa Schneider thereupon performed a number
> of stupendous triads on his cello. . . . Only Roisman went quietly on
> with his part, untouched by the pandemonium around him, playing
> Beethoven with his noble tone and elegant bowing. Before long his
> impeccable performance in the midst of bedlam stopped the others, and
> Alexander Schneider laughed so hard that I began to fear he might drop
> the Betts. . . .
>
> In the third movement, he and Kroyt had a short argument while
> both continued to play. The members of the Budapest Quartet are able
> to play a difficult passage, carry on a running conversation, and point
> out a musical accent in the score simultaneously. They played only
> excerpts from the last movement of the Beethoven, but they rehearsed
> the entire Brahms A-Minor Quartet.

As they played the Brahms, Sasha sang out the notations—
"Dolce," "Sempre mezza voce e grazios," "Lusingando." When he
reached a rest, he danced a czardas around Roisman, who played
some delicate spiccato passages with such élan that Sasha and Boris

Mischa Schneider (seated, right foreground) *with fellow cello students and their* teacher, Julius Klengel, in Leipzig in 1922. (Courtesy of Natasha Schneider Furst)

Original members of the Budapest String Quartet with the second of six second violinists who would join the Quartet over its fifty-year existence: (from left) Istvan Ipolyi, viola; Emil Hauser, first violin; Imre Pogany, second violin; and (in foreground) Harry Son, cellist. Son was a Dutchman; all the others, Hungarian.

The Schneider brothers in 1929, when Mischa was twenty-five years old; Sasha, twenty-one. (Courtesy of Natasha Schneider Furst)

A critical split occurred in the Quartet when it was composed of two Hungarians and two Russians. Here, in a photograph taken in Berlin in 1930, are (from left) Imre Pogany, Mischa Schneider, Emil Hauser, and, as he originally spelled his name, Josef Roismann. (Courtesy of June Schneider)

Three Russians and one Hungarian. The Quartet in Ithaca, New York, in 1934, two years after Sasha Schneider joined the group: (from left) *Roismann, Sasha, Ipolyi, and Mischa.* (Courtesy of Natasha Schneider Furst)

The four Russians. A jubilant Budapest String Quartet shortly after its historic March 20, 1938, concert in Town Hall, New York. Second from left is Boris Kroyt, who joined the Quartet as violist in 1936. (Courtesy of June Schneider)

Benny Goodman joins the Quartet in a practice session for the Mozart Clarinet Quintet that they recorded for RCA Victor at a single session on April 25, 1938. (Courtesy of Yanna Kroyt Brandt)

Setting a precedent, Quartet members donned white Palm Beach suits for after-noon concerts at the Library of Congress—"And oh, boy! do they look swell!" declared acting Music Division chief Edward N. Waters. The ensemble was the first quartet-in-residence at the Library, performing there for more than twenty years. (Library of Congress)

A light moment at a recording session in the 1950s. (Sony Classical)

A serious moment. Listening to the playback with recording director Howard Scott. (Courtesy of Yanna Kroyt Brandt)

The myth that the Quartet members did not speak to one another, much less sit together, was reinforced by this photograph taken by Sasha's friend Gjon Mili. Mili posed the four Russians as they waited to emplane at the Seattle airport in 1957. Its appearance in Life *magazine gave visual credence to the fabrication.* (Gjon Mili, *Life* Magazine © Time Warner Inc.)

Pablo Casals joins the Quartet for Schubert's Quintet in C at Jerusalem's Binyanei Ha-ooma in September 1961. (W. Braun)

Rudolf Serkin joins the Quartet for the Brahms Piano Quintet in F Minor, re-corded at Marlboro, Vermont, in 1963. Following Sasha's lead, Mischa and Boris spent summers teaching and performing at the music school and festival. When unable to perform, Mischa became the festival's recording director. (D. Hunstein/ Sony Classical)

The Schneider brothers sometime in the 1970s. Mischa was about seventy years old and unable to perform any longer; Sasha was in his late sixties. (Courtesy of Natasha Schneider Furst)

stood up and bowed to him while Mischa called out, "Bis! Bis!" That set off a competition to see who could play spiccato runs better. When things calmed down again, Kroyt played a solo phrase on open string, which Mischa took exception to:

"That sounds awful, Boris. An insult to my ears."

"I was playing that open-string tone when you were still a baby," said Kroyt.

"I wouldn't remember," Mischa Schneider said coldly. "I wasn't brought up a *Wunderkind,* Herr Kroyt."

"That's been oblivious to me for some time," said Kroyt.

"You mean obvious," said Alexander Schneider.

"Obvious *and* oblivious!" shouted Kroyt.

"Gentlemen! Gentlemen!" said Roisman.

Another theatrical display was touched off when Walter Trampler appeared for the rehearsal of a viola quintet. Sasha started playing "O Sole Mio." Kroyt responded with the Kreutzer étude that was comedian Jack Benny's trademark, while Mischa plucked away on his cello:

At that point, even Roisman broke down, and began playing his fiddle between his knees, like a cello. Poor Brahms went down ingloriously.

Trampler dissolved into laughter. "You know, they are really smart," he said at last. "They know that monotony is the worst enemy of a quartet rehearsal. Anything to beat monotony. They have fun and they argue about musical matters, but they are beyond bitter, personal fights. They have learned to compromise." . . .

On the stage, a violent argument, in Russian and German, had broken out between Kroyt and Mischa Schneider over an esoteric musical question in the finale of the Brahms. They would shout at each other until they ran out of breath, and then Alexander Schneider would say, *"Messieurs, faites vos jeux!"* Roisman shook his head sadly but kept silent. Then, as Kroyt and Mischa Schneider shouted louder still, he said, in his gentle voice, "Gentlemen, *please!,"* and almost immediately the argument faded away. The four men repeated the end of the last movement.

"Without Roisman there would be no rehearsal at all," Trampler remarked. "He rarely speaks, but when he does, they all listen to him."

Roisman suggested that they play the beginning of the finale once. All went well for a while, and then Alexander Schneider motioned furtively to his brother and Kroyt, and the three of them gradually played more and more softly, until they were just going through the motions and only Roisman was audible. The rehearsal ended on a note of general merriment. I asked Trampler whether it was always like this.

"Anything goes at rehearsal," he said. "That's the rule."[16]

Trampler as well as Rudolf Serkin joined the Quartet for a concert on October 7, 1957, held to celebrate Mrs. Whittall's ninetieth
birthday. It was a gala event. They performed a Haydn quartet and
quintets by Mozart and Brahms. The original manuscripts of the
works they played, also gifts of Mrs. Whittall to the Library of Congress, were displayed in the pavilion named for her adjoining the
Coolidge Auditorium. At intermission, Spivacke brought her onto
the stage, where she was surrounded by the musicians and deluged
with gifts, including a silver cigaret case from the Quartet, which
also sent ninety-one American Beauty roses to her Shoreham apartment. She kissed Joe, Mischa, Boris, and Sasha—Serkin and Trampler, too. They would have played "Happy Birthday" for her, Spivacke explained, but the song was under copyright, and Mrs. Whittall herself would have had to foot the $1.09 royalty fee. "Would
Wagner have charged Cosima for the Siegfried Idyll? Would Don
Giovanni have sent a bill along with his serenade to Elvira's maid?
The possibility is absurd. 'Happy Birthday' is out of the question!'"[17]

Twenty days later, on a Sunday afternoon, the Quartet made
television history by appearing over WCBS-TV (Channel 2) in New
York. The hour-long local program included Wolf's "Italian Serenade," movements from Debussy and Dvořák, and the entire Beethoven Quartet in E Minor (Opus 59, No. 2). There was a great deal of
concern whether anyone would watch the program. It was being
sponsored by the Metropolitan Educational Television Association
(META), a forerunner of New York's public station, WNET (Channel
13), which did not have a studio of its own and was forced to rely on
air time and studio facilities donated by commercial stations. META
was so poor that it did not have the two hundred fifty dollars necessary to make a kinescope of the recital, so there is no record of the
show. The Budapest program was sandwiched between a repeat of
the 1939 film *News Is Made at Night* and *World News Roundup*. It
was scheduled to start at 3:30 P.M., running smack in the middle of a
full lineup of programs on CBS's competitors. That same hour,
Channel 4 was presenting an interview with the Reverend Dr. Martin Luther King, Jr., and a documentary on American doctors. A
feature film with Ronald Reagan, *Nine Lives Are Not Enough*, was
already under way on Channel 5. *The Corpse Came C.O.D.* was on
Channel 7. Channel 11 had begun a western, and Channel 13 (then a
commercial station) was showing a number of shorts. Furthermore,
that Sunday was a brisk, clear autumn day, when many New Yorkers
could be expected to be outdoors, taking strolls, going to museums,
or visiting relatives. Anyway, Mischa had wondered in an interview

with *Time* magazine six years earlier, "Why would people want to sit in the living room and see only four men sitting on chairs pulling bows?"[18]

"Many hundreds of thousands" viewed the broadcast, META's president wrote Kroyt, whose daughter had worked on the program.[19] Jack Gould, television critic for the *New York Times*, said the Quartet "had proved conclusively that there is more than one measure of television's usefulness."

> Even for the viewer whose familiarity with chamber music is decidedly limited the concert was a stimulating experience. The total absorption of the members of the quartet in their work was in itself contagious. . . . The set-owner found himself under their spell. . . .
>
> The sway of the bodies of the instrumentalists, the almost poetic implementation of the meaning of the music by their changing facial expressions, completely held one's attention.[20]

The *Times* music critic, Howard Taubman, called the program "an illuminating example of how stimulating it can be to see as well as hear a group of musicians play absolute music like a Beethoven quartet, even though, strictly speaking, mechanical transmission was used." Taubman said that even a recording of the Beethoven "could not match the impact of the performance on television." The Quartet, he said, "managed to give the E minor Quartet a physical dimension. A close-up of a string player shaping the lovely song of the slow movement created the illusion that he was modeling sound as if it were a tangible thing. . . . If music is ever to get any measurable attention on TV, it could well be that chamber music would provide the most attractive avenue. Its essence is intimacy; it was designed for the home."[21]

The Quartet performed twice more on television, with both performances recorded. WCBS-TV carried their concert from the Frick Collection on Sunday, December 1, 1958. And on a Tuesday night, April 10, 1962, the CBS network carried in prime time a program, *Festival of the Performing Arts*, that featured the Budapest playing Beethoven's Quartet in E-flat (Opus 135) and Schumann's Piano Quintet in E-flat with Rudolf Serkin. The program "was even allowed to finish a couple of minutes past its scheduled time," noted Alan Rich in the *Times*. "Arturo Toscanini and the President of the United States have enjoyed the latter privilege on the air, but few others." Television, Rich was pleased to say, "made one of its rare gestures toward a small, intelligent minority, and treated that minority with respect."[22]

But it was always with Haydn, Mozart, and Beethoven, or Brahms, Mendelssohn, Schubert, and Schumann that the Budapest was associated—with the classicists and the romanticists. The young, spirited Juilliard Quartet, formed in 1945 and the first truly all-American string quartet, was known as the champion of contemporary composers. What happened to the reputation the early Budapest String Quartet first enjoyed for playing modern music? Or to the members' own predilections? "We insist on playing contemporary music," Kroyt told an interviewer in 1956. "We offer works of Prokofieff, Hindemith, Bartók—whose chamber music is considered the best of his work—Milhaud and the Americans Piston, Barber and many others," said Kroyt, whose Anbruch Quartet in Germany in the 1920s favored avant-garde composers. "We believe that this music should be heard in order to be known."[23]

If what he said was true, how come the Budapest was known as a conservative quartet?

15

What the Public Wants

Boris believed, quite correctly, that chamber-music societies were responsible for restraining the Budapest Quartet from including more modern works in its repertoire. But societies were not alone in not wanting modern works. What is true today was true then. Concert managers, who were concerned about filling a hall, also did not want them, because many concertgoers shied away from contemporary pieces and either did not purchase tickets or, as subscribers, walked out when a modern work was played. In fact, in the 1930s and early 1940s, a program solely devoted to string quartets was often considered too cumbrous for the average American music lover. It was not uncommon for the Quartet to be paired on a concert program with other performers who played a solo work or sang lieder—Efrem Zimbalist, Rose Bampton, or Nan Merriman, for example. When the Quartet did appear on its own, to perform three quartets in a recital, they started with "a light quartet"—a Haydn, for instance—and purposely left a major one, such as a late Beethoven, for last. "It was not until later," Sasha said, "that we could play three serious quartets on a program."[1]

There was another reason for the emphasis on the staples of classical music—what one observer in the *New York Times* called "cultural consumption." This was a trend away from amateurism toward professionalism that resulted in a broader, more passive audience—listeners instead of participants. Music-appreciation courses in schools and symphony orchestras, in particular, by promoting pops concerts and children's concerts reflected this trend. Orchestras, which multiplied in number from seventeen at the time of World War I to two hundred seventy by World War II, needed to broaden their audiences to fill their halls. The so-called "music appreciators" who helped promote this movement snubbed any music that was not "certified masterpieces—invariably written by dead Europeans. They had no use for new music, or American, or popular music." What was performed, especially with regard to orchestra music, was the familiar, easy-to-like "masterworks that could be endlessly recycled. The result was a vast and manipulable New Audience for concert music—provided it was old, famous and European."[2]

Each year, the Budapest tried to vary the scope of its programming, and each year it collided with this trend toward popularization of the classics that had become an epidemic sweeping through symphonic concerts. The Quartet had become the role model for the way Beethoven, Mozart, Schubert, Brahms, and others should be played. No other quartet could perform the European masters as well. Accordingly, no matter where it toured, everyone wanted to hear the Quartet perform the so-called "classics." "It seems that we have endless trouble again with programs," Annie Friedberg informed the Quartet in 1947 in a typical letter dealing with scheduling.

> *Utica* now asks for the following, although Mr. Shute said himself that it is not good program making but that the people want very much to have Brahms and the late Beethoven. . . . It seems that they have quite some trouble getting the right program and he said he thought it would help matters very much if the Quartet could give them a program "packed full of meat," as he calls it.[3]

Ordinarily, during the summer Mischa would ask the others to state what pieces they preferred to play in the upcoming concert season. The Quartet members were not shy about suggesting contemporary works. "In general," Roisman admitted, they tended to be conservative, but they "made concessions to modern times."[4] Julius Levine recalled rehearsing Egon Wellesz's octet with them in 1959. "With a new piece, they didn't kid around. They made sure we had enough work to do some justice to it."[5]

After consulting the other members, Mischa drew up five or six program choices, each consisting of three quartets, from which sponsors—or "presenters" as they are called—could select. "I juggle them around every year, you know," he said. "We mix in a little bit green, a little bit red, a little bit this and that."[6] They were flexible, though, always willing to substitute pieces if asked. But the truth was, Joe said, that they did not receive many requests for modern works.

When the Budapest did schedule a modern quartet on a program, it had to be positioned after an opening work and before the intermission—an attempt to keep the audience from walking out. That is still the practice today. Only college students in America or the avid music lovers of Buenos Aires, Paris, and Japan seemed to thirst for the new. Before the Budapest came on the scene in America, the Pro Arte Quartet ran into the same problem. After the Pro Arte performed Bartók's second quartet for the Buffalo Symphony Society, a subscriber "ostentatiously walked down the center aisle with thumbs down," and several others threatened to quit "if anything like that Bartók happened again." One society member suggested that if modern music was to be performed in the future, the piece should be scheduled either at the beginning of the program or at the close so that "uninterested subscribers might then come late or leave early."[7]

The problem was not confined to contemporary music, but, it seems, encompassed any works written after Debussy. Every year, for instance, the Quartet played a single concert in New York for the Institute of Arts and Sciences at Columbia University. In 1946, the institute's administrative office informed subscribers that instead of its selecting the Budapest program that year, they would. A poll was taken. The Quartet had sent Columbia five different program choices. One with a Piston quartet between a Beethoven and a Dvořák got seven votes; a Bartók with Schubert and Schumann garnered eleven votes; a third with Milhaud played between Mozart and Schubert received twenty-two votes; and a Hindemith sandwiched between Haydn and Beethoven got twenty-five votes. The winner, though, was the program with quartets by Brahms, Mozart and Mendelssohn. It received 116 votes.[8]

During the winter of 1958–59, the Quartet appeared in a five-recital Saturday evening series at the 92nd Street Y. Each of its programs included a contemporary work—by a composer of different nationality—Milhaud (French), Bartók (Hungarian), Prokofieff (Russian), Piston (American), and Hindemith (German)—that the Budapest Quartet had "tried out and found attractive to audiences."[9] But subscription renewals were off, and the usual attendance the Quartet drew at the Y fell so dramatically that the Y conducted a survey to find out what had happened. There were three major reasons that subscribers had not renewed—the cost of the series, the fact that the concerts were on Saturday night, and because concertgoers disliked modern music.[10] The next year the Y scheduled an entirely traditional series of programs without lowering its ticket prices and without changing the performance dates from Saturday night; the Quartet attracted record attendances averaging 895 persons per concert.[11] It got so monotonous, always being asked to perform the same works, that Mischa thought of writing a book titled in honor of one of the quartets that was most persistently requested. It would have been called, he said, "Beethoven Opus 59, No. 1."[12]

The 92nd Street Y always had the reputation of being conservative in its programming; even the rather traditional work of the contemporary Jewish composer Ernest Bloch, whose piano quintet the Quartet performed, "was a little difficult to swallow."[13] But the Library of Congress tried not to be. Spivacke let it be known as early as 1942 that he thought "it might be a good time to begin introducing into the Whittall programs an occasional modern work, even if a little radical. The earliest works of Hindemith for instance."[14] But then he backtracked. He told Mrs. Whittall that "I should like to see some of our programs include one 'conservative modern.' I was thinking of works like the first two or three quartets by Hindemith, the early Bartók, the quartet by Bloch and others; in other words, those so-called modern works in which the melodies are more apparent than the later so-called experimental works." He wanted, he said, "a mixed program with some modern works"—but, he hastened to remark, "modern works which are not too radical."[15]

Actually, outside of concerts at colleges and universities, the Quartet performed more contemporary works at the Library than anywhere else—pieces by composers as diverse as Americans Charles Tomlinson Griffes (an impressionist), Benjamin Lees (a proponent of the twelve-tone scale), and John Alden Carpenter (who favored melodic lines); folk-music advocates Zoltán Kodály of Hungary and Alberto Ginastera of Argentina; and the Russians Nikolay Lopatnikoff (an atonalist), and Nikolay Medtner (a traditionalist). In 1943, the Budapest commissioned Paul Hindemith, then at the height of his influence as a composer, to write his Quartet No. 6 in E-flat, which they premiered at the Library. While in the midst of composing it, Hindemith told them that he believed the work would be "decent, but in any event it will be a somewhat weighty piece of music." (No fee had been discussed, so Hindemith tried to bring up the subject tactfully. "This is not certainly blackmail," he said, "on the other hand I think, however, that here a composer—and surely not by accident—also has to have a teaching position." Would the

Quartet "find it inappropriate if I suggested to you that I get $8 for each performance?")[16]

That same year in Buffalo, the Quartet premiered Ernst Křenek's Quartet No. 7, Opus 96. Křenek, an early advocate of the twelve-tone idiom, could not be present for the performance, but he heard it three months later when the Budapest visited Hamline University in St. Paul, Minnesota, where he taught, and performed it for free. "You know that in the last few years I have not been spoiled by too many performances of my music, especially in the field of chamber music," he said. "For some time I felt the fact that my Sixth Quartet has never been played quite depressing."[17] Křenek offered to send the Quartet a score by a student of his, "knowing that you are interested in new works and that you may need new interesting works by American composers."[18]

David Van Vactor was also unable to hear the Budapest perform his Quartet No. 1 when they first played it at Mills College in 1947, but he received a recording of it. "It was a perfect performance!" he wrote them. "It is a great experience for a composer to have his music played with such understanding . . . with so much care and artistry."[19]

Each summer, the Quartet tried out scores that composers sent them. They would read them, and those that sounded promising they would play through. They had one rule, though, no matter who the composer was: they all had to like a piece before adding it to their repertoire. They tended to favor neoclassicists and compositions with a strong melodic line. "The Budapest," said Edgar Ortenberg,

> could permit themselves to ignore those composers who wrote music to be played on an empty bottle of Pepsi Cola—like John Cage. This kind of shit—excuse me—we could permit ourselves not to play. I hate to go to concerts with a piece of paper and pencil and solve some mathematical problem, some theoretical problem. I go to hear good music. Beethoven was very criticized at the beginning of his career, but that doesn't prove some contemporary idiots would also be future Beethovens.[20]

Boris felt the same way. "Now they have 'the crazy music'—you bang on a table and chop up food, or gargle. In my opinion, this music is simply a case of talentless people. They always try to create something sensational."[21]

Artur Schnabel, who also wrote music but was far from being considered radical, was one of the many composers who sent the Budapest a quartet. They did not like it, but they did not want to hurt the pianist's feelings. Boris, who knew him well, was asked to write him and let him down gently. Because of its busy schedule, said Kroyt, "All the new quartets" that the Quartet "played lately were *short pieces* in comparison."[22]

On the other hand, the members of the Quartet sought out Walter Piston, whose quintet for flute and string quartet they had premiered in 1942. They wrote to him in Vermont, saying they also wanted to play one of his quartets. "I have written two," Piston replied. "The second is I believe a little better and has not been much played, perhaps because it is not published."[23] Piston got his publisher to send the Quartet a score and parts, and it performed the piece at the Library of Congress in 1945. It went on to perform his third quartet in 1949. By then they had approached Prokofieff, too. His publisher was just in the process of printing his Quartet No. 2, which the Budapest performed in 1947.

In all, between 1938 and 1960, the Quartet performed more contemporary pieces than any other ensemble. Among the modern music it performed, thirteen works were played for the first time by the Budapest, three of which were dedicated to it. Five of those thirteen were written by Darius Milhaud, with whom the Quartet members developed a close relationship while summering at Mills College during and after World War II. The most amazing were Milhaud's fourteenth and fifteenth quartets, composed during the summer of 1949. Milhaud's polyphonic compositions ordinarily drew a lukewarm response unless he was in the audience. But when he was there, sitting in the back of the auditorium, confined to a wheelchair because of severe arthritis, the audience would react wildly. Henri Temianka, the first violinist of the Paganini Quartet, believed the composer "exuded an invisible, powerful magnetism."[24]

Milhaud had been given an unused 1848 music notebook with eight staves. He decided to use it to write a "crab canon." He filled the notebook to the last five-line staff with the music for two quartets—the fourteenth and the fifteenth—which could be played either separately or together as an octet for strings. The Budapest was going to premiere the fourteenth; the Paganini, the fifteenth; then both were to perform the two quartets together. The Paganini was the closest thing to a rival that the Budapest had—at least in the eyes of Temianka, a British violinist who had studied in Berlin and at the Curtis Institute in Philadelphia. Temianka formed the Paganini in 1946 with the help of a wealthy widow who purchased for his quartet four Stradivarius instruments that had once been owned by Paganini.

Temianka remembered the premiere performances of the Milhaud quartets/octet as a "strange affair." At a rehearsal with the Budapest, Temianka asked Milhaud which part should predominate. "I want to hear everything," the composer said.[25] When the two groups came on stage, facing each other across their music stands, people in the audience thought they detected the musicians exchanging hostile looks, but the performance went off without a hitch. Later, the Budapest members recorded the octet on their own; they first played the fourteenth quartet, then, with earphones on, listening to the playback, recorded the fifteenth, while Milton Katims—a violist they often performed and recorded with and who later became conductor of the Seattle Symphony Orchestra—kept time for them. (Kroyt later claimed that, with such recording technology, he could have performed six different roles in the octet, playing both viola and all four violin parts.)[26]

The Milhaud octet was the most modern work they recorded, chiefly because of Columbia's insistence that the Budapest stick to the tried-and-true. In 1942, at a concert at the University of California, San Francisco, the Quartet played the works of four budding composers—Norman Suckling, Normand Lockwood, Alexander Tansman, and Frederic Balazs, the last a pupil of Zoltán Kodály. "Who is Balazs—how is 'the Balazs'—to say nothing of Lockwood and Suckling?" asked the befuddled Goddard Lieberson, head of Columbia. The reason for his letter was to inform the Quartet that he did not want to record a Shostakovitch quartet they had suggested: "I didn't even know it was in your repertoire."[27]

Later in 1942 at New York City's Town Hall, the Quartet premiered three works expressly written for the twentieth anniversary of the founding of the League of Composers—a Milhaud quartet, Louis Gruenberg's "Five Variations on a Popular Theme (Including Three Apologies)" and the Piston flute quintet. After studying the three pieces for weeks on end and performing them once for the league, they were never asked to play any of the works again. Roisman, for one, got tired of spending so much time learning new works that few people wanted to hear. "It was a waste of time for us." Instead, he said, they should have been practicing their regular repertoire. "It is very strange," he commented many years later after a number of such experiences. "We never played Berg or Webern. Even Schönberg only the first and second, the one with voice, very good. [He forgot that the Quartet also performed Schönberg's "Verklärte Nacht"]. Many so-called modern works we played as necessity, in the middle of the program—and," he added, "if it would have been for me maybe we wouldn't have done that either."[28]

By and large, the critics were not much help. The anniversary concert of the League of Composers, for example, drew a tactful put-down from Howard Taubman in the *New York Times*. The "most attractive work" on the program was Milhaud's quartet, while the quintet by Piston, a neoclassicist, "was all dressed up, but apparently had no place to go," and Gruenberg's piece "found the composer in a sportive mood."[29] A Boston reviewer was less charitable when they played Quartet No. 7 by another neoclassicist, Quincy Porter: "To say the worst first, [it] is more an association of ideas than a mastered organization of them."[30] An Ithaca, New York, critic thought Milhaud's Quartet No. 12 "sounded disjointed, meaningless, and rather barren."[31] Piston's Quartet No. 3, said a New York *Herald-Tribune* reviewer, had "stresses, tensions, and accents peculiar to our time . . . [that] did not seem to be quite in focus."[32] A Cleveland critic thought Roy Harris's arrangement of four fugues from Bach's "Art of the Fugue" offered "a certain sense of monotony."[33] Eight years after the Budapest introduced the Hindemith quartet that it commissioned, Glenn Dillard Gunn in the Washington *Times-Herald* still was not persuaded "of the value of this Hindemith composition." He called it "calculated music" that "often omits those qualities of sensibility and emotion that are the most important factors in the musical address. Such music rarely endures beyond its generation."[34] Quartet No. 7 by Austrian-born Ernst Křenek "failed," another reviewer said, "to stir the emotions as once did, for example, the music of Dvořák on his contact with America."[35] A Buffalo reviewer found the same Křenek work "interesting" but "it seemed effortful and uninspired in comparison with the Ravel and the Mozart, K-387."[36] After hearing Porter's Quartet No. 8, a Seattle critic summed up her reaction by saying, "We know this: Quincy is no relation to Cole."[37]

The critics were kinder to Easley Blackwood, Jr., when the Budapest premiered his Quartet No. 1 in Indianapolis in 1958. Blackwood, who had studied with, among others, Paul Hindemith at Yale and with Nadia Boulanger and Olivier Messiaen in Paris, was in the audience, as were his parents. His father was the bridge columnist for the Indianapolis *Times*, whose reviewer tried to be gentle: "Whether you find it agreeable or not, whether it speaks to you or sings to you, you realize it is part of a new musical language from which we cannot retreat. . . . I would personally find it difficult to improvise mentally in any such idiom as Mr. Blackwood's."[38]

There were, to be fair, positive reviews, very often of the same modern works that were censured, but the raves were far fewer in number than the rants. A Chicago critic liked Křenek's seventh quartet; the "three-themed fugue" in the third movement, he said, "could not have been set down by any but a thoroughly schooled composer. Nor was there absent at moments a perception of lyricism, as lyricism is understood by the average music lover."[39] Paul Hume in the Washington *Post* described Porter's Quartet No. 8 as an "eminently beautiful score."[40] A Pittsburgh critic noted that Schönberg's Quartet No. 2 for String Quartet and Soprano, with Uta Graf singing the vocal part, "was supposed to create rebellious uproar" but "was received not only with calm but liking."[41] Hume overheard a backhanded compliment from a concertgoer during intermission at the Library of Congress after the Budapest performed Lukas Foss's Quartet in G: "Well, you can tell them that if they have to torture us, at least that middle quartet was not so bad as some we have had."[42] A Chicago critic realized that Bartók's Quartet No. 6 "will, of course, continue to need 'breaking in' among listeners who are new to it," but the "key" to it "is, perhaps, an awareness that the center of the intellect and of the nervous system is one and the same brain."[43] A Hartford reviewer, who heard the Budapest perform Heiter Villa-Lobos's Quartet No. 17 two weeks after the lyrical Brazilian composer's death in 1959, said it "stole the show." He called it "distinctly modern in its sonorities but richer than many modern compositions in its melodic content."[44]

Besides the controversies that erupted over performing contemporary compositions, the Quartet also had to contend with criticism of its programming, even when concert halls or chamber-music groups were responsible for selecting the works. Sometimes the criticism was justified, sometimes it was pedantic, and sometimes, especially when it came to modern works, it was ludicrously out of touch with the American music scene. Two Mozart divertimentos in one evening were too much for one reviewer.[45] A Cleveland critic regretted that a program of "classics of so much the same emotional vein"—Schumann, Schubert, and Mozart—"did not contain a broader contrast that might have been provided by including a more modern work."[46] A Nashville *Tennessean* reporter said he thought the audience would have appreciated "several short works" instead of the Brahms, Mozart, and Dvořák they played.[47] A Chicago critic complained that the Schubert Octet in F "ran an hour with repeats and all, and tho there was plenty of inspired Schubertian melody there also was ample evidence that this composer didn't always know when to end. Here was a perfect example of that kind of chamber music which provides fun for performers, but a good deal of public boredom in open concerts." He said that scheduling the Schubert together with a Beethoven trio "may be classed as a bonehead play."[48] An Indianapolis concert program of Haydn, Barber, and Beethoven was called "a bland kind of program" that "raises a question about the value of having imported artists endlessly doing standard repertoire." Seemingly unaware of audience reaction to contemporary works, this reviewer urged that "visiting artists" be asked "to trot out their latest achievements."[49] A London critic wondered about ending a recital with Beethoven's Quartet in C, Opus 59, No. 3, because the work is "comparatively calm."[50] The combination of works by Honegger, Martinů, and Dvořák was a "stylistic mixture" that "is best forgotten," a Washington reviewer said.[51] Amazingly, Glenn Dillard Gunn of the *Times-Herald* carped when the Budapest played the brisk rondo that Beethoven substituted, at the urging of his publisher, for his Opus 130 instead of the fugue originally composed as the sixth movement—the fugue that the Budapest, and just about every other quartet, played separately as the *Grosse Fuge*.[52]

Only rarely did anyone bow in the direction of the programming—though that might be because, more often than not, good programming goes unnoticed. A Buffalo critic was so enthused by a three-concert festival of music by Haydn, Schumann, and Bartók that he remarked on "the splendid balance and rightness of these three," which "together, amount to an inspiration in programming."[53]

Of course, all the Budapest members had their own preferences. Roisman said his favorites were Mozart's quartets, which "worked easily, naturally. As we played, we enjoyed it." On the other hand, he said, "though I am a Russian, I never had a great affinity for slavic composers."[54] Mischa always disliked English composers; their compositions were, he thought, "like a tempest in a teapot."[55] Depending on when you asked him, Mischa said he preferred Beethoven, Haydn, Mozart, and Brahms but had no particular favorite piece, *or* he singled out three Mozart quartets (the D, the B-flat, and the F), Beethoven's Opus 59, No. 1, and Haydn's Opus 20, No. 6—all pieces with exciting cello parts. He sometimes added a Barber quartet to that list for the same reason. "You say while you play one work, you say that that is my favorite. But then you play next time another one of the Beethovens and you say that is my favorite."[56] Years later, when very ill and dying, Mischa gave his preferences as simply Mozart, Beethoven, and Bach.[57]

Like Joe and Mischa, Kroyt liked Mozart—"every note is a gem."

When the Quartet played Mozart, he said, "I always think I hear angels singing." But Boris's special favorite was Beethoven. "Very often in a performance," he said, "I have moments of inspiration—in the same work which I have performed fifty or sixty times, I will discover one second of inspiration, I will hear something I didn't hear before. At this moment I feel that I have reached perfection." But Boris also realized that "to be prepared to listen to the master of Bonn requires a sophisticated sense of music appreciation. The Grand Fugue . . . this is not a work that is easy to appreciate. It presages much of the modern atonal music."[58]

Sasha liked Beethoven, too, though at one point, while recording the cycle, he cursed about having to play him so frequently. "I'm sick to death of it," he complained.[59] But Sasha's tastes were eclectic. "Haydn was a romantic composer," he insists, "Mozart too—and Bach."[60] To appreciate Mozart fully, Sasha believed that a listener had to read Mozart's letters. "To me, Mozart was the greatest romanticist. In his simplicity, he requires so much fantasy. Oh, we hear too many charming performances of Mozart—but they lack the tragedy, the freedom and fantasy!"[61]

Works by Haydn, Mozart, and Beethoven outnumbered the works of other composers that the Budapest Quartet performed over three decades, from 1936. In all, they played more than 265 different pieces—some of them, like the Gruenberg work written for the League of Composers' twentieth anniversary, only once; others, like Beethoven's Opus 59, Nos. 1 and 2, countless times. A goodly number of the pieces they played called for assisting artists. The early Budapest had conspicuously avoided such works, and actually, even after 1936, the Quartet preferred not to play with guests because of the special rehearsals that entailed during their busy concert tours. But they did so anyway because performing with guest artists enabled them to broaden their repertoire, primarily into piano quartets and quintets and viola, cello, and clarinet quintets. In all, they performed with more than 135 different musicians—pianists, violists, cellists, and clarinetists, in the main, but also double bass players, flutists, horn players, bassoonists, and oboists—and even with four symphony orchestras (in such works as Martinů's Concerto for String Quartet and Orchestra). They were often asked to perform at universities with faculty members or other local artists, but they tried to discourage such arrangements. "When you once start and then do not keep on using them," said Mischa, "they get offended."[62] Some artists were willing to play with them for nothing, or next to nothing, just to be able to say that they had performed with the Budapest String Quartet. Pianist Edward Kilenyi was willing to trade his fee for a hundred dollars' worth of tickets for performing a Bloch quintet at the 92nd Street Y in 1942. He planned to hand out the tickets to concert managers, agents, and friends. But the Y expected that "if the success of the past season is an indication of what we may expect next year, the house will be sold out by subscription."[63] The issue became moot when Kilenyi was drafted. Clarinetist Mitchell Lurie offered to play with the Quartet for free if the Library of Congress would pay his transportation costs from the West Coast, but Lurie was in the army and, for some strange reason, Spivacke said his military service precluded his joining the Quartet at the Library.[64]

Most musicians who did accompany the Budapest speak of the facility with which they were able to adjust to the Budapest style of playing and the way they were accepted with open arms. "I felt like a member of the Quartet," said double bassist Julius Levine.[65] "Occasionally they wanted me to do this or that," clarinetist David Oppenheim recalls.

> But mainly it was like going to a store and putting on a jacket—and it's a perfect fit and you say, "I'll take it." You didn't have to work at bringing two widely divergent views together. They were there with you. And you felt them with you. And on the stage, in performance for the first time, you felt you could take the widest latitude, that they were with you. They might argue with you or object later, but you couldn't lose them. They were wonderful to play with. It was less work relative to the performance than anyone else I ever played with. The Budapest gave you the freedom to express yourself as long as you were in the range that was acceptable.[66]

There was, to be sure, the occasional flare-up between temperamental musicians. Sharp-tongued Clifford Curzon grew impatient in a recording session while waiting for Sasha, Boris, and Mischa to get an introductory passage in a Brahms piano quintet correct. Finally he said, "Why any village violinist would know how to play a phrase like that." Roisman, who was not involved in playing the musical passage and usually said little, took the reprimand personally. "I'm not from no village. Odessa is a big town."[67]

Mischa said the Quartet always accommodated itself to a guest pianist's interpretation. "You let him take the lead. He is left to do the interpreting."[68] Whether the pianist actually did take the lead depended on who he or she was. Autocratic George Szell, who played at both the Library and Ravinia with the Budapest, tried to exercise control even over what piece they would play. "I have decided for the *Brahms* Quintet," he sanctimoniously announced to Spivacke at the Library of Congress in 1945, "which after a period of being fed up with it and a subsequent period of rest turns out to be not such a bad piece after all."[69] Szell performed with the lid of the piano on short stick—that is, raised only slightly. Rudolf Serkin played with the lid all the way up. Yet both were perfectly matched with the Quartet.

Artur Balsam's experience with the Quartet was different from Curzon's. "I didn't have anything to tell them," he said. "Everything was natural. We hardly ever stopped in rehearsal." The Quartet, he was surprised to discover, "didn't like to repeat. We played without repeats. Unusual at the time." But "their intonation was always perfect. The tempi were a little fast, maybe, but in a minute you were with them, if you know what I mean. They forced you to feel that you loved it."[70]

On the other hand, Serkin once rebelled against them. Walking out on stage at the Library for the second of a repeat-night set of performances, he announced for all the members of the Quartet to hear, "Now we play my way!"[71]

Fellow string players were treated especially well. "They included me," said violist Milton Katims, "in their very democratic method of resolving any musical disagreements during rehearsal." Katims said that when he first tried out for the Quartet—in Mischa's room at the Great Northern Hotel in the mid-1940s—"I felt as if I had always been making music with them. It was a very natural musical marriage." The Budapest members referred to Katims as "the fifth member of the Quartet."[72] Walter Trampler inherited the title when he succeeded Katims in the 1950s as their usual accompanist in viola quintets. "Their musicality was universal," he said. "You couldn't say they played Beethoven better than Mozart, or anything like that. With some quartets today, you can say, 'Yes, they understand the late Beethoven quartets beautifully, but Mozart maybe not so good.' I never heard anybody say that about the Budapest Quartet. I certainly didn't feel it."[73]

Cellist Gregor Piatigorsky not only played a series of concerts with them at the Library in the fall of 1960 but also joined them on the spur of the moment at concerts in Louisville and Pasadena. Both those times, Piatigorsky was in town to give a solo recital and went to hear the Budapest perform. When the tall cellist appeared backstage before the performance to visit with his friends, they prevailed on him to send for his instrument and join them for their concert; they simply dropped a scheduled string quartet in favor of a cello quintet. Paul Katz, later cellist with the Cleveland Quartet but then a teenage student, was at the Playhouse in Pasadena when the change in program to Schubert's Quintet in C was announced because of "a dear friend in the audience that day who agreed to play with them." It was, he said, "a big thrill for me."[74] Other guest cellists, like Benar Heifetz, always took the second cello part. Piatigorsky was the only one to whom Mischa would cede the lead cello.

A reverse incident occurred with Milton Katims. He once flew to Indianapolis to play three viola quintets with the Quartet, but Kroyt suddenly took ill. The concert was about to be cancelled when someone suggested that the Budapest switch their program to three string quartets, with Katims taking over Boris's part. There was "barely enough time to talk through the music," Katims recalled—"repeat here—no repeat there et cetera. I had the time of my life 'sight-reading' a concert with the great Budapest String Quartet." A local newspaper could not resist making a bon mot: "Budapesters Carry a Spare."[75]

"Budapesters"? The Quartet members did not think of themselves as Budapesters. The four Russians cringed when they heard themselves referred to as Budapesters. However, when the Quartet first toured America in the early 1930s, and even later, many people thought they were Hungarians. Critics, whom one would think would be better informed, called them "the four famous Magyars," "the Hungarian foursome," "the boys from Budapest" and even "this little orchestra from Budapest" and "the Budapest chorus." As late as 1950, Clive Barnes—later of the *New York Times*—described the Quartet members in a London newspaper as "four Americans of Hungarian parentage."[76]

For some time it was common for true Hungarians to seek out the musicians after a concert. Most times, they were immigrants who were proud of the Quartet's achievements, but the Library of Congress attracted numerous diplomats, too. They all greeted their "fellow countrymen" in Hungarian and tried to strike up conversations with the bewildered Quartet members until it finally dawned on them that they were not Hungarian. "Tell me," a young woman asked Sasha in English after a concert, "which part is more beautiful, Buda or Pest?" Sasha did not know what she was talking about. Of the four Russians, only Boris had ever been to Budapest, in 1923, when he performed a concerto there. "You know," she said, "there is a river which runs between them." But Sasha, with great assurance, said, "There is no river!"[77]

A lot of other funny things happened to them on the way to fame.

16

Opus Oops!

If the Budapest String Quartet had one flaw, it was their penchant for playing bridge. In their first years together, they were veritable addicts. On their lengthy tour of Australia and New Zealand in 1937, they filled in their off-hours between rehearsing and performing by starting to play cards, until, as Sasha confessed, they got "more involved in playing bridge than playing quartets."

"It came to the point," he said, "that we would play bridge up to the last minute before being picked up in the car for the concert and we no longer accepted invitations to any parties after the concerts, telling people that we were exhausted and had to go back to the hotel immediately to sleep. Actually, there was always a table set up for us with four chairs, four big sandwiches and beer, so that we could continue playing bridge where we left off—mind you, in evening dress. We didn't even bother to change we were so involved in the game."[1]

One night during the Australian tour, the Quartet had to break off in the middle of a game, with Mischa about to throw the first card out, to go to the concert hall. He pondered which card to play all the way to the hall and during the first movement of Schubert's Quartet in G. When the movement finished, Mischa got up, bowed, and started to walk off stage, to play his card.

Mischa's *faux pax* failed to deter them. "It was crazy," he said. "All the time someone loses and someone wins."[2] The games went on. So much money was changing hands on that tour—Mischa was able to pocket eighty Australian pounds—that they decided to pool all the winnings and purchase new suits when they returned to

Europe. That never happened, however. Acromonious disputes between partners were routine, but one day matters got out of hand.
Joe, partnered with Mischa, bid seven no trump, the highest you can
bid in bridge—a grand slam if they could make all thirteen tricks.
Boris was furious. He had a good hand and did not want Joe and
Mischa to play theirs. So he bid an impossible "Eight heart."[3] It
suddenly dawned on all four how ridiculous the situation was and
how obsessed they had become with cards. It was the end of their
bridge playing, temporarily. When Jean Giraudoux joined their boat
enroute to the Dutch East Indies, Sonya Kroyt—a compulsive bridge
player herself—discovered that the French writer was an avid fan of
the game, so a truce was called and the bridge games resumed. Several years later, Sonya got livid when she learned the games were
interfering with the group's rehearsals. Boris had made the mistake
of babysitting again for his daughter Yanna. He brought her to the
Library of Congress for a Budapest rehearsal. When the young girl
returned home, Sonya asked her what the Quartet had played; meaning, of course, which piece of music. "They played bridge," said
Yanna.[4] During rehearsal? When they were supposed to be practicing
on the Strads? Sonya had visions of the Library of Congress cancel-
ling the Budapest contract. Maybe, though, someone at the Library
already suspected the lapse. A cartoon in *Saturday Review* magazine
showed four men on a concert stage seated around a card table,
playing bridge. A member of the audience in the first row is leaning
toward his companion and saying, "It doesn't look like the Budapest
String Quartet to me."[5]

Sonya and Boris enjoyed a relationship as stormy as that among
the members of the Quartet. Boris, whose love of gadgetry extended
to electric razors and cameras—he had at least a dozen of each—
returned from the Quartet trip to Japan in 1952 with a new Nikon.
But knowing full well what Sonya would say—how many cameras
does anyone need, after all?—he asked Mischa for a favor. Mischa
was to say that he had bought the camera but had decided he did not
want it and had given it to Boris. The ruse did not work. As expected,
Sonya was angry. Boris's only recourse was to yell back at her for
smoking too much.[6]

Actually, there was a childish streak in all the Quartet members.
Double bassist Julius Levine was on his way to a rehearsal with them
in Manhattan of Schubert's "Trout" Quintet when he passed a street
vendor selling little wind-up monkeys that played cymbals and
drums. Though new to the Quartet, Levine wanted to show his
appreciation for being asked to join them. He purchased four of the

toys and wrapped them individually. When he arrived at the rehearsal hall, the Quartet was already on the stage, finishing a run-through of a quartet. Levine left the toys at the front of the platform and went backstage to take his bass fiddle out, embarrassed now by his presumptuousness and wondering if perhaps he might be insulting the four Russians. When he came back on stage, he was astonished to see Joe, Mischa, Sasha, and Boris down on the floor, winding up and playing with the toys.[7]

Each Quartet member was responsible for bringing his own music to a recital. At Washington Irving High School in Manhattan one night, Boris forgot his part for a Beethoven quartet that was on the program with a Haydn and a Brahms. He asked the audience whether anyone had a score that he could follow. Young Samuel Rhodes, a student at the High School of Music and Arts, was there and could have kicked himself. Rhodes, who later became violist with the Juilliard Quartet, possessed a viola part but had left it at home. The Quartet made up the omission by substituting another Haydn that, Rhodes said, "was so vivid and wonderful" no one in the audience complained.[8]

Rhodes was again present when an odder incident occurred at Washington Irving during another evening Budapest concert. The four musicians reached the conclusion of a Brahms quartet when Sasha suddenly turned a page and stopped playing. The last page of his music had fallen off. "I could have faked it," said Sasha, "but I didn't want to do this to my colleagues." Sasha remembered hearing the Kolisch Quartet, which played from memory—"all four of them nervous wrecks and my getting wet with perspiration from nervousness listening to their playing and making mistakes." While his brother, Joe, and Boris looked at each other curiously, Sasha left his chair and went backstage, to search for the missing page. But he could not find it, so the Quartet promised to play the movement as an encore at their next performance at the school, and Sasha vowed that he would play a concert there every year; he kept his promise.[9]

Washington Irving, incidentally, was the Quartet's favorite hall in Manhattan. Tickets for the high school auditorium were purposely priced at twenty-five cents to enable students and low-income families to hear good music. The Quartet always took a lower fee there than at any other hall where they performed, because the members all felt it attracted the most appreciative audience. "The higher uptown you go," said Mischa, "the colder the audience gets." When the Quartet performed at Washington Irving, Mischa said, "we played with more gusto."[10] Boris felt the same way about

New York audiences. The least appreciative, he said, were at the
Metropolitan Museum of Art; although the hall was fully sub-
scribed, many upper East Side couples routinely skipped performances.[11] Only audiences in Cleveland—where many of the concertgoers were doctors, lawyers, and faculty members from Case
Western Reserve University—matched those at Washington Irving.

Washington Irving's auditorium held twelve hundred persons
and was always sold out for Budapest concerts. It was one of the
larger halls that the Quartet regularly performed in. But before the
Quartet was established and in great demand, the four musicians
accepted bookings wherever they could get them. Once they performed for only three persons—a rich Southern widow and the local
reporter and his wife, whom she invited to the performance in her
house. They also played in the garden of a Portland music enthusiast, while his guests sat, stood, or reclined on an adjacent terrace.
Before the Buffalo Chamber Music Society found a home of its own,
the Victorian mansion of Cameron and Jane Baird was the scene of
many of their recitals in that city. When Baird died in 1960, they
played at his funeral. Joe and the Schneider brothers broke a rule
about getting involved in each other's personal lives to perform with
Mieczysław Horszowski at the wedding of Boris's daughter Yanna.

Mischa seemed to be the one most beset by one particular slip-
up—losing his place in the middle of a piece. It happened to Boris
once; he got so mixed up in a solo phrase that it took him four
measures to work out of it. But such embarrassing moments happened more than once to Mischa. At the Library of Congress one
night, he was "fit to be tied," because he momentarily got lost and
failed to start a repeat section in a Mozart quartet.[12] Another time, in
a difficult section of the last movement of Beethoven's Opus 59, No.
2, when each instrument comes in one after another, Mischa missed
his cue "and the whole business was shaky," he recalled, "just like a
storm. But we kept on, because you are a professional, you know,
you kept on playing, until we came together. And we felt so awful,
especially I felt so awful."[13]

Things sometimes went awry because of the Quartet's busy
travel schedule, especially in the 1930s in Norway, where the four
often had to catch ferries after a concert to proceed to the next town
on their schedule. Once while on tour there, the departure time for
the boat they had to catch on a certain night was moved up one hour.
The concert program listed the three quartets they were to play, but
not the movements, so in order to get to the boat on time, they
played one movement from each of the three quartets and a fourth

movement as an encore. At another town in Norway, the members were not sure when a ferry they had to take was scheduled to depart. They asked a bellboy at their hotel to come to the movie house where they were playing to let them know when the boat left. In the middle of their performance, while they were playing, the bellboy came out on stage and announced out loud that the ferry was leaving in an hour.[14]

The most ludicrous experience of all, though, occurred when they were on tour in South America. This time, they were concerned that they would make a midnight plane flight after their concert, which was scheduled to start at 9 o'clock; however, audiences in South America routinely arrived an hour and a half late. Fortunately, the concert-hall manager was sympathetic. "I have sold out the house and to tell you the truth, I would like to teach them a lesson for being so stupid to always come so late to concerts." So, in order for the Quartet to be able to get to the airport in time, the concert began as scheduled, at 9 o'clock; only Pola Roisman and Sonya Kroyt were in the audience.[15]

The darnedest things happened sometimes when they played. Humidity was a problem at recording sessions held for a time in an old, abandoned church on East 30th Street in Manhattan. Resonance in the church, which was made of wood and plaster, was perfect, allowing for what recording technicians call "a long decay, a beautiful natural violin sound." But the sound was always dry and wiry on hot days and seemed to be better on rainy ones, so a humidifier had to be installed in the church, and the problem then became the whir of its engine.[16]

More annoying when the Quartet performed on stage before an audience were ventilator fans rattling, heating pipes whistling, and doors somewhere being slammed. Buffalo seemed to have a premium on such distractions, no matter where in the city they played. The "small, gilt-covered chairs" in the ballroom of the Hotel Statler, where the Quartet first played for the Buffalo Chamber Music Society, were not only uncomfortable but "squeaked during string passages of quiet ecstasy."[17] A motor in an air-conditioning unit at Baird Hall at the University of Buffalo started to clatter like "a lawn mower," so the Quartet halted playing and "exchanged meaningful looks—mutual exhortations to courage and resignation."[18] (Adolf Busch had been plagued by an air-conditioning unit in Buffalo, too, at Kleinhans Hall, another recital hall where the Budapest also performed. First, an electrician beamed a purple spot into Busch's eyes as he was about to start playing with his quartet. He dropped his bow, put his hand to his face, and rushed off stage. When he returned, the electrician forgot to turn off the air-conditioning system, so Busch had to grapple with his music stand, using his bow, hands, and even nose to keep his music from blowing away.[19])

The Library of Congress was not immune to these types of distractions. The roof in the vestibule of the Coolidge Auditorium started to leak during a thunderstorm in the middle of a concert. Spivacke and an assistant rushed there and stood under the torrents, cupping their hands, to reduce the noise as the water hit the floor. Needless to say, they got drenched.[20]

Noise, whether man-made or machine, was always distracting. A *New York Times* critic marveled that the "quiet" at a concert of the Quartet at the 92nd Street Y "was almost palpable. Nowhere else in the city can one draw so many angry looks from just shifting in his seat."[21] That may have been true of the audience, but not always of the staff. Sasha once felt compelled to interrupt a concert at the Y to stride backstage and bawl out the noisemakers.[22]

A different problem in the early years was the lack of sophistication of concertgoers in some cities. Once, after Joe first joined the Quartet, a woman came backstage following a performance, eager to see Joe's instrument because, she said, she had never seen a second violin before.[23]

Joe, by the way, was then playing on an instrument made by Domenico Montagnana, an apprentice of Stradivarius. He, as well as the other members, owned a variety of instruments over the years. None ever owned a Strad, although Boris performed on the so-called Tuscan Strad from 1960 on; it was loaned to him by the widow of Cameron Baird of Buffalo, a friend of the Quartet and amateur violist who died that year. Many violinists, especially soloists like Paganini and Heifetz, prefer instruments made by Guiseppe Guarneri, which are more rugged than Strads. Roisman owned an unusual violin that he thought was either a Guarneri del Gesu or one made by another member of the violin-making family, Pietro Guarneri, but it was actually neither. It was a viola that had been cut down to violin size—an unusual but not-unheard-of refashioning. Emil Hauser sold the instrument to him during the war, telling him that it was a Guarneri at one time owned by Joseph Joachim and played continuously since only in quartets. The instrument, as Joe learned many years later, was originally made by another Cremona luthier, Lorenzo Storione, with a Guarneri scroll apparently added when it was reshaped into a violin.

Before Boris took to playing on the Tuscan Strad, he owned variously a viola made by Karel Van der Meer, a Grancino, and an instrument made by Michael Deconet (a pupil of Montagnana). Sasha played a French-made Vuillaume and later a Guarneri del Gesu. Mischa had a Carlo Testore cello in the 1930s, later a Guadagnini, and then the instrument that was most associated with his playing, a Gofriller.

Another problem the Quartet had when touring in the early years was audience manners. Twice it abruptly broke off playing before an Atlanta audience because of chattering, refusing to continue until there was absolute silence. They halted after the first movement of an early Beethoven quartet, sitting motionless and without saying anything for several moments until the talking subsided, and then resumed playing. Shortly thereafter, during the third movement of a Brahms quartet, "the sound of creaking boards, stomping feet and creaking doors filled the auditorium," and so they stopped again. "Seldom before has any artist or group of artists resorted to such drastic action to get silence," a local newspaper reported, "but it certainly produced the desired results."[24]

The Quartet ran into a similar problem in Miami, prompting a critic to comment, "The Budapesters themselves, affable and lovable people, probably trust that when next they visit this community no one will be seated or applaud between movements, or slam doors on the final notes."[25] In fact, applause between movements was so annoying that a number of concert halls, including Town Hall in New York, printed notices in their programmes asking, "Please Refrain From Applauding Between Movements." Sometimes they added, "There Will Be No Encores," though the Quartet—especially outside of New York—often did play encores in its first years in the United States.

Noise, birds, weather, and bugs always made playing at Ravinia unexpectedly eventful. Despite the promises of the North Western Railroad to reduce service during concerts, trains still ran on tracks alongside the festival park during concerts, and locomotive engineers often honked as they went by. A Chicago critic wondered if "we can ask them to silence the horn which turns an octet into a nonet and has music lovers begging, 'No, No, Nonet.'"[26] If it was not a train going by at Ravinia, it was the birds—"to compete with diesels and the sparrows is not unlike using your silver tea service at a barbecue," said another Chicago reviewer.[27] And then there was the notorious Ravinia heat and humidity—what Mischa called the "heat and hell of Ravinia"[28]—which caused intonation problems for the string instruments. "The tone of the quartet seemed to fade out before it could reach the back rows," a reporter noted.[29] The Quartet members also had to contend with a "plentifully, not to say excessively, present" world of insects—"mosquitoes, gnats and an assortment of other larger flying objects."[30] Another reviewer wrote, "There were Haydn, Schumann, Mozart, humidity, and mosquitos at Ravinia last night, with the Budapest Quartet playing the first three and the audience seeking whatever victory it could put together over the others."[31] "As a hedge against hot weather," Don Henahan of the Chicago *Daily News* noted, the Quartet was moved "outside to the air-cooled pavilion," but then the weather turned cold. "At any rate, the Budapests . . . have learned after more than thirty years together how to warm up an audience," reported Henahan, who later, using the byline Donal Henahan, was chief music critic of the *New York Times*.[32]

If it was not the heat, it was the cold. The Quartet was always on the road, touring through the Midwest, during the coldest months of the year. Despite a stormy night in Buffalo, a local wit said, "Neither rain nor gloom of night will stay these chamber courtiers from the swift completion of their appointed rondo."[33] "The outdoors last night was not fit for any man, on foot or carried," said a Toledo, Ohio, reporter who braved a storm to hear the Budapest perform at the Museum of Art. "Still there were some 200 vigorous souls who got as far."[34] On the other hand, the Quartet members themselves never made it to a recital in northern Illinois. They were all in a car with Boris driving on Armistice Day in 1947, when the car skidded on an ice-covered back road. Kroyt braked sharply but hit a tree, tossing everyone forward. Joe suffered a broken collarbone, but fortunately he was unable to play for only a month; only a few other concerts had to be cancelled—most were rescheduled. One aspect of the incident did eventually provide a humorous headline for one Washington newspaper. Joe had to sue Boris to collect medical expenses from Boris's insurance company. As it turned out, on the same day that a marshal served Kroyt with the lawsuit papers, two other marshals appeared at his apartment in Washington—to present him with notification of a rent increase and to give him notice to appear for jury duty. "Plagued by Law, Viola Artist Plays on," said the headline in the Washington *Star*.[35]

Joe stayed behind one night when Howard Scott of CBS Records introduced the others to baseball. Scott took Mischa, Sasha, and Boris to a Washington Senators' night baseball game and spent "a hysterical evening" trying to explain what each ball player did and why a base runner could not just run straight across from first base to third. The Schneider brothers stuffed themselves with hot dogs and beer, while Boris tried to figure out the meaning of the peculiar signaling between the "pisher" and the "cocker." The next morning, instead of recording, as they were supposed to do, they regaled Joe with stories about the game.[36] They became such fans that several lunchtimes at the Library found them in the employee lunchroom, watching the World Series on television.[37]

At one point, to keep their egos in check, Scott had to outwit them. When the Quartet first recorded at the Library of Congress, only one microphone was used. It was placed on a chair on one side of the stage, with the Quartet lined up on the other side. However, they insisted on sitting in their normal positions when, with the advent of stereo, they recorded again at the Library. Ordinarily the Quartet balanced their own sound. "They were extremely sound conscious," said Scott, "and, of course, extremely balance conscious. They were perfect because they did it all themselves. We didn't have to sit and raise a fiddle, lower the cello, or any of that stuff." One day, Scott decided to use three mikes, one on each side of the Quartet and a third hanging directly overhead. But Boris felt that the sound of his viola was at a disadvantage because the *f* holes on his instrument faced away from the mike on his side. "It's not fair," he said. So Scott positioned a mike in front of Boris. Now Sasha was annoyed. "So what's the matter with me?" he asked. So Scott positioned a fifth mike in front of Sasha, and the recording session went on. What Scott did not tell them was that two of the mikes were dead. While they were playing, Scott had Sasha's and the overhead one turned off.[38]

One difficulty no string player can avoid is the breaking of a string on his instrument during a performance. It happens all the time and veteran concertgoers are not surprised when one pops. It happened, however, to both Milton Katims and Benar Heifetz during a sextet at a Budapest concert at Town Hall, causing a "gust of laughter" when the second one went.[39] The laughter was louder and longer when Jac Gorodetzky tried to leave the stage at Ravinia to replace a string that broke during a performance. He could not open the door. He stood there, pulling on the doorknob and banging on the door. Considering how well the Quartet performs, a reporter said, "it hardly seems necessary to enforce the contract by locking the door leading offstage while they are playing."[40]

Alert concertgoers noticed that every so often Boris would smile between movements as he adjusted the music on his stand in preparation for the next movement. That was Sasha's doing. Always the prankster, he once delayed an opening phrase a second or two, just to see the expression on the others' faces as they waited for him to start.[41] But if Sasha was notorious for anything, it was for inserting photographs of young, nude, nubile young ladies inside the pages of his colleagues' music that would appear while they were playing. Joe and Mischa were above such antics. Sasha, who ordinarily carried a nude photo in his violin case, once put it in Joe's music, but Joe refused to react and simply went on playing from memory.[42] Boris was a better foil. He learned not to smile when he came upon a nude picture in the middle of a movement, but at the end of the movement you could count on him to grin. Boris, who kept the famous nude photo of Marilyn Monroe on display at home, tried slipping a similar picture into Mischa's music. Mischa's eyebrows went up when, turning a page, he came upon it. He slammed the music shut and played from memory until he reached the next page. After joining the Quartet for several concerts, Julius Levine felt comfortable enough to get into the act. This time Boris could not hold himself back from breaking out in a broad smile in the midst of playing. Instead of a nude photo, Levine had slipped into Kroyt's Beethoven a picture of ninety-year-old Mrs. Whittall.[43]

They all could afford to smile as 1960 approached—as Joe, Mischa, and Boris were approaching their twenty-fifth year together, and Sasha his fifteenth with the Quartet. They were the most popular and well-known chamber-music group in history, in any country. Columbia had by now issued more than fifty-five Budapest albums and had sold more than two million copies of their recordings, a total not exceeded by any other Columbia artists except major symphony orchestras. Their concerts were routinely sold out. Their Beethoven cycles at the 92nd Street Y were a fixture of the New York musical scene, and a similar annual series was started in Buffalo in 1955. They commanded fees no other American quartet could hope to get. They made annual spring trips to Puerto Rico to take part in the Festival Casals. They flew from San Juan to Israel in 1959 to be the nucleus of a chamber-music festival that Sasha arranged at the urging of violinist Isaac Stern, donating their fees for all their appearances there. The next year they toured Italy, France, and England again. They played at Aspen and Tanglewood. In Buenos Aires, they drew thirty-five hundred people to the largest opera house in the world, the Teatro Colon. Everywhere, people knew them, recalled Robert Mann of the Juilliard String Quartet, "even airline stewardesses."[44] The Budapest String Quartet's name had become so recognizable that the *New Yorker* magazine could run a cartoon showing four suspicious-looking hoods with instrument cases leaving a bank, while a police officer confidently told his partner, "They're OK, Sarge—it's the Budapest String Quartet."[45] Writing facetiously in the *Saturday Evening Post* about the beneficial side to being "flaming, hackle-rousing, toe-curling" angry, humorist H. Allen Smith said that "perhaps" the most hostile person he knew was a

> man quite prominent in the entertainment world who hates the Budapest String Quartet. He believes that all four members of the group are hambones without equal anywhere in show business. "It has eaten its way right inside of me," he says. "One look at those four musicians and I feel like screaming. It's the way they wobble and wag and jerk their heads and their torsos. I tell you it's not only hammy—it's cornball!" He asked that I not use his name for fear that he will be waylaid and beaten up four times in rapid succession.[46]

The world of chamber music was no longer elitist. Thanks in good part to the Budapest, it was undergoing a transformation. It was becoming part of the mainstream of classical music, a popular source of pleasure for myriads of people.

17

"Mr. Chamber Music"

In the late 1940s, after World War II, there were perhaps three or four major string quartets active in the United States—the Juilliard, the Paganini, and the New Music, as well as the Budapest. Ten years later, a dozen or more were concertizing. "I can state with certain authority that the interest in chamber music is growing by leaps and bounds," Henry Colbert, a music manager, said in 1957. He said that he could count between five hundred and six hundred "outlets for chamber music ensembles in the U.S.A. and Canada, almost half of which present nothing else."[1] Henri Temianka of the Paganini Quartet claimed that same year that there were "now a thousand-odd" community concert associations, "an astonishing development" that had occurred from 1952 to 1957 alone. "In Dallas, where we have played annually for the past ten years, we have now been asked, for the first time, to play concerts on two successive days, a sure indication of an increasing audience. A similar request came from Seattle."[2]

A major reason was the interest created by the Budapest, whether because of favorable reviews or by word of mouth. Their fan mail came from all over the United States and from abroad. One fan who masked herself as "Viola" wrote Boris, "I know you love me. If you did not, you wouldn't keep me tucked under your chin for so many hours every day."[3] A California woman said she and a friend stood in a crowded train for two hundred miles to hear the Quartet play the Beethoven cycle at Mills College—"the major musical experience of our lives."[4] Another woman, the mother of a child with a "very serious heart condition," thanked the Quartet for permitting her daughter to attend a rehearsal at Mills—"You are fortunate men,—you who can contribute to humanity this beauty it so badly needs. Upon our imperfect world of savage confusion & pain, you can impose a perfect world of harmony & order."[5] Supreme Court Associate Justice Abe Fortas, who played the violin, said he was "looking around for somebody to write a string quartet for two second violins. That would take care of Sasha and allow me to participate."[6] A student at Kanazawa University in Japan wrote, "I like music very much, but I didn't know the string quartet was wonderful this way. I cannot understand music but I feel something with listening wonderful music. When I was listening your music I forgot present, and past too. I felt like weeping and many dreams come and go."[7] A minister said he played the Quartet's recording of Beethoven's Opus 131 at the final evening of a summer camp for nine-year-olds, one of whom asked him afterward, "Gee, what was that music? It sounded like God talking."[8]

When the Quartet first toured Japan in 1952, there were only two chamber-music societies in the entire country. When they returned less than two years later, there were ten.[9] Wherever they went, music societies seemed to sprout up or, if they already existed, breathe with new life.

A friend of Mischa's, Dr. Ernest Bueding, thought Cleveland in the late 1940s was on a "starvation diet" when it came to chamber music. Bueding, a physician on the medical faculty of Case Western Reserve University, decided to try to correct the situation. The Quartet played for informal music groups that he and friends organized there in the winters of 1947, 1948, and 1949. By 1950, because of "the great success of these concerts," the Cleveland Chamber Music Society was officially established, and for the first fifteen years of its existence, the Budapest was an almost annual visitor.[10]

Bueding left Cleveland in the early 1950s to teach at Louisiana State University and helped found the New Orleans Friends of Music. To Bueding, it seemed only natural to ask the Budapest to appear at the organization's opening concert, on January 27, 1956, the two hundredth anniversary of Mozart's birth. The concert drew a thousand persons and was "so successful" that "already there is talk of expansion for next year's series."[11]

Some music lovers complained that chamber music was not meant to be played in large halls before so many people. But Sasha pooh-poohed them. "It is a silly idea to play just for a small group," he told an Arizona reporter. "It is a matter of listening. It is better to play in a big hall not entirely filled up, than in a small hall that won't hold all the people who want to get in." Chamber music, Sasha said, "was written with much more warmth and dedication than other works. . . . It was not written for size."[12]

People, many people, wanted to hear the Budapest, wanted to sample Beethoven, Mozart, and Brahms, wanted the opportunity to relish music that was the finest a composer could write. Thirsting for the experience, people began crowding into Budapest concerts as early as 1940. "The jam-packed audience" at the Civic Theater in Portland, a newspaper reported in June 1942, helped to lay to rest "a couple of ancient rumors for all time: (1) nobody, especially not chamber music addicts, wants musisc [sic] in the summertime; (2) chamber music is a bore."[13] The Lecture Hall of the Detroit Institute of Arts "all but burst its seams and it was necessary to open the windows, which give on the surrounding corridors, and permit die-hard customers to listen with their bodies outside and their heads poked in."[14] "That sound" from the Veterans' Building, a San Francisco newspaper said, "was not a football rally, but merely an over-flowing audience expressing its appreciation."[15] The same newspaper remarked in August 1943 on the "huge attendance the Budapest has drawn this season."[16] Because of the Quartet's popularity, it was not unusual to have seats placed on the stage with them when they performed, as happened on numerous occasions when they played in Boston's Jordan Hall. It got so, an Indianapolis critic said, that "a season of chamber music without the Budapesters would be like Christmas without Santa Claus: A season that lacked an essential personality."[17] An Ithaca, New York, journalist said, "We longed for a 10-foot snowfall so that the Budapest Quartet would have been marooned, and thus would have played for us again." The "four members," he said, "collectively deserve the sobriquet of 'Mr. Chamber Music.'"[18]

In the summer of 1948, instead of going to Mills College, the Quartet spent a month at the University of Minnesota in Minneapolis, teaching and playing. They had to arrange extra concerts to handle the press for tickets, and at one recital, on the July Fourth weekend, "even though the mercury hit 100 degrees, Schott Hall auditorium was filled with perspiring but thoroughly happy music lovers." Minneapolis "chamber music addicts" were in such a "state bordering on frenzy" that one of the Quartet's concerts was shifted to the university's huge Northrop Auditorium, attracting "probably the largest audience for a chamber music event . . . the town has ever mustered."[19]

By 1955, with Sasha back in the Quartet, *Newsweek* magazine was calling the Quartet's performances at colleges and universities "a healthy sign of growing U.S. musical maturity."[20] And two years later, *Life* proclaimed that "the admirers of chamber music have multiplied from a cult to a mass audience." The "busy Budapest," it said, "is finding new fans in the Montana ranch lands, playing the same long-hair programs in Missoula as in New York. . . . The music that Haydn, Mozart and Beethoven wrote for performances in court circles of Vienna is played by the Budapest Quartet in high school halls and basketball courts before ranchers and college students."[21] The *Christian Science Monitor* declared, "How times have changed! Now it is the younger set that forms the majority of Budapest hearers."[22] An Alabama reviewer could not recall, "to the best of my memory," when so many people filled "the concert-room of the Barbert Institute, Birmingham, as sat, stood or sprawled there last night."[23] A Buffalo critic noted that, because of the Budapest Quartet, many concert agencies were now devoted exclusively to chamber-music ensembles: "Nothing like it existed in America a generation ago."[24] Another Buffalo critic credited the Quartet with playing "a leading part in the extraordinary modern revival of interest in chamber music."[25]

The Quartet performed more concerts for the Buffalo Chamber Music Society than for any other society—forty-five in all between 1931 and 1965. It saved the society from extinction during the 1934–35 season, when the society could afford to offer only one concert. "In a sense," a history of the organization declares, "the Budapest *was* the Society."[26] For a long time, the chairman of its executive committee was Cameron Baird. A violist, Baird had studied in Germany with Paul Hindemith, and Hindemith first lived at the Baird home when he fled Germany in 1938. Another chamber-music enthusiast in Buffalo was Frederick Slee, an accomplished amateur string player who was known as the Niagara Frontier's best-known corporation lawyer. Slee had his own ideas about the order in which the seventeen works in the Beethoven cycle should be played, though he never explained his rationale. When he died, he left enough money to have the cycle played in six concerts every year. The Budapest was the first to perform the Slee Bequest and continued to do so through 1964. The sequence "was odd at first," says Mischa, "but then it started to make sense."[27]

The Ravinia Festival, started in 1904, was originally a summer showcase for symphony orchestras and opera performances. A four-day chamber-music series was started in 1940, but it was treated as a stepchild of the festival and scheduled after the usual six-week ap-

pearance of the Chicago Symphony. The first quartet to perform was
the Pro Arte, which drew, a concertgoer who was there remembered,
"only a handful of people." Chamber music was "not a popular
affair" at Ravinia until the following August, when the Budapest,
which had already replaced the Pro Arte at Mills College earlier that
summer, first appeared, in place of the Pro Arte.[28] Though the appearance with Benny Goodman at one of their recitals helped to
shoot attendance up to what festival administrators thought—
"much to our surprise and pleasure"—was "an unbelievable" 7,594
for the four concerts,[29] the Quartet drew almost as many persons
when George Szell performed with them two years later. By 1951
they were attracting almost fifteen thousand persons for their four
appearances. Chamber music became such a popular feature of the
festival that performances were moved from the end of the season
and integrated into the festival throughout the summer. Considered
a vital part of Ravinia, the Quartet performed a special concert for
the festival staff and members of the Chicago Symphony Orchestra; Pierre Monteux, its conductor, took the second viola part in
Mozart's Quintet in G Minor.

It would be wrong to insinuate that the United States was devoid
of chamber-music societies or that there were no chamber-music
fans at all before the Budapest Quartet, but their number was limited. The University Musical Society of the University of Michigan
in Ann Arbor, which was established in 1879, started a chamber-
music festival in 1941. The Budapest began appearing there in 1945
and for the next twenty years performed there more often than any
other ensemble. The Peoples' Symphony Concerts at Washington
Irving High School in New York—which the Quartet members loved
to play for—began in 1900, when the concerts were first held at
Cooper Union and then at Carnegie Hall; from 1914 on, Peoples'
Symphony began offering soloists, dance recitals, and quartet perfor-
mances by such ensembles as the Kneisel and Flonzaley quartets.
Cornell University's concert series began in 1903; between 1931—
when the Budapest played there on its first U.S. tour—and 1959, the
Quartet performed there thirteen times. The Coleman Chamber
Music Association in Pasadena, California, a routine stop on the
Budapest's western tours, was founded in 1904. The New Friends of
Music, for whom the Quartet performed after their Ellis Island ad-
venture, started during the 1935–36 season. The 92nd Street Y began
offering chamber music in the 1937–38 season, when the Quartet
first appeared. To the chagrin of Y staffers, William Kolodney, who
was in charge of its music programs, went on a half-day schedule in

1954 and spent the other half day working about a dozen blocks away at the Metropolitan Museum of Art. The Quartet had played a single concert in the museum's Morgan Wing in 1946, but with the opening of the Grace Rainey Rogers Auditorium in the mid-1950s, they became a staple. Kolodney signed the Budapest Quartet for yearly series at the "Met," though he made a point of not scheduling the same works as those the Budapest played at the Y.

One problem that the Quartet continually had to wrestle with was fees. They steadily, but cautiously, increased them. In comparison with hiring soloists, the cost of engaging the Budapest was relatively inexpensive. When they played at the Y in 1938, for example, the four musicians had to split a concert fee of three hundred dollars,[30] while Efrem Zimbalist was getting more than twice as much, six hundred fifty dollars, for a solo violin recital.[31] Even seven years later, when they were firmly established as the nation's leading string quartet, they were getting six hundred dollars a concert, while Nathan Milstein was asking a "minimum of $1,000."[32]

That same year, 1945, Luther Marchant, who arranged the twelve concerts that Mills College presented on its campus and at the San Francisco Museum of Art, reported that the trustees had voted to raise the Quartet's fee from $4,800 to $5,300—"the best we can do"—but that meant that Mills could not afford to engage violist Milton Katims to perform quintets with them: "The money we could have paid him must go toward your increase in salary." Marchant added, "You realize that last year was the first time in fifteen years that the concerts have paid for themselves."[33]

A flurry of reactions of dismay was touched off when the Quartet raised its fee to eight hundred dollars two years later, in 1947. A Seattle concert manager, Annie Friedberg said in a letter to the Quartet members, "writes that he can not pay" eight hundred dollars for a single concert, "so are you willing to go to Seattle for just one concert between your Portland dates, for $600?" A Pittsburgh manager, she said in the same letter, informed her "that it would be quite a hardship for them to pay $800. Are you willing to make that a special price or not?"[34] A Denver Symphony Society official said he "personally shall be very sorry if the quartet cannot be signed here," but he saw "little chance of it" because of the increase in their concert fee.[35] The University of Chicago was interested in engaging the Quartet for three recitals, but "their chamber music series is operated on a deficit which must stay within certain limitions [sic]. . . . perhaps you would be willing to take $700 instead of $800.

Everybody," Friedberg added, "is coming down in price so I have to do the best I can."[36]

Princeton University was a regular stop on their annual tour of the Northeast, and physicist Albert Einstein, a regular concertgoer sitting in the first row. But the head of its recital program, Friedberg told the Quartet, "says that they do not want to give you up and if you insist, they will pay your fee this season but do not know whether they would not have to make other plans for the season following, as they can not raise their own admission prices."[37] The Budapest decided "under the circumstances, and confidentially, to accept $700."[38] They made the same adjustment for the Mozart Society in New York, whose head wondered, "would it be possible for you to play for us for 600 instead of 800 this year. We are only a small group at best . . . [and] as soon as we are more firmly established, which I hope will be the case next year, there will be no question of that any more."[39] Despite all the negative reaction to the eight-hundred-dollar fee, Friedberg wondered whether she should ask nine hundred dollars a concert "in most cases" for the 1949–50 season. "I certainly think that you should have it, as everything is higher in price, and I do not doubt that people would be willing to pay the higher price."[40]

By 1960, the Quartet's standard fee had risen to fifteen hundred dollars, though it asked a lesser amount for its annual series at such places as the Library of Congress and the 92nd Street Y. Fifteen hundred dollars is a paltry sum by modern standards, but then, in the years before the severe inflation caused by the Vietnam war, it was a rather large amount and more than any other American quartet earned. When the Budapest was getting $1,350 from the Buffalo Chamber Music Society in 1964, for example, the Juilliard and the Kroll quartets were making $1,000 a concert; and the Lenox, $850.[41] In fact, the Quartet was the bellwether. As its fees rose, those of other American quartets followed suit. In the mid-1950s, members of the New Music Quartet, reacting to the thousand-dollar fee that the Quartetto Italiano charged during a brief American tour, met with members of the Budapest to try to convince them to raise their fee. If the Budapest did, the New Music could charge more, too. The Budapest, however, was loathe to do so. It was always wary, afraid that recital halls could not manage the increase.[42] "We are realists," said Mischa. "Even if the greatest quartet in the world, you can only ask so much."[43]

Although Mischa, Joe, and Boris planned to cut down on their crowded tour schedule when Sasha rejoined the Quartet, they still played ninety-nine recitals in the 1956–57 concert season and more than eighty concerts each year after that. They were so much in demand that during one typical two-week period they performed thirteen concerts on thirteen consecutive nights, swinging from Washington up to New York City and into New England and returning home only for Thanksgiving.

Tours like that could be exhausting. Their overall schedule may not have been as taxing as in previous years, but they were no longer young men who could hop from city to city every day, squeezing a nap in between an afternoon rehearsal and an evening performance, packing, unpacking, and rushing to airports or train stations to get to the next engagement. Mischa began to "hate" to go on tour; he could not "stand it any more."[44] The Quartet had crossed the Atlantic to New York sixteen times, he counted, and had made the trip to Australia and Indonesia eight times.[45] It was different, he said, when the Quartet members were "young," though even then, it was difficult to be "always going away for two months, suffering all the time, having nostalgia, always dreaming how good it would be to come home." At that time, he went on,

> I always had a terrific longing to go back home and to be together. But I said, "Well, what am I going to do if I give that up, what is going to be, what will happen to me? I will go and play in an orchestra, sit in an orchestra." And that was this fight between your profession and your private life. I can't remember that I ever was absolutely happy on a tour, because always I was thinking of home.[46]

The jet age only made matters worse: "One has no time for anything but the plane voyage, checking into the hotel, a rest before the concert, the concert, then late to bed because of parties after the concerts, and the next day again the plane, hotel, et cetera. And the life is so lonesome."

Mischa was certain that "Roisman, or Boris, or my brother," felt the same way—"but we never talked about it."[47] But Boris, for one, shared Mischa's growing disaffection with touring. He tried to recreate some semblance of home in whatever hotel he stayed. He would unpack, cover the dresser with a piece of fabric, and studiously place on it his writing utensils, comb, brush, and an assortment of gadgets—a travel alarm that also contained a compass and barometer and told the time of day around the world, an elaborate combination knife-and-cutlery set, and the electric water heater for his tea. When he was finished, the room looked like his bedroom at home, but it was no substitute. Boris said his worst fear was that if he went to hell, his eternal chore would be to pack and unpack in one hotel room after another. Now a grandfather, Boris was writing home, "I miss you all very much! Some Times I feel painful lonely after 'the little ones'! My dear grandchildren! (and I miss Mutsi!) This Tours are getting now more difficult for me than ever."[48]

They were older, less able physically to cope with long stretches of travel. Boris was going on sixty-three in 1960; Joe, nearing his sixtieth birthday; Mischa was fifty-six years old; Sasha, going on fifty-two. Something was bound to give.

18

Silence in the Library

Joe did not tell anyone at the time, but when he and the other Quartet members settled in America in 1939, he took a routine physical examination in order to apply for a life-insurance policy. The doctor warned him that he had high blood pressure. That was scary enough—after all, Joe's father had died of a heart attack at the age of fifty, and Joe was always conscious of his own health problems. But what the doctor went on to tell him was more frightening: "Every time you are excited it is a nail in your coffin."[1] So Joe, as reserved and undemonstrative as he ordinarily was, became even more introverted.

Only Pola knew about Roisman's condition, though every so often Joe left a clue: when his blood pressure went up, his intonation went off. In the midst of a performance, Edgar Ortenberg remembered, Joe's pitch would go up "one thirty-second of a note and we would all go up with him."[2] It is not unusual for a player's intonation to go off; it happens to string players now and then, so evidently none of the others ever suspected anything serious was the matter. Besides, because Joe suffered so many illnesses and accidents, minor variations in his performance were to be expected and hardly bothered the others.

In the late summer of 1945, for example, Joe contracted Rocky Mountain spotted fever while vacationing at Lake Tahoe and had to be hospitalized in Reno. Two days after he returned to Washington, he suffered a relapse with a temperature over 105 degrees and again was hospitalized. The Quartet postponed its opening concerts at the Library of Congress that season because Joe's doctors said his condi-

167

tion "showed signs of deterioration."[3] But Ira Hirschmann, who had scheduled a series of piano quartets and quintets for the New Friends of Music at Town Hall, did not believe them. In fact, Hirschmann, who had used his influence with Fiorello La Guardia to get the Quartet members out of Ellis Island in 1938, was unreasonably upset. The Budapest asked Hirschmann to eliminate from the programs works with pianists with whom they had never before performed. Joe said his doctors "warned me that I must avoid the strain which comes from extra rehearsals."[4] Instead, the Quartet offered to play viola quintets with Milton Katims. But Hirschmann did not believe Joe was that ill. He feared losing subscribers and suggested that, inasmuch as six of the piano works required only one violin, Ortenberg could handle those pieces. Without explaining the problems the Quartet was having with Ortenberg, Joe rejected what Hirschmann thought was a "fair and logical solution" to the problem. That incensed Hirschmann even more. He accused Joe of a "last minute inability to comply with your moral agreement."[5] It was not until Hirschmann actually met Joe that November in New York and saw how frail he looked that he appreciated the seriousness of Joe's condition, and then he was all apologies. "Having been a victim of malaria I know what you are going through," he said.[6]

Each time Joe's intonation went off, the problem was quickly picked up by critics, though they never realized what the cause was. They jumped on the flaw because the Quartet had a reputation for perfect intonation. And when Joe's intonation went off, it seemed to happen in splurges. One series of incidents occurred in 1944, when Alice Eversman wrote in the Washington *Evening Star* of Joe's "faulty intonation and rather strident tone."[7] A Chicago critic chided his "jiggy restlessness" at a Ravinia concert,[8] and two days later another reviewer called Joe's tone "shrill and inexpressive."[9] The difficulty carried over into the first part of the next year, 1945, when a Pittsburgh critic said he heard "an occasional off-pitch note from the first violin."[10]

Joe's difficulty recurred after his bout with Rocky Mountain spotted fever that fall. A concert at Town Hall "surprised" one critic because of Joe's "lax intonation and roughness of tone,"[11] and another spoke of his "tiny slips."[12] As might be expected, Joe suffered several lapses after he broke his collarbone in the car accident in 1947. "In some of the strong measures," said Eversman, "the first violin wavered below the pitch."[13] Another critic reviewing one of the New Friends of Music recitals, said Joe's violin tone in his solo passages "was impure in the early movements, but gained steadiness as the concert wore on."[14]

Amazingly, after he broke his left wrist in Japan in 1952 and suffered through a grueling retraining of his fingering hand, Joe's playing did not prompt any adverse comments. In fact, no problems with intonation cropped up again until 1959, when Joe went through another period of faulty pitch. That February, a Los Angeles *Examiner* critic called attention to "occasional lapses of intonation—worthy of mention only because they occur so rarely in Budapest Quartet recitals."[15] And in San Francisco, a reviewer remarked that Joe "exceeds the legal limit so far as notes out of tune are concerned."[16] Of the same concert, another critic said, "The tone was not as suave as we remember it, and the more than occasional harshness, sliding and bad intonation were definitely things to complain about."[17]

Almost as suddenly as they began, the intonation problems disappeared, despite the still heavy concert schedule that Joe had to face. The season of 1959–60 was a busy one for the Quartet, with eighty-six concerts in all, including twenty-two at the Library of Congress and eighteen recitals in a swing through Italy, France, and England before returning to the United States to perform the Beethoven cycle at the Library in the spring. The Quartet was at the height of its second period of peak playing, and the response was enthusiastic. Three recitals at the 92nd Street Y attracted nearly forty-eight hundred people. Their performance in London was "masterly," said the *Times*, "and always the playing was crystal clear and the manner forthright."[18] An Italian critic said they were the "proven masters in the excavation of the most aristocratic of musical treasures."[19]

There was no hint of a recurrence of any problem in the fall of 1960 either, when, at the start of the new concert season, they played twelve recitals at the Library before setting off on a round of tours on the East Coast and in the Southwest. "At this stage in their career it is unnecessary to point out the extravagant perfection which the Budapest lavishes on every work in their repertory," the New York *Herald-Tribune* declared.

> They do not play a false note—not by so much as a microtone. They read every phrase as though they had written it themselves. Their rhythmic stability is incredible, as is, as well, their ability to find an appropriate string color for every dynamic level from the most tentative pianissimo to the most clamorous forte. And they sing. They never

shape a line that is not informed with the breath of strong song, their intuitive realization of a composer's melodic gift being one of the wonders of the music world. In short, the Budapest represents the ultimate in chamber music performance.[20]

In the winter of 1960 between Christmas and New Year's eve, Joe suffered a mild heart attack. His recovery was short and swift, but the psychological effects were deep and disturbing. By the middle of February, when the Quartet was on tour in California, Mischa was able to write Harold Spivacke at the Library of Congress: "Joe is O.K. We played all the concerts except 3, when the schedule was too tight." But Mischa was worried about Joe's mental state. A Library staff worker they all knew, Richard Hill, had recently died. Knowing how superstitious Joe was and how anxious he was about his heart condition, Mischa said, "I have not told Joe about Dick."[21]

Roisman grew even more introspective and reclusive. Finally Mischa went to him. "What's the matter, Joe," he asked, "you sit there and don't say one word?"

"All right," Joe replied, "I am going to tell you." He then told Mischa about the physical examination he had taken more than twenty years earlier and what the doctor had told him. The heart attack had scared him so that Mischa thought, "He's so afraid of life. He thinks he is the sickest man in the world." Joe, he believed, was turning into "such a hypochondriac."[22]

You would have thought that the Quartet would drastically cut its concert tours because of Joe's illness, but it did not. Perhaps Joe did not want to be responsible for a severe cutback in the earnings of the others. Mischa, for example, had two teenage sons at home to support. The Quartet toured in Pennsylvania and throughout the Midwest in the winter of 1961, played twelve concerts again that spring at the Library of Congress, appeared twice at Ravinia, performed at Tanglewood, and, in late August, returned to Israel for the second time. They played the Beethoven cycle in Tel Aviv in five concerts that attracted fifteen thousand people, performed with Pablo Casals and pianists Eugene Istomin and Rudolf Serkin in Jerusalem, and appeared in Haifa—in all, playing nine concerts as part of a chamber-music festival that *Jerusalem Post* critic Yohanan Boehm, himself a composer and conductor, called "an outstanding musical experience."[23]

But every so often prior to Christmas 1960 something was off in the Quartet's playing. Maybe it was an omen that foretold Joe's heart attack, but in the few months before he suffered it, Joe's blood pressure must have gone up and down because he was beset again with sporadic intonation problems; and the problem spread to the others like an epidemic. Day Thorpe, music critic for the Washington *Evening Star* and a friend of Sasha's, received a vicious anonymous letter attacking the Budapest Quartet as well as "Heifetz, Rubinstein et al." as "vulgar pretenders." The Budapest, the letter writer said, was

> a repulsive quartet . . . sans pitch, timbre, subtlety, that distorts entire passages, that groans, scrapes, attacks in fury, keens like drunken gypsys [sic] and does nothing with beauty, sympathy, or delight; that, in short, is one of the most despicably over-rated groups of beastly butchers on this continent or any other.[24]

Such a letter might be dismissed as the rantings of a crank, but the Washington *Post* started publishing letters to the editor that were critical of the Quartet's "off-pitch playing."[25] Even Paul Hume, the critic for the Washington *Post* and one of the most ardent champions of the Quartet, started to criticize their performances. "In the face of the power of their readings," said Hume after a concert at the Library in March 1960, "it becomes less important, if no less disturbing, that problems of intonation are often present, and that in reaching for the largest effect, they pass beyond the boundaries that fine tone allows. Is it possible to have both technical perfection and equal musical insight? From the evidence of past performances from these men the answer is 'yes.' It was often present last night. Perhaps that is all we should expect. But it [is] not all we hope for."[26] A week later, Hume took all the Quartet members to task: "The evening's playing was even and easy but I seem to notice more than usual this spring the somewhat grainy sound that comes from the Budapest when they use as heavy pressure on the bows as they are now doing regularly."[27]

Mrs. Whittall was frantic. Nobody in Washington had ever talked about her "boys" in this way before. But the negative reviews were only the tip of an iceberg of complaints she already had. What had happened since that night nearly four years ago, when, on her ninetieth birthday, everybody was all smiles and kisses? The Library, Mrs. Whittall, and the Quartet were inseparable then. The Quartet members were family. Everyone—all the Quartet members and every member of the Music Division from Spivacke on down—visited together, came to musicales held at Spivacke's home, cared about the others, always asked about the others' children and spouses. Sasha had hugs for every woman staffer as he made his way down the corridor to the Music Division. When Joe celebrated his twentieth anniversary with the Quartet in 1947, the Library arranged a special commemorative program in which the Quartet played the same pieces that were played at Joe's debut with the Budapest in 1927. The same was done for Mischa in 1950 and for Boris in 1956.

Ever since Sasha's return to the Quartet, unsettling things had happened. Sometimes his personal schedule conflicted with the Quartet's appearances at the Library, and programs without him had to be arranged. "About the Schubert Octet there is trouble," Mischa wrote Spivacke in 1955, "first he [Sasha] cannot play with us the last pair of concerts (28, 29 of April) because he has the Schubert Festival at Dumbarton Oaks and plays the Schubert Octet with the same men we played last Fall, second: it would not be good for the Library to repeat the same work in a space of one week. . . . Here are the dates that Alex can play with us. . . . We are sorry to cause you all the trouble and we hope you will find a good solution."[28]

Out of deference for Sasha's personal concertizing, in 1961 the Library for the first time dropped from its contract with the Budapest the stipulation that the Quartet members had to practice certain proscribed hours on the Stradivarius instruments.[29] It was a concession to reality. Sasha, Boris said, "protested against rehearsing endlessly."[30] Instead of getting together to practice on the Strads on the Monday, Tuesday, and Wednesday before concerts on Thursday and Friday, they now rehearsed only Wednesday. Sasha would fly in to Washington for a day's rehearsal, play the concerts, them immediately fly out.

Moreover, despite what the concert programmes said about the Quartet members performing on the Strads, Sasha was not doing so. He was playing on Fritz Kreisler's Guarneri del Gesu, which Kreisler donated to the Library in 1952. "Nobody knew," said Sasha.[31] But that is impossible. The Kreisler Guarneri was kept under lock in the Whittall Pavilion along with the Strads. Ordinarily, when the Strads were to be used, an assistant reference librarian and another staffer were in charge of turning off the alarm in the pavilion and taking the instruments to the Music Division office, but neither ever handled the Kreisler for any member of the Quartet.[32] Someone else had to have opened the display case; someone had to have known that Sasha was using the Kreisler violin. Spivacke? His assistant, Ed Waters? Even if he did not personally do it, Spivacke must have known about the substitution.

It all came to a head one day after another mention of Joe's having an intonation problem during a Library recital. Upset, Mrs.

Whittall stormed by Spivacke's administrative assistant and into Spivacke's office. The assistant could not hear what was said, but the upshot was that, although he "didn't like to do it," Spivacke had to inform the Quartet members that after the 1961–62 season, they were no longer wanted.[33]

The Quartet members were astonished. So, too, were all the Music Division staffers at the Library. The Quartet resented Spivacke for the way he handled the situation. "It started to be, you know, like the professor in his home place is not appreciated," said Mischa. "They treated us—the management—like an old log. I think they thought it was enough, and we personally thought, too, that it was enough." Mischa believed the Library did not want to accede to the Quartet's having "a few months' free to go on tour."[34] But the Quartet had always been able to travel throughout the United States and to Europe, South America, and the Pacific without upsetting its close relationship with the Music Division.

The parting of ways, when it happened, was bittersweet. The Library staff held a special farewell luncheon for the Quartet, but Mrs. Whittall did not attend. She did send each of the Quartet members a silver tray as a present, but they never thanked her. Though a cause of many of the problems, Sasha was especially bitter. After performing at the Library since 1938—after 465 concerts there—there was not one penny in pension money—"nothing whatsoever"—the Quartet could count on. "It was a sad moment in the Budapest Quartet's career," he said, "when we realized that the Library of Congress uses you for its own purposes, then drops you when it doesn't need you anymore." Sasha hoped that "the same thing doesn't happen" to the quartet that succeeded the Budapest, the Juilliard.[35]

Officially, the word circulated was that the Quartet was leaving the Library of Congress in order to be able to tour more. "We want to have some more freedom," Mischa was quoted as saying.[36] But that was nonsense. With Joe's illness in mind and Sasha's busy schedule a fact of life, they wanted to do less, not more.

Be that as it may, the Quartet played its final two repeat-night concerts on March 29 and 30, 1962, to standing ovations. "There was something special in the air," an *Evening Star* reporter said. "There were persons in the audience who were at the first of these concerts. There were others, now capable quartet players themselves, who were not yet born when the series started."[37] A classical radio broadcaster likened the "Iron Men of Music" to a football team: "May

theirs be happy travels and music-making. Roisman, two Schneiders, and Kroyt. What a team!"[38] Ironically, it was Paul Hume in the
Post who provided the most touching "eulogy":

> Many of us can remember standing in the falling snow on G Street,
> waiting in line for the precious tickets—two to a customer—that would
> let us hear the Budapest Quartet play Mozart and Haydn, Beethoven and
> Brahms, or Debussy, Ravel and Bartok, in the Coolidge Auditorium.
>
> For nearly a quarter of a century these men drew from the Stradi-
> varius instruments in the Whittall collection such sounds as no other
> quartet had made. Their tone, their phrasing, their style, their knowl-
> edge entered into us and became for us the essence, the fiber, the very
> meaning of Beethoven, of Mozart, of Schubert.
>
> We cannot forget the texture of their playing any more than we can
> forget the whispered excitement that swept over the Coolidge Audi-
> torium when they came on the stage.
>
> Beauty will come again to the quartet concerts at the Library. But it
> will not be the same.[39]

The Quartet's leaving the Library sparked an idea in the mind of
their good friend in Buffalo, Cameron Baird, head of the music department at the University of Buffalo (soon to be State University of
New York at Buffalo). They had performed at his home, in concert
and for fun, where Baird had joined them on the viola. Would they
like to be the quartet-in-residence at the university? To teach and
play before, between, and after concert tours? With the status of
professors? They were all amenable. After performing in Buffalo for
more than thirty years, they knew many people in the city and felt
comfortable with both the university administration and the local
chamber society. Kroyt, for one, was flattered. "Herr Professor" was
an honored, respected title in Germany. Mischa even went so far as
to sell a home he had purchased in Bethesda, Maryland, and move to
Buffalo. Boris rented a suite at a local hotel. Joe and Sasha flew in to
town when they were needed for master classes or recitals. And
when they were not in Buffalo, they were in New York, recording
again works they had done before, in stereo this time, or off on tours
around the United States and in Europe.

They told a Buffalo journalist that their "barnstorming" days
were over, but a look at their schedule belied that statement.[40] They
were to make more than eighty-five appearances in the 1962–63
season, when yet another calamity befell Joe. The Quartet was on
tour in Europe in the fall of 1962 when suddenly Joe could barely get
out of his hotel bed or stand erect. His back pained him terribly. Pola

managed to get him to a doctor. Joe had suffered a slipped disc in his spine and was barely able to move.

The other members simply rearranged the Quartet's programs again. "It was impossible to replace him," said Boris. "We didn't even try."[41] Mischa said, "It is just that we have played together for so long that we have the same feeling for the music."[42] So, while they waited for Joe to recover, the Quartet substituted trios for quartets or, as in the case of a series of recitals at the University of Michigan, they played piano quartets with Eugene Istomin. The performances gave Sasha a unique opportunity to play first violin—one that Joe had always denied him—but he was not always well received by the critics. One in Louisville thought "Joseph Roisman, the missing member of the Budapest Quartet, keeps a tighter rein on things when he is first violinist of the group." He said that having Sasha in the first chair

> wrought slight changes in the Budapest style. It was still intense, taut, and profoundly expressive in slow movements. But Schneider is never one to understate an emotion. . . . He gave himself free rein in a manner that smacked more of gypsy camps than Vienna. It was amusing to hear the more moderate approach of his colleagues bring him to heel. It was as if an extraordinarily talented "enfant terrible" were being disciplined by his patient elders.[43]

Joe, meanwhile, was planning to return in time for a much-heralded return tour of Australia, their first there in more than a quarter of a century. "Let's hope that next season we can again work in complete health and harmony," he wrote William Kolodney at the 92nd Street Y in January 1963. "I am steadily improving and, God willing, may play again in a month from now."[44]

The Quartet did return to Australia that spring, and aside from a slight case of gastric trouble that caused him to quit playing in the middle of a Brahms quartet, Joe performed without any difficulty.[45] There was no recurrence of his back trouble. Pola, of course, traveled with him to Australia. Ever since his heart attack in 1960, she was his constant companion, carrying his violin and portfolio of music, arranging for porters to handle their luggage, making certain there were no hitches in their travel and hotel accommodations, protecting him from interruptions so that he was able to take his afternoon nap. She pampered him so much, especially after Joe suffered the back problem, that it disturbed Mischa: "You know, people who don't have any children and don't have any responsibilities, they don't focus on anything else except themselves. And Pola, that's her baby. It is her husband, it is her baby, it is her lover. Can you imagine a woman lives like that!"[46]

The Australian tour was a resounding success, so popular that the government afterwards issued a postage stamp with their picture on it.[47] In the twenty-six years that the Quartet members had been away from Australia, they had matured, and it showed in their playing. As Joe put it, when the Quartet members were young, in the 1930s, they "generally" played "faster than the way it was played before."[48] Now, they had matured. Their tempos were slower, their sound richer, their interpretation more profound. All their years together and what they had been through—the terror of a Germany turning Nazi, marriages and divorces, the profitless early performances in the United States, their almost overnight success, the never-ending tours, and Joe's illnesses and accidents—all had an effect on the way they now approached Beethoven and Mozart and Schubert and Brahms. A critic in Melbourne, Australia, who had heard them perform in 1937, said, "Years of experience have allowed them to reach the stage where each individual instrument speaks as freely and as eloquently as is possible."[49]

For the first time, the Quartet was serious about reducing its concert schedule. Only fifty-two recitals were scheduled for the 1963–64 season, so few that, despite his distaste for playing cello recitals, Mischa appeared in one in April 1964 in Buffalo. But even the abbreviated scheduled seemed too much for Joe. As the concert season wound down, Joe on May 1, 1964, wrote similar notes to Mischa, Sasha, and Boris:

> I just want to tell you that I have decided that the coming season (1964–65) shall be my last one.
>
> I suppose that I could play for a few more years—but the travelling is becoming more and more difficult for me, especially to the hard to get places.
>
> I hope that this way I will be able to save myself too much wear and tear.[50]

Joe said he had made his decision "after very careful consideration." The "last 4 years I have been hit very hard, yet I have continued our schedule as if nothing would have happened. This, whitout [*sic*] any doubt, put a great deal of strain on my health. I remember very well, how after a recording day in New York, I was lying in my hotel room unable to move my sore back." He was embarrassed to mention money "when the most important thing should be satisfaction in Quartet playing," but "financial rewards were very negligible, since I had double expenses—Pola travelling with me for the last 4 years."[51]

Mischa suggested an alternative. Suppose they restricted their future performances only to New York and Buffalo and continued making recordings "provided the sessions are not intermixed with the N.Y. concerts." Joe said he had been thinking of the same solution, "but coming from *me* it may have had a touch of an ultimatum, which I was trying to avoid."[52]

So, a compromise was reached. Joe would continue to play; they would continue to make recordings; the Quartet would fulfill its 1964–65 commitments—fifty-nine concerts—but take a sabbatical the following season, playing only in Buffalo, and then appear only in New York and Buffalo after that.

The Budapest's future—for Mischa, Sasha, and Boris—might have looked rather limited and predictable, but they had discovered a new, exhilarating outlet for their musical talents on the campus of a small, out-of-the-way college in southern Vermont.

19

The Marlboro Men

The ever-energetic Sasha burst onto the Marlboro scene like "an electrical storm."[1] He made things happen, pushed young musicians to use their talents, ranted, raved, and clowned his way into being one of Marlboro's unforgettable characters. And with him, he brought the others, to make Marlboro the breeding ground for a new generation of chamber-music players.

Sasha first visited Marlboro in the summer of 1955, after trying to keep the South Mountain music festival in Massachusetts going following the death of Elizabeth Sprague Coolidge two years earlier. He was immediately impressed with what he saw. The Marlboro Music School had been founded in 1950 by violinist Adolf Busch and flutist Marcel Moyse and their families as "a place where musicians could come to play chamber music together, to exchange ideas, and to experiment with music in a relaxed atmosphere." It was a school, music festival, and summer retreat "rolled up into one" and had, Sasha says, "all the musical forces and more for classical and contemporary music."[2] The music school uses the facilities of Marlboro College, a liberal-arts institution that dots a hilltop several miles outside Brattleboro, Vermont, with an assortment of very New England–looking white, wooden buildings that house classrooms, dormitories, and a dining hall. Driving up the macadam road that reaches the highest point on the campus, where the dining hall and many of the rehearsal rooms are, one can hear the strains of half a dozen different musical works wafting through the air. "Caution: Musicians at Play," a sign announces. Because there was no auditorium in the first years, the musicians played concerts in the dining hall. Wednesday night concerts restricted to the participants are still held there.

Busch had died by the time Sasha first saw the campus, but his son-in-law, Rudolf Serkin, a good friend of the Quartet, was now the director. Serkin immediately invited all the members to join the summer sessions:

> Dear friends, all the time since Sascha [*sic*] came last summer for a short visit to Marlboro, and seemed to like it here, I have been day and night dreaming about next summer, about the possibility of spending part of the summer with you all and making music together here in Vermont. . . .
>
> I don't know if you know about Marlboro. . . . How it has grown last summer to a considerable size . . . with all the hope and promise to fill a needed place in music. . . .
>
> I think a firstrate Music festival could be built in Marlboro. And this, together with my great desire to be together with you, gives me the courage to ask you if you would like to play and teach here, and if yes, do you see any possibility to make it possible! Sometimes dreams do come true.[3]

Sasha accepted and immediately left an unmistakable imprint on the school and the musicians. He purchased an old schoolhouse nearby and spent the next twenty summers at Marlboro. Just his being there attracted a legion of young musicians. He convinced Pablo Casals to participate in 1970. Sasha, violinist Felix Galimir remembered, insisted that the older musicians play with the younger musicians. Sasha himself always took the second violin part in quartets with the younger musicians, and the other veteran professionals followed his example.[4] He "galvanized" young players, double bassist Julius Levine recalled. He was a "mover and shaker," said cellist David Soyer.

Sasha lured his brother Mischa to Marlboro in 1962, and the following year the entire Quartet spent the latter part of August there, after the festival was over, recording with Rudolf Serkin Brahms's Piano Quintet in F Minor. Boris joined the school the next year, 1964, but Joe was concerned about his health and did not want to tax himself with rehearsals every morning and afternoon during the hot summer months. Anyway, he said he preferred "cement sidewalks to trees and grass."[5]

Those summers were what many people consider "the golden years" of Marlboro. The Quartet members were part of the *"alte cockers,"* as the older musicians called themselves, that the festival attracted—violinists Felix Galimir and Isidore Cohen; Adolf Busch's

brother, cellist Herman Busch; violist Philipp Naegele; and pianist
Mieczysław Horszowski. The younger players—many of them on a
solo-career track—included Ruth and Jaime Laredo (she, a pianist;
he, a violinist); violinists Michael Tree, Arnold Steinhardt, John Dalley, and Shmuel Ashkenasi; cellists Leslie Parnas and David Soyer;
Samuel Rhodes and his wife Hiroko Yajima (he, a violist; she, a
violinist); cellist Paul Katz and his wife Martha Strongin (a violist);
and young Peter Serkin, a pianist like his father—to mention just a
few. They were audacious, fired-up musicians, eager to learn, to
play, to excel. It was so different from Buffalo, where Sasha had
resigned his professor's postition because the students "were pretty
bad, hardly gifted, and had no interest whatsoever in learning."[6]

Strange to say, considering how verbal they were, none of the
three—Sasha, Mischa, or Boris—felt fully comfortable expressing in
words their thoughts about playing chamber music. Joe had, however. In an interview in 1954 with violinist Michael Tree's parents,
who were writers, he talked in great detail about the problems faced
by four musicians playing together in a quartet—bowing, fingering,
vibrato, and intonation—how when he played *piano*, he preferred to
have the others "play a bit below," or how when a pianist accompanied the Quartet and played *piano* he would play "double *piano*."
Tempi, he said, was "one of the most difficult problems" chamber-
music groups faced. "There is much danger," he continued, of playing slow movements "too sluggishly." Musicians, he felt, "must get
away from the thought that they must make something of every
phrase, of every bar. If the music is performed simply and very much
as it is written, the desired end will be achieved. Many times I hear
musicians who do so much with every phrase that when a climax
arrives the whole point is lost!" Joe was just as emphatic about
playing *allegro* movements. "We hear too much fast playing!" And
he warned against taking "liberties" with the dynamic marks of
Beethoven and Brahms. "I feel that the dynamics should be carefully
followed. Brahms, as well as Beethoven, knew just what he
wanted!"[7]

Sasha, Mischa, and Boris taught by example. They never talked
about the music, said Jaime Laredo, "It was all in the playing." If a
violinist did not play a phrase correctly, Sasha would pick up his
instrument and play the notes the way he thought they should
sound. "Don't rush!" he constantly told the young players. "Articu-
late!" When playing, Sasha tended to exaggerate in order to ensure
that the musicians understood him. If a crescendo was called for, he
gave it the maximum amount of expression. He emphasized accents,

too, and hated it when others played timidly. "Don't play orchestra!" he would shout—the worst insult to apply to a musician that he could think of, since in his view, orchestra players were automatons, without any musical ideas of their own.

Despite Sasha's rough edge, Laredo credits him for "a lot of my musical values. The most important thing I learned from him was that music is not music without life, that there's no life to the music if there's no energy to the music. First of all, you have to play with love. You can fuse energy into what you're doing. Any phrase that you play, anything, any piece of music that you play, if it doesn't have energy, if it's not coming from the heart and really has no bite, as Sasha would say, it just sits there. It has no life."[8]

Sasha's method of teaching reflected a student–teacher relationship, and some of the young players could not cope with him. He could be dogmatic and blunt, threatening to give it to them "over the head." He had no patience, especially with insecure or timid musicians. He was, a Marlboro participant remembered, "very, very frank—'You play out of tune,' 'You never phrase,' 'You never make dimuendos.' 'You don't do this, that,' whatever it was. And if you weren't ready to accept that and take it, try to grow from it, he could turn you off. I remember instances of people being totally inhibited and tied up." Sasha yelled at a musician auditioning for the Festival Casals, "How dare you play like that for me! Where are you at school? Who is your teacher? Leave school! Join an orchestra! Do something with your life!"[9]

Mischa and Boris were different. Their instruction was more along the lines of a partnership of equals. They, too, showed by example, but they did not criticize anyone's playing. "They didn't sit with a score in their hand and pontificate," Michael Tree remembered. "They got right into the nitty-gritty of the music, and we just talked and discussed as we played, or played as we talked. Well, as young kids we had to play over our heads very often to keep up with these guys. It was a way of imparting their experience, the information through the vehicle of the work itself, the music, rather than words."

Tree, who later became the violist with the Guarneri Quartet, learned "a very wonderful lesson" from Boris when performing a viola quintet with him. Though a violinist then, he took the first viola part in the quintet. Nothing untoward happened in rehearsal, but when they went on stage to perform the piece, Tree got "the shock of my life." Boris, playing the second viola and sitting to Tree's right, had a solo passage. In the seating arrangement that the

Budapest and most other quartets followed, the *f* holes on the instruments of the first and second violinists as well as those of the cello face the audience, and their sounds project throughout a concert hall. The violist's instrument, on the other hand, faces the back of the stage. But Boris developed a special hallmark to his playing. He always turned toward the audience when he had a solo passage, bending to the left as he phrased the notes, so that the *f* holes of his viola faced out toward the audience and the sound projected. He suddenly did so in the midst of performing the quintet. "I'll never forget it," said Tree.

> Suddenly he wheeled around and I thought he was going to knock me off my chair—and he almost did. You know, the adrenalin was going. He wheeled around and almost played in my lap. Boris was right. Just those few extra inches of exposure causes the full sonority of the quartet to change. If he had sat in the normal position he would have sounded muffled. It would have sounded somewhat distant. It isn't only a question of volume. It's also a matter of presence—the presence of sound. There's more to sound than just sound. There is a core—a presence, to use that word again—that somehow projects with as much closeness as loudness. Boris compensated for the inherent danger of being swallowed up by allowing the instrument to speak to the audience directly, as the violinists and cellist do. A viola has to play—and now I go out on a limb—but a violist has to sound a little too loud at all times within the quartet in order that he sounds equally loud or equal to the others. Because, after all, we're not playing for ourselves, we're playing for the listeners, and we almost have our backs to them.[10]

Boris was willing to learn, too. He welcomed new ideas, said Jaime Laredo. "I used to marvel when I played with Boris. I used to marvel at the energy that he had and the enthusiasm that he had." If someone suggested a different way of phrasing a passage, Boris would say, "Let's try it."[11] Mischa was awed; he had never seen Boris work as hard.[12] Boris, in fact, was having the time of his life. "It was like playing with a kid, someone younger than me," said Laredo.[13] During Boris's first summer at Marlboro he played a trio that he had performed with the Schneiders when Joe was ill, Beethoven's Serenade in D, Opus 80. This time, his partners were violinist Sergiu Luca and cellist Robert Sylvester. "It was refreshing," Boris said. "It was new and it was exact. I enjoyed myself more than I ever enjoyed myself before."[14]

The Young Turks were enjoying themselves, too. Playing Mendelssohn's octet, they "started doing things that Mischa thought a bit alarming and amusing at the same time," Tree recalled:

Exaggerating. And there were some bowings we took in the last movement that were a series of repeated notes at a fast clip that we decided almost on the spur of the moment to play all on down bows, by the quick ticking of the bow. Well, Mischa saw that and I remember his eyes were like saucers. He had never seen anything like that and he thought we were out of our minds. But he came to like it. In other words, he was willing, as was Boris also, when we worked with him, to adapt and adopt the way the younger players do. And it was a great tribute to them that they simply did not tell us, "No, it can't be done." And it's also a great tribute to Marlboro, because I can't think of other festivals, or schools for that matter, where there isn't a strict line, a demarcation, between student and teacher.[15]

Jaime Laredo recalled playing a Mozart viola quintet with Mischa, who had played the piece "thousands of times and recorded it already three times. A new edition of the score had come out—very different from earlier ones—different notes, articulations, bowings, et cetera. He was anxious to try it all. I thought that was amazing. He didn't agree with a lot of things, but that's all right, neither did I."[16]

They were like "uncles" to pianist Ruth Laredo, who was a pupil of Serkin's. Every morning during her pregnancy with her daughter Jennifer she would have breakfast with Mischa. He had, she said, "a great vision of a music piece as a whole." She learned, she said, "how to listen to the strings, how to play with the strings." There was "a certain feeling that I got from all the members of the Quartet that the music had to sing and every note had an expression to it. There was no such thing as a note without meaning to it. No filler. Everything had to fit into a whole and it had to express something. And I think of that all the time."

Ruth Laredo relished "being near them, for year after year after year, at close range, and seeing them at work and hearing what they had to say, playing for them, playing with them, being given advice about your playing, and hearing what they had to say about their lives and what they had gone through as young musicians and seeing the world through their eyes."

Looking back on the early 1960s at Marlboro, Ruth Laredo marveled at the "whole spawning of string quartets, the Renaissance of string quartets, ever since those years."[17] Jaime Laredo went on to become the artistic director of the chamber-music series at the 92nd Street Y. Sergiu Luca founded the Chamber Music Northwest series in Portland. Shmuel Ashkenasi organized the Vermeer Quartet; Rhodes became violist with the Juilliard; Strongin and Katz were founding members of the Cleveland Quartet. Being at Marlboro, said Katz,

> meant everything to me. Just hearing Boris talking about the Opus 135—and what made the most enormous impression on me was here was a man in the twilight of his career who had lived with these pieces for forty years and more, and his passion and his love and his enthusiasm for them—it was bursting, it was fantastic. The first movement of Opus 135 is almost like a kaleidoscope full of little short motifs darting and flitting here and there. It turns very quickly from light to dark, from something that's gay and light to something that's brooding and *mysterioso*. And Boris was so sensitive to that, and it meant so much to him that one felt these moods and these changes and the way he would just pause before a particular harmony or just had a twinkle in his eyes. Those things have a lot to do with the way I feel the piece today.[18]

With Sasha's nudging and encouragement, Tree, Steinhardt, Dalley, and Soyer formed their own quartet—the Guarneri, a name suggested by Boris, who had been in the Guarneri Quartet in Germany. "I give it to you," he said.[19] Sasha warned the four musicians to avoid playing the late Beethoven quartets—"not for many years, because you could play like God possibly—not very likely, but possibly—and they'll kill you."[20] Mischa said they should live on their reputations as soloists and chamber-music players. "Now you are a quartet, the best thing I would advise you is not to play a note in public," he said facetiously.[21]

"It was rather a poignant moment in both our careers, in both quartets," said Tree, who volunteered to switch from violin to be the Guarneri's violist. "The Quartet was clearly ending their concertizing and they may or may not have taken a rather paternal interest in us. I think they did. And without that I think we would have been just that much further from having felt courageous enough to start. After all, we all had to change our life styles, we have to commit ourselves."[22]

The Guarneri, most aficionados agree, became the musical heirs of the Budapest, for a number of reasons; their close relationship at Marlboro, for one thing. They worked side by side, practicing and performing together. They sat elbow to elbow at meals in the dining hall, talking, discussing music, regaling one another with jokes and stories about music and musicians. The young musicians shared their aspirations with the older ones. The older musicians shared their experiences with the young ones. Steinhardt met his wife at Mischa's house. He even eventually purchased Joe's violin, the same cut-down viola that Hauser sold to Roisman in the 1940s, so it has continued to be played in a quartet since the days of Joachim.

Boris, said Tree, "comes to mind very often. I hear Boris in my ear as I think of certain passages, having heard him play them and having imagined how he would have played them. Sure, we try not to imitate as such. But we are all a product of what we've heard through the years of listening to great players. Whenever I hear quartets play today, I think of Mischa, because for the most part that feeling of support is lacking. He provided the Quartet with a unique feeling of bottom, of base, of support."[23]

"The Budapest Quartet," said Soyer, "was the epitome of string quartets—the peak, the absolute top. They were the first modern quartet in the sense of impeccable ensemble, good intonation, the fact they were a democratic organization, in the sense of being musically democratic. This was the sound of a string quartet as it should sound. Their interpretative ideas—the way of playing Beethoven, or thinking about Beethoven, or Mozart, or what-have-you—I would think that any quartet that ever came after the Budapest Quartet would have emulated them, or would have been greatly influenced by them. Not that we copied them, but nevertheless we heard that as students. This was the way it was done. This was the best possible way it could be done, and so as an adult player, you unconsciously come to those things."[24]

"We owe a tremendous debt to the Budapest Quartet," Tree added. "It doesn't seem to rob us of our individuality. We happily acknowledge the debt we owe."[25]

20

Coda

The final years before the Budapest String Quartet disbanded were sad ones in many ways. The members barely saw each other any more, except to perform one of the increasingly dwindling number of concerts they had or, in the case of Sasha, Mischa, and Boris, to see one another at Marlboro during July and part of August. Mischa continued to live in Buffalo; Sasha, in New York; Joe and Boris, in Washington. "The Quartet doesn't speak now at all," Boris lamented.[1] Mischa was upset, too. "No artist can do what we are doing—it's dangerous, and soon it's going to be the end."[2]

Always circumspect in the past, careful to avoid any talk about their personal relationships, they began to voice recriminations. And too often their performances suffered.

The Quartet continued to draw sell-out crowds to their concerts, and their records continued to sell well. Their recording of Schubert's "Trout" Quintet with Mieczysław Horszowski and Julius Levine was nominated as the best chamber-music recording of the year in 1963. Six months in advance of the 1964–65 season, the 92nd Street Y sent out ticket-renewal notices "because of the great demand for subscriptions."[3] Hearing the *Grosse Fuge* in Los Angeles, a concertgoer remarked, "How was this music ever thought to be difficult for the listener?" Critics spoke of the "poetry" of their performance, their "grand sweep," the "warmth, spontaneity, and meaning" of their playing.[4] The Quartet, one New York reviewer said, "is to chamber music what the King James version of the Bible is to the English language."[5] But there were omens, too.

Mischa was never satisfied with his own performances—"I can't help it, that's my character, I am never satisfied"—but the allusion to the Bible, he thought, was ridiculous. "That was a concert I found we played so badly," he said.[6]

A concert at the 92nd Street Y in 1962—"an autumn ritual, almost as old and revered in New York as the World Series"—did not, a *Times* critic wrote, "always maintain the standard it once proudly carried." There were "things to marvel at. . . . But the concert was uneven."[7]

The problem was fundamental. For one thing, there was no thought about replacing Joe in the Quartet. The others were too old to break in a new player. They did not have "the desire or the energy," said Mischa.[8] But as might be expected, Joe wanted to avoid lengthy rehearsals, or even rehearsing at all. Sasha was as busy as ever with his own career as performer, conductor, and concert promoter and did not have much time for practicing. At recording sessions, the members barely talked except to say hello and good-bye.[9] The Quartet no longer performed new works; they did not have time for the extensive rehearsals a new composition demanded. "Like the new Carter quartet," said Mischa. "It would take three, four months and an entire new technique. We don't have it, not that we wouldn't have it."[10]

Boris was not sure the Quartet really needed to rehearse even their standard repertoire. "We used to overpractice," he said. "You practice and practice so much that when you are on stage you don't think about the music you are performing. But this has now changed." Boris believed the Quartet had matured to the point where rehearsals were unnecessary. "We now go out on the stage and make music with a devil-may-care attitude. If anything goes wrong, it goes wrong."[11]

Sasha expressed the same attitude in an interview with a *New York Times* reporter in 1962. "Now we play with a freedom we never even thought possible thirty years ago. You know Schnabel said he wished music had no bar lines. After a while you can forget bar lines. But this is not possible when you are young. You must learn to stop worrying about whether every note will be perfect; about whether the whole world will be destroyed if you play a passage wrong. After a while you don't think about whether or not you are projecting; about whether or not every note is right; about whether or not your Beethoven is going stale. You just go out and make music. I think we've reached that point."[12]

But Mischa disagreed with both Boris and his brother. "We matured, that is right. We could have never done the things we are doing now ten or twelve years ago, never—the freedom, the freedom to play. But if you haven't rehearsed for such a long time you forget what it was to make music, sometimes you play against." Mischa was distressed that the Quartet did not practice at all. "We don't rehearse," he said. "When we have a good concert, we have a good performance, we are still the best. When we don't play well, we are still performing and it always has a sweep and a picture. But there's a lot of dirt there that you never clean out. How could you have a picture that has not been cleaned out for four years? It has so much dirt. It is necessary to clean. We don't clean."[13] Mischa felt so badly about the way the Quartet performed at one concert at the 92nd Street Y that when he returned to the stage for a bow he pretended he had a broom in his hands and brushed the stage clear of wrong notes.[14]

David Soyer recalls joining the Quartet to play Dvořák's sextet at the 92nd Street Y in December 1964. At rehearsal, Soyer, who had studied the score beforehand, wanted to correct something.

> Three of them turned their heads and looked at me like I was out of my mind. Sasha thought it was riotously funny. Here's this young guy comes in and starts to tell these guys how to play. So we went on with the rehearsal, and we came to the last movement, the variation movement that starts with a viola solo. And Boris started to play the theme, and as he was playing the theme, Joe Roisman said, "You know, Boris, that's much too slow."
>
> And Boris said, "It has to be like that."
>
> And Roisman said, "No, it's much too slow."
>
> And Boris said, "All right, what about that fingering you took in the Haydn quartet last month." That took care of the argument and the discussion. I remember Mischa standing up and saying, "Why do we always make a ritard in this place? For twenty-five years we always do this. Why?"
>
> And Roisman looked up at him and said, "All right, so let's not make a ritard." There was no discussion, no argument. If you want to make a ritard, make a ritard. You want louder? Okay, louder. You want lower? Okay, lower. I think by that time in their lives, they could not discuss anything. They could just play.[15]

Mischa blamed Boris for being too lazy to practice. Boris, meanwhile, was angry with Sasha. "He sits there and makes jokes, because he is not interested, he thinks on something else—on bills, or on his love affairs or something. When Alex came back, for example, he used to make so many jokes, he used to laugh so that we got sometimes letters from the audience complaining about this. When we played at the Y we got a letter from a lady, she was complaining that Alex comes out and makes a face like he is going to perform some clowning on the stage."[16]

Sasha's relationship with Joe became tense at times, too. On his return to the Quartet in 1955, Sasha was able to instill in the others his energy and enthusiasm—they came alive again after ten years with Ortenberg and Gordodetzky—but he felt that he was often unsuccessful when he tried to share with them the musical ideas he had learned while away, especially the nuances he had picked up from Pablo Casals—"the freedom of expression" and "musical conviction" not to "rely on the printed page of music."[17] He had progressed, Sasha believed, while they had stood still. Sasha suggested that they play a minuet movement in three beats instead of one, but Joe emphatically said "No!" At other times, Joe would play a phrase in a specific mood or expression, but Sasha, on repeating it, would insist on his own interpretation. At a recording session, Sasha was shown a newly discovered edition of "Eine Kleine Nachtmusik," with Mozart's own annotations. Sasha was excited. Why play someone else's version of the piece when you had the composer's original intentions? "It says here . . ." he started to say, but Joe shrugged his shoulders, belittling his excitement and refusing even to look at the music.[18] Deflated, Sasha would just play his part as expected and then bolt from the studio without bothering to listen to the playback. The situation worsened after Joe's heart attack. When he wrote the Quartet members about his desire to retire in 1963, Joe added in his note to Mischa that "even" the satisfaction in playing quartets "is rather questionable at the present time and has been going on for some years. You know the situation as well as I do—it is not a very pleasant one."[19]

Boris was now irritated with Joe, also. "He plays everything in the same mood. For example, his Mozart was exactly like the Beethoven and Beethoven was exactly like the Brahms and Brahms—you know, it was exactly performed like we played Debussy."[20]

And yet, for all their bickering, they still basically respected one another. It was as though they were a fussy, old, tired married couple, stubborn, rigid, griping about trivia, trying to rationalize the fact that they were no longer "whipper-snappers." The complaints were an aberration. In their hearts, after nearly thirty-five years of knowing each other as musical colleagues, they still admired one another's skills. Sasha called Roisman "a wonderful man and the most magnificent *primarius* I have ever known."[21] Boris acknowledged Sasha's growth as a musician and his "terrific driving ambition."

And, for all Joe's faults, said Boris, "I prefer him a thousand times to any other violinist which fiddles around."[22] Mischa thought Boris "a fantastic viola player, a wonderful musician," and Joe, he said, "could do anything. He had such command." It was "a great miracle for the Quartet," Mischa added, that Joe, like Hauser, was not a dictator, as other first violinists had been. Even Sasha said he could not have been the first violinist that Joe was.[23]

With the number of their concert appearances decreasing, Mischa and Boris started branching out from the Quartet. Joe refused to think about performing without the others. "You mean," the one-time café *primo geiger* said, "I should walk out there without my colleagues and play *standing up?* Never!"[24] Mischa had reacted similarly when he was asked to play a cello sonata by Rachmaninoff in 1952, during a program devoted to the Russian composer at the Library of Congress. Mischa got out on the stage, looked around, and saw none of his colleagues. He felt "strangely isolated" and was "scared to death."[25] Nevertheless, to everyone's surprise, Mischa agreed in April 1964 to play a cello recital—sonatas by Brahms, Shostakovich, and Beethoven—in Buffalo. It went off quite well, according to the critics, and he played two further recitals, one at the Library of Congress that November and the other again in Buffalo in May 1965. The November recital was his first appearance at the Library since the Quartet left three years earlier, and "an ecstatic capacity audience heard a performance which was a major triumph in every sense."[26]

Late that December and into the first week in January 1965, the Quartet made its last recordings for what was now called CBS Records—Dvořák's "American" Quartet and one of the works that the Quartet played when Boris made his debut in the Quartet in 1936, Smetana's "From My Life." It was a grueling twelve days of work. Although he had disliked recording sessions in the past, Joe was now willing to do more of them because he did not have to dress up or face an audience. But he had good days and bad days. Mischa wanted to take advantage of the good days and record as much as possible. But Joe now was having constant intonation problems, and Mischa was having trouble, too. "There is a woof in my cello," he told a musician friend.[27] Tom Z. Shepard, who directed the sessions, was able to splice together an acceptable rendition of the Dvořák, and it was subsequently released. But he had difficulty with Joe's intonation in the Smetana, and the Quartet vetoed the idea of making the spliced-together version public. It was never released.

Mischa and Boris had taken the second cello and viola parts in

1965 when they joined the Guarneri Quartet in performing Tchaikovsky's "Souvenir of Florence" Sextet at the 92nd Street Y, and later they recorded the work with the Guarneri at an old ballroom on East 11th Street in Manhattan that had been turned into a recording studio. As they listened to a scherzo section with a Russian-like theme during the playback in the engineer's booth, Boris could not contain himself. "I can't stand it," he said. He went out on the dance floor and started prancing around the mirror-lined ballroom like a ballet dancer, doing pirouettes, in a kind of waltz. The Guarneri members laughed so hard that they cried. "There was something grand about it," Arnold Steinhardt said, "something very beautiful, very touching, the essence of the Russian spirit."[28]

That recording session was the last time Mischa ever played the cello. He had been experiencing pain for some time. Boris's daughter Yanna saw him trying to practice, "struggling to play, willing himself to move his arms and fingers in a constant battle with pain. His usually placid face was covered with sweat. And no sound came out of the cello."[29] A few days after the recording session with the Guarneri, Mischa went into a Buffalo hospital for an operation on his spine. The problem was one he had lived with for more than thirty-five years, though he had never complained about it. He could remember to the exact day—July 15, 1930—when he first felt back pains. "How familiar that awful cramped feeling has become since!" Mischa wrote in his unfinished autobiography.[30] The problem never went away. When he and June Holden were married in 1947, she did most of the driving when they traveled across the country to Mills College and back to Washington. If Mischa drove, she sat behind him, massaging his neck. He could not turn to look at the side mirrors. When they had children, he could not pick them up to hug them; they sat on his lap instead.[31] Over all his years with the Quartet, however, he never made a fuss. Maybe that is why he thought Joe was "such a hypochondriac."

The operation was not a success. Mischa came to New York for a second one, but it, too, failed to alleviate the problem. The Quartet was scheduled to perform the Slee Bequest Beethoven cycle at the State University of New York at Buffalo in late January 1966, but the cycle had to be rescheduled to March, and then it was cancelled altogether.[32]

Mischa was not even able to play the Quartet's last concerts—three recitals at the Albright-Knox Art Gallery in Buffalo, performed on February 15, 17, and 20, 1967. Leslie Parnas took Mischa's chair as cellist. The critics' reception of several of the works they played was chillingly negative. The first two nights, the Quartet members played trios and sonatas as well as a piano quintet with Leo Smit, but no string quartet. One reviewer was put off in the first concert by Sasha's "facial maneuvers" when he played a Beethoven sonata. "He treated the initial Allegro assai roughly and was rather uneven in the final Allegro vivace." A Brahms quintet "was marred by Roisman's inept performance; they played like virtual strangers."[33] In the second concert, another reviewer said, a Beethoven trio with Sasha, Boris, and Parnas "somewhat disappointed." The tempo "in all movements was too slow, lacked impetus, and in many spots it was notably devoid of the sense of humor explicit in the score."[34] The variations in a Mozart divertimento, played in the third concert, "went on and on."[35] The "trio became a struggle and the music suffered, particularly the Adagio which lost the excitement of its melancholy." Then in its second season, the Guarneri Quartet, this critic pointed out, had performed the night before the Budapest recitals began. "Despite . . . the unimpressive playing of Josef Roisman, the Budapest String Quartet, with the invaluable aid of Leslie Parnas and Leo Smit, provided three evenings of entertaining chamber music. But the kudos go to the Guarneri String Quartet, the lesser known group that played better."[36]

It was a sad finale for a spirited, inspiring, and unprecedented chamber-music ensemble.

It is ironic that it was the Library of Congress that went to some length to celebrate the fiftieth anniversary of the Quartet. A special exhibition was mounted in December 1968—a year after the actual anniversary and more than a year after the Budapest's last performance. A billboard display was set up, with programs and photographs from the Quartet's history, and the Juilliard Quartet, its successor as the Library's quartet-in-residence, performed a concert in their honor.

Joe, then sixty-eight years old, was there. "It sounds strange," he told an interviewer, "but I am not going to do anything."[37] Instead, he and Pola led a quiet life. They spent their time going to antiques auctions, adding to his pipe collection, and building a coin collection. They visited what family she had left in Hungary. "Imagine," he wrote back, "a member of the Budapest at last in Budapest!"[38]

Mischa, sixty-four, sold his Gofriller cello, now that he could not play anymore. But he refused to retire. While he was able to, he taught at the Curtis Institute of Music in Philadelphia and at the California School for the Arts outside Los Angeles. He was the mentor of the young Cleveland Quartet, when it succeeded the Budapest for the Slee Bequest Beethoven cycle in Buffalo. He continued to spend his summers in Marlboro, a magnet for the children of young musicians, who doted on his "Mischa cookies." He had a suite of rooms with easy access for the wheelchair he was forced to use. It was always filled with visitors, who would drop by to talk music and baseball, which had become Mischa's passion. Every day he worked out on an exercise machine in an effort to prevent his muscles from deteriorating further. For years, he lived on aspirin, the only medicine he took to relieve his constant pain. A young assistant—and one year, his granddaughter from Denmark—drove him around the campus and saw to his needs. At every concert, ensconced in his wheelchair backstage at the concert hall, Mischa directed the festival's performance recordings, as much a stickler as ever for perfection.

After more than twenty years at Marlboro, Sasha left abruptly in 1977, selling his house and refusing to talk about why he left. A spate of rumors circulated as to the reason for his sudden departure— some young musicians had rebelled against his authoritarian manner; he made a disparaging remark about Serkin's father-in-law, Adolf Busch, in front of Serkin's wife, Irene; he and Serkin disagreed about whether a certain work was ready to be performed in public; or Irene Serkin was angry at Sasha's encouraging her son Peter's rebelliousness. Sasha's explanation, in his autobiography, is cryptic. He talks of "a time when concessions enter the picture," that the world is made up "of compromises and dishonesty." Serkin, he said, "should not constantly have the burden of solving Marlboro's problems nor should he have to compromise as a soloist or in life."[39]

Neither Sasha nor Serkin ever provided the answer, but it must have been a serious disagreement. "When Sasha blows, Sasha blows," said a musician who knew him for many years.[40] Yet Sasha never hid his affection for Serkin. The two happened to be together in the 1940s when Sasha received a call from Mischa, telling him about the fate of their mother and sister in Auschwitz. "Rudy was right there when I heard, and I think there was something very profound established between us at that moment, and something very Jewish. . . . the feeling of deep brotherly love which grew between us."[41] Sasha finally returned to Marlboro in July 1991, when, a few months after Serkin died, he directed the festival orchestra and Serkin's son Peter in a Mozart piano concerto that was part of a commemorative program in Serkin's honor.

Sasha was always interested in Peter Serkin's career. He was instrumental in having Serkin, then only seventeen years old, play with the Budapest in a concert in Boston in 1964. Boris's protégé was another teenage pianist, Murray Perahia, who first attended Marlboro in 1966. Like Mischa, Boris also started to perform viola recitals before the Quartet folded. His first took place in April 1965 in Buffalo, and he, too, returned to the Library of Congress in March of the following year, prompting a reviewer to comment, "It is beginning to look as if the Budapest Quartet is returning to Washington one by one."[42] Boris paid a second visit to the Library in February 1967, when he performed with Perahia and clarinetist Harold Wright. The recital was recorded by the Library and later released on Vox Records.

In all, Boris performed in eleven recitals between 1965 and 1968, including a trio recital with Sasha and Horszowski in Buffalo and a concert with Ruth and Jaime Laredo in Buffalo in 1968. In addition, he took the violist chair in the St. Louis String Quartet in October 1967 when the violist, Takaoki Sugitani, a young musician Boris knew from Marlboro, took ill. The following year, Boris himself fell ill with stomach cancer. Sometimes his hand trembled along the fingerboard of his viola, and yet, playing a Bach sonata at home one day, he astounded himself by how well he played, better than he ever had before.[43] Boris underwent an operation and had to shelve plans to record Brahms sonatas with Perahia and to tour with a group of Marlboro musicians. But he did feel well enough to perform in a Beethoven cello quintet for the Chamber Music Society of Lincoln Center at the recently opened Alice Tully Hall. It was his first appearance at Alice Tully, but it was also his last performance. Gaunt and ailing, the once-robust Boris died on November 15, 1969, at the age of seventy-two. He was buried in a cemetery in Washington Township, New Jersey. His wife Sonya, who continued to take part in the Marlboro Music School as its social director, died on January 8, 1980, and was buried beside him.

Joe suffered a heart attack in his apartment in Washington on the morning of October 9, 1974. He was seventy-four years old. His body was cremated, and his ashes, in an urn, deposited at a cemetery in Mount Vernon, Virginia. His wife Pola died six years later, on October 30, 1980, at the age of seventy-eight. Her ashes were deposited alongside his.

Mischa once said, "The most beautiful thing would be to die on stage, while playing."[44] But his wish was denied. He was bedridden during his last days, and could not bear to listen to music any more. He destroyed most of the journals he had so faithfully kept over his years with the Quartet. Mischa died in Buffalo at the age of eighty-

causes. His body was cremated, and the ashes were taken by his son Greg.

Over the years, Sasha remained as busy as ever, hopping planes to appear all over the world, conducting, performing, putting together music festivals, always, it seemed, on the move. "Sasha is Sasha," a friend said.[45] In his eighties, he still helped arrange concerts at the New School of Social Research and led the performances of the high-school students' orchestra he founded that played every Christmas Eve at Carnegie Hall. He took the orchestra to the Kennedy Center in Washington, and after its performance, he conducted waltzes in the lobby. He helped to found the Mostly Mozart festival in New York. In 1982, after much reluctance and soul-searching, Sasha put aside his resentment and returned to the Library of Congress, to play a recital with Peter Serkin that he dedicated to Joe and Boris. In 1988, he was a recipient of a Kennedy Center Honor.

In many ways, however, Sasha was not the same Sasha. He lost vision in one eye and suffered from bad circulation in his legs and heart problems. Wracked by his aches, still affected by the death of his brother Mischa, his gruffness sometimes expressed itself as bitterness. Those who knew him found him cantankerous, and he sometimes lost old friends by his caustic remarks. He railed against what he called "all the compromises and dishonesty which used to be the sole property of politicians and courtesans, but has become a fact of musical life as well."[46] Although he did not amplify on what he meant, he evidently was critical of the way music is treated as a business nowadays, the sacrifice of performance to monetary considerations, and the importance attached to technique over interpretation.

Back in 1948, Sasha wrote Elizabeth Sprague Coolidge, "I still hope some day to get married and really have a lot of children and grandchildren."[47] But both Sasha's marriages failed—his second, to actress Geraldine Page, lasted but three years—and he never fathered any children. He kept a house in Provence, in southern France, where he went every year since he studied with Pablo Casals in 1949. In Manhattan, he lived on the second floor of a building he owned on East 20th Street, in the midst of a business area north of Greenwich Village. On the ground floor was a hardware store. For all the friends he made over the years, as a musician and through his travels, he was, in the eyes of many of them, a lonely man. He died, alone, of heart failure on February 2, 1993, at the age of eighty-four. His body was cremated.

21

The Legacy

How do you measure the influence the Budapest String Quartet has had on chamber musicians performing today? In what way can you describe the impetus the four Russians gave to spreading the enjoyment of chamber music throughout the United States? What was their contribution? What is their place in musical history?

There are no reliable statistics that you can point to, no comparative studies, just bits and pieces of information—and a wealth of remarks by musicians and critics that attest to the impact the Quartet had on the world of chamber music and, in particular, on string-quartet players performing today.

Nobody kept count in the 1930s, but there evidently were only a handful of radio stations then devoted to classical music. Now there are some 250 such stations.[1] The number of regularly performing, touring ensembles devoted solely to playing quartets grew from less than a handful in the late 1930s to fifty by the time the Quartet disbanded in 1967, indicative of an enormous increase of interest in the musical form. By then, the Washington *Post* editorialized, "music once reserved for the chambers of a titled elite has become a delight for the many."[2] The membership of Chamber Music America, a professional association formed in 1977, included seventy-six string quartets in 1984, one hundred fourteen only six years later, when the association estimated there were actually a total of at least one hundred ninety such ensembles concertizing.[3] The most recent figures of attendance at chamber-music concerts of all types—duos, trios, quartets, and chamber orchestra—are at least ten years old, but indicate that eight million people attended such concerts in

1980.[4] That is likely to be an overestimation. Chamber Music America, which conducted a survey of its membership in 1991, said the figure is more like four and a half million people, which is still impressive.

Was the Budapest Quartet responsible, even in part, for such an explosion of numbers in performing groups and attendance? That is impossible to prove, although it is obvious that their popularity undoubtedly made Americans conscious of an entire world of music hitherto all but ignored, if not unknown. Adolf Busch complained in the early 1940s, at about the time the Budapest Quartet settled in Washington and became the quartet-in-residence at the Library of Congress, that in the United States "the whole attitude to music is quite different from what we are used to and what we love. The virtuosos have ruined the country in *this* sense. Every young person tries if possible to play even faster or louder than the famous X, or Y, or Z, and thereby to deserve to earn more money and have a more impressive career than his colleagues. That one masters one's instrument so as to make good and beautiful music is something that most of them still have to learn."[5] Busch, whose own well-known quartet was often joined in concert by his son-in-law Rudolf Serkin, was especially upset by the state of chamber music in the forties:

> The quartet engagements aren't enough to live on. One would have to play for so little money that one could have *many* concerts—there are too few well-paying ones. The concert situation here is so completely different from what it is in Switzerland or Europe in general. Aside from the hullabaloo of agents, who are in control of everything, as there are hardly any associations (concert societies), and whose possible sole interest is making money, the lack of chamber-music societies and above all the lack of smaller halls is extremely important. Here in this country everything has first of all to be big. . . . However since chamber music is always everywhere intended for a small, though cultivated audience, but the programs have been set for decades by managers and virtuosos (with bad taste and lust for the American dollar), the audience has to suffer, and *does* suffer, quite literally still today.[6]

Yet, some twenty-five years later, when the Budapest was still performing, Howard Taubman could ask rhetorically in the *New York Times*, "Who listens to chamber music, indeed? . . . We are everywhere—in large cities and small, in hills and plains, in the United States, and Europe and Latin America. We have not lost our capacity to be stirred by the monumental climax in Beethoven's Ninth or in Wagner's 'Gotterdammerung.' But we do not require many of these grandiose moments. For continuing satisfying nourishment, we prefer a Beethoven quartet, a Mozart quintet, a Mendelssohn trio."[7]

One thing is indisputable. The Quartet inspired an entire generation of chamber musicians. The Budapest was "the landmark" in violinist Felix Galimir's eyes: "They gave a stamp to quartet playing that has ever since been the criterion of how one plays string quartets." Their appearance on the concert-hall scene, he said, "was the first time that someone noticed the string quartet."[8]

In the words of clarinetist David Oppenheim, recently retired dean of the New York University School of the Arts who both performed and recorded with the Quartet, the Budapest "was stylistically the first modern quartet. It was to quartet playing what Heifetz was to violin playing. Other younger quartets, who may not now play like the Budapest, play the way they do because there was a Budapest Quartet to set the standards, to inspire, *and* to take quartet playing out of the 19th century."[9]

Violinist Jaime Laredo agreed. The Budapest members were "the fathers of all quartets. You can talk about this great quartet or that quartet, but then there's the Budapest Quartet. They absolutely set the standard, they really did."

Violist Samuel Rhodes pointed to the Budapest as the "bridge" between quartets of the old school of playing with their expressive emphases and those performing today, which are so technically proficient:

> They had a particular combination of a perfectly schooled, impeccably, technically trained first violinist who floated above the rest, tremendously dynamic inner voices and a wonderful rhythmic and expressive sense in the base line. And all of these elements interacted with each other. In a fast movement, it could be very, not driven, but very dynamic and full of fire—*con brio*. When they played Prokofieff's first quartet, the virtuoso qualities of each of the members stood out, they were unsurpassed. Yet when it came to a late Beethoven, or a Brahms movement, they had the depth of expression also. So they had both sides in their way of reacting in their personality.

To Rhodes's colleague in the Juilliard Quartet, violinist Robert Mann, "The Budapest Quartet, a little bit like Toscanini, had an unerring sense about time and tempo character which even though they didn't play all the tempos that Beethoven indicated with his metronome markings which is becoming fashionable now, of course, they played with a certain sense of flow and onward-goingness that actually made quartets much more exciting than in the old days." The Budapest players, he said, were "not four clones of the same person," but "four different but deep feeling people who know how to come together in a conversation. They were, and still are in my mind, an amazing ensemble."[10]

For Julius Levine, the double bassist who began performing and recording with the Quartet in the late 1950s, the yardstick for whether a performer is great is whether you would want to listen to him many years later. "If you can imagine a musician thirty years from now and the fingers a little slow, would you still want to do and hear him play?" he said. "When I got to play with the Budapest, some of the fingers were already slowing down and I loved them."

Cellist Leslie Parnas talked about the time when he was a student and how "they were tremendously vivid to me—all of them playing those late Beethoven quartets—that was the education of the gods for me as a kid to hear them playing that. I'll never forget an Opus 132 that they played. I almost felt the presence of Beethoven on that stage. My hair would stand up on edge at some of those performances, it was so marvelous."

To Parnas, the Budapest, through its radio broadcasts and recordings, made playing quartets a performance media. "You know you could always find things that you would disagree with. Even some out-of-tune notes here and there perhaps. But as far as their unique place in the world, there was no question in my mind that they had achieved it."

Every note might not have been perfect in their last years, said violinist Arnold Steinhardt, "but it was still a revelation." As a student, he was attracted to their style of playing—an amalgam of German and Russian training. "Up to then, I only knew the Russian school of Auer, which was a little bit more 'heart on sleeve,' emotional, played for theatrical flair. There was a kind of subtlety and sophistication in their playing that defies imitation. They opened up a vision of music that many of us students had no idea of. I have a sense that I was listening to the Beethoven Quartet not the Budapest Quartet, and I mean that in the highest terms."

Critic Paul Hume expressed the same opinion. After the Budapest performed for so long, "it was inevitable that the playing could not always remain on the Everest-like eminence that had, for so long, been their hallmark. But there was never an evening when the rewards to be enjoyed by hearing those four men join their combined understanding and love of music did not produce something which has not been duplicated since they disbanded."[11]

What was the Budapest's influence on expanding the audience for chamber music? Back in the 1950s, many concert managers were worried what effect long-playing records would have on attendance. They were sure audience figures would drop precipitously when music lovers could stay at home and listen to their favorite compositions without the troublesome and annoying need to flip a record every four minutes. But Harold Spivacke, for one, found that even though "some of the old concert-goers bought hi-fi sets and stopped coming" to the Library of Congress, "many young people who started listening to the Budapest records suddenly discovered the need to see them too. The theory that the mass media destroy audiences was not borne out in our experience—in the long run they stimulated attendance at our live concerts."[12]

One of those whose appreciation of music was stimulated was critic Robert Parris. He recalled that "when, as a boy, I used to pester the music librarians in the Philadelphia Public Library for scores and records of Beethoven played by the Budapest, it was with the sense of requesting the Last Word."[13] Another critic, J. Fred Lissfelt of Pittsburgh, believed that it was "invaluable" for students to listen to the Quartet. "They hear the scores ideally played and can apply such criteria to their own work. For the music lover, there can be no greater joy."[14]

Michael Tree was one of those students who heard the Budapest perform when he was studying to be a string player. He was impressed by "the aura about them" even before they played a single note: "There was something so masterly and controlled and something very European about them. Some people arrive at their seats a little early, or sit down more abruptly than others. They had a great feeling of calm and suaveness on stage. The way they carried themselves onstage, the way they sat, gave one a feeling of great authority."

And, when they picked up their bows and began to pull them across their instruments' strings, "the Budapest String Quartet knew how music should be played," said critic Harold Schonberg. "They knew that God did not intend musicians to be metronomes. They didn't worry too much if a composer didn't write a ritard and they felt a ritard was necessary. They played a ritard. And it was always within the meaning and structure of the music. They had a fine feeling for the structure. They handled the Beethoven quartets, for instance, with a kind of freedom that I think has just about vanished from the earth. And with a beautiful sound. They were crackerjack instrumentalists."

Lon Tuck of the Washington *Post* believed the Quartet's many

years with the Library of Congress made Washington "uncontesta-
bly big-league in chamber music—opening a path toward musical
maturity that continues today. Even more important, though, the
unprecedented possibilities of broadcasting and recording that accompanied the Budapest's activities created a worldwide audience
for the matchless literature of the quartet. That changed the face of
music, and may well be the most lasting of the Budapest's many
achievements."[15]

The importance of the Quartet's residency at the Library worked
both ways. Both Joe and Mischa agreed that it was one of the most
important factors in the Budapest's success. It was, Joe said, "the
turning point" both in the life of the Quartet as well as in the lives
"of individual members."[16]

One tangible legacy the Quartet left is the large number of recordings that they made over nearly forty years. You can still hear
the Budapest, be stirred by their playing, discover a cornucopia of
insights into the way not just Beethoven but also Brahms and Bartók,
Schubert and Debussy, Mozart and Ravel can be performed. Pressings from the 1930s, 1940s, 1950s, and 1960s have been reissued over
the years since the Budapest disbanded, and now compact discs are
being released by Sony Classical. In addition, the Library of Congress
is hoping to issue recordings of Quartet performances. In 1990, it
drew on its vast collection of such recordings to sponsor for National
Public Radio a series of programs that featured many of the Quartet's
finest concerts.* Listening to them, wrote critic Alan Rich, it becomes clear why "you hear your grandparents talk of hearing the
Budapest in the old days at the Y.M.H.A. or in the New Friends of
Music concerts at Town Hall, and talk about how their breath nearly
stopped and how the tears ran down their cheeks."[17]

Depending on whom you read or talk to, some say the recordings
of the early years are the best; others point to those made in the
1950s, or even 1960s, despite Joe Roisman's intonation problems.
They fault the few recordings made when Ortenberg was second
violinist and are generally critical, too, of those made when Gorodetzky replaced him. Those who prefer the early recordings speak
about the vigorous attack and youthful exuberance they detect in
the members' playing; those who prefer those of the later years talk

---

* As this book was going to press, the Library of Congress announced that it planned to
release in the spring of 1993 a compact disc of an all-Rachmaninoff program performed at the Library in April 1952 by the Quartet with pianist Artur Balsam. Included on it will be Rachmaninoff's two unfinished string quartets, Nos. 1 and 2, and
his Trio élégiaque for violin, cello, and piano.

of their rich sonority and the maturity of their interpretative ideas. "Nothing is ever definite, least of all in a quartet," said Roisman, trying to explain the striking differences between the recordings of the 1930s, and those of the 1960s. "When I listen to some of our early recordings, I am puzzled. We used to play Hugo Wolf's 'Italian Serenade' very fast, in bravura style. Now we play it slowly. We *feel* that it should be slow. The exuberance of youth is behind us, I suppose."[18]

Reviewing a reissue of recordings from the 1950s, critic Irving Kolodin wrote, "The Budapest Quartet, of golden fame, played . . . from the heart. The four hearts beat with such unanimity and rapture in this reissued version of performances by which many musicians of the Fifties and Sixties lived and died that the sound, especially in the slow movements, flows on and on, with the steady, unhurried but relentless natural undercurrent of a great river. . . . There are riches here that no other quartet has ever mined."[19]

Summing up the various pros and cons of those who reviewed the recordings, discographer Burnett James wrote, "Although one may criticise the Budapest Quartet from time to time; find some shortcomings in their most ambitious and comprehensive undertakings; there is no reasonable doubt that in the musical life of our times the group has occupied, and continues to occupy, a unique place. Four men dedicated to a single end—and attaining it with remarkable consistency."[20]

Without boasting, the members of the Quartet understood their place in the history of chamber music. They realized that their style of playing—the unique union of their four instrumental voices—their interpretative nuances, and fulsome sound were milestones. A whole "new generation of quartet players," Boris said, "are molding their play after our performance." Moreover, as Boris pointed out, before the Quartet, there "never was a quartet of such duration, never a quartet which had such success." The Budapest was the first quartet to rely solely on performing to earn a livelihood and the first to make money on recordings. "After the Quartet's experience, many quartets saw you could make a living playing quartets."[21]

"We were the vanguard," said Mischa. "Some people said we made chamber music in this country. I'm not that conceited, you know, to say that we have. I will tell you what helped—the Library of Congress and the radio programs. People in North Dakota, in South Dakota, in states where they did not have chamber music, and said we have to listen to this kind of an ensemble. And that's how chamber music became popular here."[22]

Joe said that he had "a wonderful life although not very easy and it took a long time before we got to the top where we were and where we stayed perhaps longer than anybody else, but I would do it certainly all over again if I could do it because it was so satisfying—to know that you give to people and they enjoy it so much."[23]

"After listening to some of today's quartets," added Sasha, "I understand why connoisseurs all over the world are still enjoying our records.

"The Budapest String Quartet is more alive than ever."[24]

Appendix 1: Repertoire

The following works were performed by the Budapest String Quartet, or by members of the Quartet at Quartet concerts, from the season of 1936–37 through 1966.

Bach

Concerto in D Minor for Two Violins and Orchestra; Concerto in F Minor for Harpsichord and Strings; Four Fugues from *The Art of the Fugue* (arranged by Roy Harris)

Bach–Mozart

Prelude and Fugue in D Minor; Adagio and Fugue in F Minor

Balazs

Divertimento

Barber

Quartet in B Minor, Opus 11; Adagio for Strings

Bartók

Quartet No. 1, Opus 7; Quartet No. 2, Opus 17; Quartet No. 5; Quartet No. 6

Beethoven

Quartet in F, Opus 18, No. 1; Quartet in G, Opus 18, No. 2 ("Compliments"); Quartet in D, Opus 18, No. 3; Quartet in C Minor, Opus 18, No. 4; Quartet in A, Opus 18, No. 5; Quartet in B-flat, Opus 18, No. 6; Quartet in F, Opus 59, No. 1 ("Rasumovsky"); Quartet in E Minor, Opus 59, No. 2; Quartet in C, Opus 59, No. 3; Quartet in E-flat, Opus 74 ("The Harp"); Quartet in F Minor, Opus 95; Quartet in E-flat, Opus 127; Quartet in B-flat, Opus 130; Quartet in C-sharp Minor, Opus 131; Quartet in A Minor, Opus 132; *Grosse Fuge* in B-flat, Opus 133; Quartet in F, Opus 135; Quartet in E-flat (recomposed and transcribed Piano Quintet, Opus 16); Quartet in F (recomposed and transcribed Piano Sonata in E, Opus 14, No. 1); Piano Quartet (recomposed and transcribed from Quintet for Piano and Wind Instruments, Opus 16); Viola Quintet in C, Opus 29; String Trio in G, Opus 9, No. 1; String Trio in C Minor, Opus 9, No. 3; Piano Trio in E-flat, Opus 1, No. 1; Piano Trio in G, Opus 1, No. 2; Piano Trio in C Minor, Opus 1, No. 3; Piano Trio in B-flat, Opus 11, No. 4; Piano Trio in D, Opus 70, No. 1; Piano Trio in B-flat, Opus 97 ("Archduke"); Serenade in D for Violin, Viola, and Cello, Opus 8; Serenade in D for Flute, Violin, and Viola, Opus 25; Septet in E-flat, Opus 20; Variations, Opus 121a, on the theme "Ich bin der Schneider Kakadu"; Sonata for Violin and Piano in G, Opus 30, No. 3

Blackwood

Quartet No. 1

Bloch

Piano Quintet in C

Boccherini

Cello Quintet in C; Cello Quintet in E-flat, Opus 12, No. 2; Cello Quintet in E; Quintet No. 1 in D for Guitar and Quartet

Borodin

String Quartet No. 2 in D

Brahms

Quartet in C Minor, Opus 51, No. 1; Quartet in A Minor, Opus 51, No. 2; Quartet in B-flat, Opus 67 ("Pastoral"); Piano Quartet in G Minor, Opus 25; Piano Quartet in A, Opus 26; Piano Quartet in C Minor, Opus 60; Piano Trio in C, Opus 87; Piano Trio in C Minor, Opus 101; Trio in E-flat for Violin, Horn, and Piano, Opus 40; Trio in A Minor for Clarinet, Violincello, and Piano, Opus 114; Piano Quintet in F Minor, Opus 34; Viola Quintet in F, Opus 88; Viola Quintet in G, Opus 111; Clarinet Quintet in B Minor, Opus

115; Sextet No. 1 in B-flat, Opus 18; Sextet in G, Opus 36; Songs for Voice, Viola, Piano; Sonata No. 1 in F Minor for Viola and Piano, Opus 120, No. 1

Bruckner

Viola Quintet in F

Busch

Piano Quintet, Opus 35

Carpenter

Quartet for Stringed Instruments

Coleridge–Taylor

Clarinet Quintet in F-sharp Minor, Opus 10

Debussy

Quartet in G minor, Opus 10; Danses for Harp and Strings

Denny

Quartet No. 2

Dittersdorf

Quartet No. 1 in D; Divertimento in D

Dohnanyi

Serenade in C, Opus 10; Piano Quintet in E-flat Minor, Opus 26

Dvořák

Quartet in E-flat, Opus 51; Quartet in F, Opus 96 ("The Nigger," renamed "The American"); Piano Quartet in E-flat, Opus 87; Piano Quintet in A, Opus 81; Viola Quintet in E-flat, Opus 97; Double Bass Quintet in G, Opus 77; Sextet in A, Opus 48; Piano Trio, Opus 90 (Dumky)

Elgar

Quartet in E Minor, Opus 83; Introduction and Allegro for String Quartet and Orchestra

Enesco

String Octet in C, Opus 7

Faure

Piano Quartet in C Minor, Opus 15

Foss

Quartet in G

Franck

Quartet in D; Piano Quintet in F Minor

Ginastera

Quartet No. 1

Glinka

Quartet in F

Grieg

Quartet in G Minor, Opus 27

Griffes

Two Sketches for String Quartet Based on Indian Themes

Gruenberg

Five Variations on a Popular Theme (Including Three Apologies)

Handel

Concerto in B-flat for Harp and Strings

Haydn

Quartet in G, Opus 17, No. 5; Quartet in D, Opus 20, No. 4 ("The Row in Venice"); Quartet in E-flat, Opus 33, No. 2 ("Joke"); Quartet in C, Opus 33, No. 3 ("The Bird"); Quartet in D, Opus 50, No. 6 ("The Frog"); Quartet in G, Opus 54, No. 1; Quartet in C, Opus 54, No. 2; Quartet in D, Opus 64, No. 5 ("The Lark"); Quartet in E-flat, Opus 64, No. 6; Quartet in G Minor, Opus

74, No. 3 ("The Horsemen"); Quartet in G, Opus 76, No. 1; Quartet in D Minor, Opus 76, No. 2; Quartet in C, Opus 76, No. 3 ("Emperor"); Quartet in B-flat, Opus 76, No. 4 ("Sunrise"); Quartet in D, Opus 76, No. 5; Quartet in E-flat, Opus 76, No. 6; Quartet in G, Opus 77, No. 1; Quartet in F, Opus 77, No. 2; Trio No. 1 in G for Violin, Violincello, and Piano

Heiden

Quintet for Horn and Strings

Hindemith

Quartet No. 3 in C; Quartet No. 6 in E-flat

Jacobi

Quartet No. 2; Hagiographa, Three Biblical Narratives for String Quartet and Piano

Kodály

Quartet No. 2 in D, Opus 10; Duo for Violin and Cello, Opus 7

Kreisler

Quartet in A Minor

Křenek

Quartet No. 7, Opus 96

Langstroth

Four Pieces for String Quartet, Opus 20

Lees

Quartet No. 1

Lockwood

Informal Music No. 2

Loeffler

Music for Four Stringed Instruments

Lopatnikoff

Quartet No. 3, Opus 36

Martinů

Quartet No. 6; Piano Quintet; Concerto for String Quartet and Orchestra

Mason

String Quartet on Negro Themes, Opus 19

Medtner

Piano Quintet in C

Mendelssohn

Quartet in E-flat, Opus 12; Quartet in D, Opus 44, No. 1; Andante (or Variations) and Scherzo, Opus 81, Nos. 1 and 2; Piano Quartet in F Minor, Opus 2; Viola Quintet in A, Opus 18; String Octet in E-flat, Opus 20; Piano Trio No. 1 in D Minor, Opus 49

Milhaud

Quartet No. 2; Quartet No. 4; Quartet No. 6; Quartet No. 7; Quartet No. 8; Quartet No. 9; Quartet No. 10; Quartet No. 11; Quartet No. 12; Quartet No. 13; Quartet No. 14; Quartet No. 15; Octet (Quartet Nos. 14 and 15 performed simultaneously); Quartet No. 17; Cello Quintet; Trio No. 1; Cantante de l'Enfant et de la Mère

Mozart

Quartet in G (K. 387); Quartet in D Minor (K. 421); Quartet in E-flat (K. 428); Quartet in B-flat (K. 458, "The Hunt"); Quartet in A (K. 464); Quartet in C (K. 465, "Dissonant"); Quartet in D (K. 499); Quartet in D (K. 575); Quartet in B-flat (K. 589); Quartet in F (K. 590); Adagio and Fugue in C Minor (K. 546); Oboe Quartet in F (K. 370); Piano Quartet in G Minor (K. 478); Piano Quartet in E-flat (K. 493); Flute Quartet in D (K. 285); Flute Quartet in A (K. 298); Viola Quintet in B-flat (K. 174); Viola Quintet in C Minor (K. 406); Viola Quintet in C (K. 515); Viola Quintet in G Minor (K. 516); Viola Quintet in D (K. 593); Cello Quintet in E-flat (K. 614); Clarinet Quintet in A (K. 581); Horn Quintet in E-flat (K. 407); Piano Trio in G (K. 496); Piano Trio in E (K. 542); Duo in B-flat for Violin and Viola (K. 424); Sinfonia Concertante in E-flat for Violin, Viola, and Orchestra (K. 364); "Eine Kleine Nachtmusik" (K. 525); Divertimento for Violin, Viola, and Cello in E-flat (K. 563)

Nabokoff

Serenata estiva

Piston

Quartet No. 2; Quartet No. 3; Quartet No. 4; Quintet for Flute and String Quartet

Porter

Quartet No. 7; Quartet No. 8

Prokofieff

Quartet No. 1 in B Minor, Opus 50; Quartet No. 2, Opus 92

Purcell

Chaconne in G Minor for String Quartet; Fantasia No. 2 in B-flat; Fantasia No. 9 in E Minor

Rachmaninoff

Quartet No. 1 (unfinished); Quartet No. 2 (unfinished); Sonata in C Minor for Violincello and Piano, Opus 19; Trio élégiaque for Violin, Violincello and Piano, Opus 9

Rameau

"Berger Fidèle"

Ravel

Quartet in F; Introduction and Allegro for Harp, Flute, Clarinet, and String Quartet

Reger

Quartet No. 4 in E-flat, Opus 109; Clarinet Quintet in A, Opus 146; Trio in A Minor, Opus 77b

Respighi

Doric Quartet

Rieti

Quartet No. 2; Quartet No. 3

Roussel

Quartet in D, Opus 45

Le Chevalier de Saint-George

Quartet in E-flat, Opus 1, No. 2; Quartet in C Minor, Opus 1, No. 4

Schönberg

Quartet No. 1 in D Minor, Opus 7; Quartet No. 2 in F-sharp Minor with Soprano Voice, Opus 10; Sextet, "Verklärte Nacht" ("Transfigured Night"), Opus 4

Schubert

Quartet in A Minor, Opus 29; Quartet in E-flat, Opus 125, No. 1; Quartet in E, Opus 125, No. 2; Quartet in G, Opus 161; Quartet in G Minor; Quartett-satz in C Minor; Quartet in D Minor, Op. posth. ("Death and the Maiden"); Quintet in A for Violin, Viola, Violincello, Double Bass, and Piano, Opus 114 ("The Trout"); Cello Quintet in C, Opus 163; Octet in F, Opus 166; Five German Dances

Schumann

Quartet in A Minor, Opus 41, No. 1; Quartet in F, Opus 41, No. 2; Quartet in A, Opus 41, No. 3; Piano Quartet in E-flat, Opus 47; Piano Quintet in E-flat, Opus 44

Shostakovich

String Quartet, Opus 49; Piano Quintet, Opus 57

Sibelius

Quartet in D Minor, Opus 56 ("Voces Intimae")

Smetana

Quartet No. 1 in E Minor ("From my Life")

Stravinsky

Concertino for String Quartet

Tansman

Quartet No. 5

Tchaikovsky

Quartet No. 1 in D, Opus 11; Quartet No. 2 in E, Opus 22; Sextet in D Minor, Opus 70 ("Souvenir of Florence")

Tournier

Féerie for Harp, Two Violins, Viola, and Cello

Van Vactor

Quartet No. 1

Villa-Lobos

Quartet No. 2, Opus 56; Quartet No. 6; Quartet No. 17

Vivaldi

Concerto in D Minor, Opus 3, No. 11 ("L'Estro armonico")

Warlock

Quartet in G Minor; Five Elizabethan Songs for Voice and Strings

Wellesz

Octet, Opus 67

Williams

Quartet in G Minor; "On Wenlock Edge"

Wolf

Italian Serenade

Appendix 2: Sony Classical Discography

The following discography was prepared by Sony Classical, successor to the Columbia Recording Corporation and CBS Records. It includes re-issues released since 1970. Album numbers ending with the letter "K" indicate a compact disc; those ending with a "T" indicate an audio cassette. All other identifying numbers are LP's.

For recordings released before 1970, see the discographies published in the Nov. 1963 (Vol. 3, No. 3) issue of *Audio and Record Review* and the Dec. 1970 (Vol. 37, No. 4) issue of *The American Record Guide.* The latter includes the Quartet's first recordings, issued from 1926 on, when the Budapest String Quartet was under contract to Gramophone and recording for His Master's Voice. Each recording is keyed to a list of personnel who made it.

Of all the recordings the Quartet made for HMV in Germany, England, and America, only one compact disc containing three Mozart works has been re-issued in the United States as far as it is known: EMI Angel CDH 7-63697-2, which includes the Quintet in A, K 581, with Benny Goodman, and Quartet Nos. 19 and 20, K 465 and K 499, respectively. The photograph of the Quartet on the album's cover, when first issued in 1990, was inaccurate; it was taken before 1930 and includes two members of the original Quartet who had left the ensemble by the time the Mozart pieces were recorded.

KEY

A—Hauser, Pogani, Ipolyi, Son
B—Hauser, Roisman, Ipolyi, Son
C—Roisman, A. Schneider, Ipolyi, M. Schneider
D—Roisman, A. Schneider, Kroyt, M. Schneider
E—Roisman, Ortenberg, Kroyt, M. Schneider
F—Roisman, Gorodetsky, Kroyt, M. Schneider
G—Roisman, ———, Kroyt, M. Schneider
H—A. Schneider, Roisman, Kroyt, M. Schneider

Bartók

Quartet
No. 2 in A Minor, Op. 17
Group C. ODYSSEY Y4 34643; re-released Oct. 1977

Beethoven

Quartets
No. 1 in F and Nos. 2–6, Op. 18
Group F; recorded 1951–52. PORTRAIT MP2K 5231; re-released 1992
No. 2 in G, Op. 18
Group D; recorded 1938
No. 3 in D, Op. 18
Group C; recorded 1935. ODYSSEY Y3 35240; re-released Sept. 1979
No. 7 in F, Op. 59, no. 1[1]
No. 8 in E Minor, Op. 59, no. 2[1]
No. 9 in C, Op. 59, no. 3[2]
No. 10 in E-flat, Op. 74[3] "Harp"[2]
No. 11 in F Minor, Op. 95
Group F; recorded 1951–52. ODYSSEY Y3 3316; re-released May 1975
No. 12 in E-flat, Op. 127
No. 13 in B-flat, Op. 130
No. 14 in C-sharp Minor, Op. 131
No. 15 in A, Op. 132
No. 16 in F, Op. 135
Group F; recorded 1951–52. ODYSSEY Y4 34643; re-released Oct. 1977

1. Nos. 7 & 8 also recorded by Group D. SONY CLASSICAL SBT/SBK 47665; re-released Jan. 1991. Also released in 1992 as PORTRAIT SBK 46545
2. Nos. 9 & 10 also on SONY CLASSICAL MPK 45551; re-released Aug. 1990. Also recorded by Group D. SONY CLASSICAL SBT/SBK 47665; re-released Jan. 1991
3. No 10 also on ODYSSEY Y3 35240; re-released Sept. 1979

Grosse Fuge, Op. 133
    Group D; recorded 1961. SONY CLASSICAL SBK/SBT 47665; re-released Sept. 1991. Also SONY CLASSICAL MPK 45551; re-released Aug. 1990

Brahms

Quartets
    No. 2 in A, Op. 26
        Group G with Clifford Curzon, piano. ODYSSEY 32 26 0019; re-released May 1970
    No. 1 in C Minor, Op. 51
        Group unknown. PORTRAIT MPK 45686; re-released Aug. 1990
    No. 8 in E Minor, Op. 59, no. 2
        Group C. ODYSSEY Y4 34643; re-released Oct. 1977
    No. 3 in B-flat, Op. 67
        Group unknown; recorded 1932. PORTRAIT MPK 45553; re-released Aug. 1990
Quintets
    Op 34 in F Minor for Piano and Strings
        Group D with Rudolf Serkin. PORTRAIT MP/MPT 38769; re-released July 1983. Also PORTRAIT MPK 45686; re-released Aug. 1990
    Clarinet Quintet in B Minor, Op. 115
        Recorded in 1955 or 1961 with David Oppenheim, clarinet. PORTRAIT MPK 45553; re-released Aug. 1990

Debussy

Quartet
    Quartet in G Minor, Op. 10
        Group D; recorded 1958. PORTRAIT MP/MPT 38774; re-released July 1983. Also PORTRAIT MPK 44843; re-released Aug. 1990

Dvořák

Quartet
    No. 6 in F, Op. 76 "American"
        Group D. COLUMBIA M, MQ 32792; re-released Feb. 1974
Quintets
    Op. 81 in A
        Group F with Clifford Curzon, piano; recorded 1953. ODYSSEY 32 26 0019; re-released May 1970
    No. 3 in E-flat, Op. 97
        Group D with Walter Trampler, viola; recorded 1964–65. COLUMBIA M, MQ 32792; re-released Feb. 1974

Faure

Quartet
> Quartet in C Minor, Op. 15
>> Group G with Jesus Maria Sanroma, piano; recorded 1957. ODYSSEY Y 33315; re-released May 1975

Franck

Quintet
> Quintet in F Minor
>> Group D with Clifford Curzon, piano; recorded 1956. ODYSSEY Y 33315; re-released May 1975

Haydn

Quartets
> No. 1 in G Major, Op. 76
> No. 2 in D Minor, Op. 76 "Quinten"
> No. 3 in C Major, Op. 76 "Emperor"
> No. 4 in B-flat Major, Op. 76 "Sunrise"
> No. 5 in E-flat Major, Op. 76
>> Group F; recorded 1954. ODYSSEY Y3 33324; re-released May 1975

Mendelssohn

Quartets
> Op. 12 in E-flat
>> Group C. ODYSSEY Y4 34643; re-released Oct. 1977
> No. 1 in D, Op. 44
>> Group D; recorded 1959. ODYSSEY Y4 34643; re-released Jan. 1977

Quintet
> Quintet for Strings
>> Group D with Walter Trampler, viola. ODYSSEY 33308; re-released May 1975

Octet
> Octet for Strings
>> Group D with Felix Galimir and Isidor Cohen, violin; Walter Trampler, viola; Benar Heifetz, cello. ODYSSEY Y 33308; re-released May 1975

Mozart

Quintets
> No. 2 in B-flat, K 174[4]
> No. 3 in C Minor, K 406[5]

4. No 2 on ODYSSEY Y3 35233; re-released July 1978. Also on SONY CLASSICAL SM3K 46527; re-released Apr. 1991
5. Nos. 3–7, also Group E with Milton Katims, viola; recorded 1941–49. ODYSSEY Y3

No. 4 in C, K 515[6]
No. 5 in G Minor, K 516
No. 6 in D, K 593
No. 7 in E-flat, K 614
> Group D with Walter Trampler, viola; recorded 1956–57. POR-TRAIT-M3P 39663; re-released Oct. 1984

Quartets with piano
> For Piano and Strings in G Minor, K 478
> For Piano and Strings in E-flat, K 493
>> Group G with Mieczysław Horszowski, piano. PORTRAIT MP/MPT 38775; re-released July 1983. Also PORTRAIT MPK 44844; re-released Aug. 1990

Quartets
> No. 14 in G, K 387
> No. 15 in D Minor, K 421
> No. 16 in E-flat, K 428
> No. 17 in B-flat, K 458 "The Hunt"[7]
> No. 18 in A, K 484
> No. 19 in C, K 465
>> Group F; recorded 1954. ODYSSEY Y3 33324; re-released Apr. 1972
> No. 20 in D, K 499
>> Group C. ODYSSEY Y4 34643; re-released Oct. 1977
> No. 23 in F, K 590
>> Group C; recorded 1935. ODYSSEY Y3 35240; re-released Sept. 1979

Ravel

Quartet
> Quartet in F
>> Group D; recorded 1958. PORTRAIT MP/MPT 38774; re-released July 1983. Also PORTRAIT MPK 44843; re-released Aug. 1990

Schubert

Quartets
> No. 13 in A, Op. 29 "Rosamunde"[8]
> No. 14 in D Minor, Op. posth "Death and the Maiden"
> No. 15 in G Major, Op. 161
>> Group F; recorded in 1953. ODYSSEY Y3 33320; re-released May 1975

35233; re-released July 1978. Also SONY CLASSICAL SM3K 46527; re-released Apr. 1991

6. Nos. 4 & 5 on PORTRAIT MPK 45692; re-released Aug. 1990

7. No. 17 also recorded by Group D (1940) and No. 19 also recorded by Group C (1932). Both quartets are on ODYSSEY Y3 35240; re-released Sept. 1979

8. Nos. 13 & 14 also on PORTRAIT MPK 45696; re-released Aug. 1990—Group unknown

Quartettsatz in C Minor
  Group C. ODYSSEY Y4 34643; re-released in Oct. 1977
Quintet
  Quintet for Piano and Strings in A, Op. 114 "Trout"
    Group G with Mieczysław Horszowski, piano; Julius Levine,
    bass; recorded 1963. PORTRAIT MP/MPT 38776; re-released
    July 1983. Also SONY CLASSICAL SBK/SBT 46343; re-
    released Oct. 1990

Schumann

Quartet
  No. 1 in A Minor, Op. 41
    Group D; recorded 1961. ODYSSEY Y 34603; re-released Jan.
    1977
Quintet
  Quintet in E-flat, Op. 44
    Group D with Rudolf Serkin; recorded 1963. CBS MYT 37256; re-
    released Feb. 1982. Also CBS MYK 37256; re-released Aug.
    1990. Also recorded by Group F with Clifford Curzon; 1956.
    ODYSSEY 32 26 0019; re-released May 1970

Wolf

Serenade
  Italian Serenade in G Minor
    Group C. ODYSSEY Y4 34643; re-released Oct. 1977

Appendix 3: Guest Artists
(from 1936 on)

Prior to 1936, the Budapest String Quartet rarely performed with guest artists. Among the exceptions was Bruce Simonds, pianist, who joined the Quartet for a concert in Buffalo on March 11, 1935, playing with them both the Franck Quintet in F Minor and Schumann Quintet in E-flat, Opus 44.

Assisting musicians appeared more frequently on recordings that were made in Europe. The most notable one was violist Hans Mahlke, who joined the Quartet in Berlin in 1932 for a recording of the Brahms Quintet in G, Opus 111, released in 1934 by His Master's Voice. (It was later released in the United States by Victor Red Seal Records.) In addition, after Boris Kroyt joined the Budapest String Quartet in 1936, the group made several recordings in London with assisting artists. Violist Alfred Hobday and cellist Anthony Pini performed in the Brahms Sextet No. 2 in G, Opus 36, recorded in 1936; Hobday played second viola for the Brahms Quintet No. 1 in F, Opus 88, recorded in 1937; and cellist John Moore and violist Watson Forbes joined the Quartet for Dvořák's Sextet No. 1 in A, Opus 48, recorded in 1938. (All were also released by Victor Red Seal.)

All told, after 1936, the Quartet performed in concerts or made recordings with 142 different assisting artists, many of whom ap-

peared at numerous concerts with them. The Budapest also performed with one guest string quartet (for Milhaud's Octet, com-
prised of Quartets No. 14 and 15 played simultaneously) and with
four symphony orchestras (for works such as Elgar's Introduction
and Allegro for String Quartet and Orchestra, Martinů's Concerto for
String Quartet and Orchestra, and Mozart's Sinfonia Concertante in
E-flat for Violin, Viola, and Orchestra).

Piano

Guido Agosti
Claudio Arrau
Artur Balsam
Clifford Curzon
Rudolf Firkusny
Leon Fleisher
Carl Friedberg
Rudolph Ganz
Rafael González
Reginald Gooden
Friedrich Gulda
Myra Hess
Mieczsław Horszowski
Eugene Istomin
Irene Jacobi
Erich Itor Kahn
William Kapell
Louis Kentner

Emma Endres Kountz
Mischa Levitski
Marcel Maas
Miguel Graciá Mora
Eunice Norton
Paul Oberg
Egon Petri
Nadia Reisenberg
Artur Rubinstein
Jesús Mariá Sanromá
Karl Ulrich Schnabel
Peter Serkin
Rudolf Serkin
Frank Sheridan
Leonard Shure
Leo Smit
Jack Stoll
George Szell
Rosalyn Tureck

Violin

Isodore Cohen
Stefan Frenkel
Felix Galimir

Joseph Gingold
Louis Graeler
Max Hollaender
Paul Wolfe

Viola

Louis Bailly
Carlton Cooley
Robert Courte
Marcel Dick
Watson Forbes
Lillian Fuchs
Nathan Gordon
Nicholas Harsanyi

Milton Katims
Samuel Lifschey
Pierre Monteux
Edgar Ortenberg
Milton Preves
Germaine Prevost
William Primrose
Fred A. Ressel

Ralph Hersh
Alfred Hobday

Sanford Schonbach
Abraham Skernick
Walter Trampler

Cello

Herman Busch
Pablo Casals
Rudolph Doblin
Roman Dukson
Pierre Fournier
Victor Gottlieb
Benar Heifetz
Virginia Peterson Katims
John Martin
Frank Miller

Howard Mitchell
John Moore
Leslie Parnas
Gregor Piatigorsky
Anthony Pini
Dudley Powers
Milton Prinz
Daniel Saidenberg
Harvey Shapiro
David Soyer

Double Bass

Alvin Brehm
Vaclav Jiskra
Julius Levine
Georges E. Moleux

Buell Neidlinger
Philip Sklar
Anton Torello
Kenneth Winstead

Clarinet

Simeon Bellison
Kalman Bloch
Clark Brody
Augustin Duqués
Anastasio Flores
Frank Fragale
Benny Goodman
Stanley Hasty
Gustave Langenus

Robert Lindemann
Mitchell Lurie
Ralph MacLean
Robert McGinnis
David Oppenheim
Victor Polatschek
Bernard Portnoy
Harwood Simmons
James Wilson
Harold Wright

Harpsichord

Ralph Kirkpatrick

Horn

John Barrows
Myron Bloom
Alfred Brain
James Buffington
James Chambers

Mason Jones
Fred Klein
Helen Kotas
Ellen Stone

Oboe

Earnest Harrison   Mitchell Miller
Marc Lifschey   Lois Wann

Harp

Marcel Grandjury

Flute

Julius Baker   Wallace Mann
Ruth Freeman   Henry Woempner
René Le Roy   John Wummer

Bassoon

Elias Carmen   Hugo Fox
John Christlieb   Bernard Garfield

Guitar

Gustavo López

Soprano

Bethany Beardslee   Uta Graf

Tenor

James Schwabacher

Recitante

Madeleine Milhaud

String Quartet

Paganini Quartet:
   Henri Temianka, first violin
   Gustave Rosseels, second violin
   Charles Foidart, viola
   Adolphe Frezin, cello

Orchestra

Buffalo Symphony, conducted by Joseph Krips
Detroit Symphony, conducted by Paul Paray
National Symphony, conducted by Howard Mitchell
Seattle Symphony, conducted by Milton Katims

Notes

Despite all the articles written about the Budapest String Quartet in newspapers and magazines—or, perhaps, because of them—an amazing number of inaccuracies dealing with the history of the Quartet as well as of its individual members exist. I have attempted to sort out the most egregious of them.

Unfortunately, there is no complete set of concert programmes; nor does a complete set of tour schedules exist, although the Annie Friedberg Management Agency drew up a schedule each concert season. According to Lillian Knapp, who was Annie Friedberg's assistant and later booking director for the agency, the office files were discarded when the agency went out of business at the same time that the Quartet disbanded at the close of the 1966–67 season. I have compiled my information about concert programmes and schedules from a number of sources, chief of which were the programmes that Boris Kroyt saved and the schedules he also kept. Both, though, are incomplete, and even when a tour schedule is available, it may not contain all the concert dates, because additional engagements were often added after a season began. For example, matching the entries in the few diaries that Mischa Schneider did not throw away with a particular season's schedule shows that concert engagements were added to a tour after Friedberg initially typed up a schedule. As a result, it is frequently impossible to state how many concerts were played in any one season and where all of them took place.

In addition, many of the clippings of reviews that Kroyt—or, for that matter, other members—cut out of newspapers do not contain the name of the newspaper or the date the review appeared. I have frequently been able to determine the city with ease—by matching the works played against existing concert programmes and/or the name of the reviewer—and sometimes have been able to figure out the date by matching the city with a tour schedule or programme.

Kroyt's remarks in the taped interviews I made with him in 1964 and 1966 can sometimes not be taken literally. He frequently had difficulty expressing himself in English, and when he read portions of the interviews that were transcribed, he made some changes in the wording, though not in the content or substance. I have used the original taped version when it was clear what he meant. One caveat should be added: when the tapes were presented to the Music Library at Yale University and transcribed by it, a section was purposely withheld from public inspection because some of Kroyt's remarks were made off the record at a time when the Quartet was still performing. Now, a quarter of a century later, I am taking the liberty to use them, as well as comments made by Mischa Schneider under similar circumstances.

The following abbreviations are used on second reference to citations in the notes:

BQ-MDLC	Budapest Quartet, Concert Files, Music Division, Library of Congress.
Cornell	Scrapbooks, Music Department, Cornell University.
I	Interview conducted by Nat Brandt.
Kroyt Papers	Papers of Boris Kroyt, in possession of Yanna Kroyt Brandt.
Kroyt-Interview	Taped interview of Boris Kroyt conducted by Nat Brandt.
Ortenberg Papers	Scrapbook of clippings and programmes, 1944–45 season, in possession of Edgar and Tamara Ortenberg.
Ortenberg-Interview	Taped interview of Edgar Ortenberg conducted by Nat Brandt.
Roisman Papers	Interview notes and other data related to Joseph Roisman, made by Tibor Bartok and Alan M. Kriegsman, in possession of Alan M. Kriegsman.
A. Schneider-Autobio	Alexander Schneider. *Sasha: A Musician's Life.* New York: privately published, 1988.
A. Schneider-Files	Alexander Schneider, Personal Files, Budapest Quartet Collection, Music Division, Library of Congress.
M. Schneider-Autobio	Unfinished, unpublished autobiography by Mischa Schneider, in possession of June Schneider.

M. Schneider-Interview   Taped interview of Mischa Schneider conducted by Nat Brandt.

M. Schneider Papers   Papers of Mischa Schneider, in possession of June Schneider.

WC-MDLC   Whittall Collection, Budapest Quartet, Music Division, Library of Congress.

YMHA   Records of Education Department, Archives, Young Men's and Young Women's Hebrew Association, New York.

Preface

1. Boris Kroyt, "Beethoven's String Quartets: Their Performance," *Listen: The Guide to Good Music,* May 1945, 5. Kroyt appended a note to a photocopy of the article that he sent to his daughter, Yanna Kroyt Brandt. In it, he said that a writer had helped prepare the piece for him and was the author of the last several pages.

2. Paul Hume, interview conducted by Nat Brandt. (Hereafter, all interviews with individuals other than Kroyt, Ortenberg and M. Schneider will be designated I.)

3. Joseph Wechsberg, "Profiles: The Budapest," *New Yorker,* Nov. 14, 1959, 72.

1. A Close Call

1. Boris Kroyt, interview conducted by Nat Brandt. (Hereafter referred to as Kroyt-Interview.)

2. Alexander Schneider, *Sasha: A Musician's Life* (New York: privately published, 1988), 34. (Hereafter referred to as A. Schneider-Autobio.)

3. Mischa Schneider, interview conducted by Nat Brandt. (Hereafter referred to as M. Schneider-Interview.)

4. Kroyt-Interview.

5. Ira Hirschmann, *Caution to the Winds* (New York: David McKay Company, 1962), 91. La Guardia's friend who was in charge of Ellis Island was Ed Corsi.

6. M. Schneider-Interview.

7. A. Schneider-Autobio, 49.

8. Kroyt-Interview.

9. New York *World-Telegram,* Mar. 21, 1938.

10. New York *Sun,* Mar. 21, 1938.

11. New York *Herald-Tribune,* Mar. 21, 1938.

12. *New York Times,* Mar. 21, 1938.

2. A Fertile Field

1. Kroyt-Interview.
2. Felix Galimir-I.
3. R. Peter Munves-I.
4. H. J. Storer, "Chamber Music—Something About Its Present State and Developement [*sic*]," *Musician*, Vol. 9, No. 5 (May 1904): 184.
5. M. Schneider-Interview.

3. Quartet-in-Residence

1. Harold Spivacke to Annie Friedberg, Feb. 20, 1939, Whittall Collection, Budapest Quartet, Music Division, Library of Congress. (Hereafter referred to as WC-MDLC. The files are arranged by concert-season year, such as 1938–39.)
2. "Resident Quartet at the Library of Congress," *Concert Night: The Library of Congress* (Washington, D.C.: Library of Congress, n.d.).
3. Harold Spivacke to Annie Friedberg, Feb. 20, 1939, WC-MDLC.
4. Interview notes and other data related to Joseph Roisman, taken by Tibor Bartok and Alan M. Kriegsman, in possession of Alan M. Kriegsman. (Hereafter referred to as Roisman Papers. Some of the material in the papers is typed, much of it is not; some of the material is paginated, most of it is not. Ergo, the lack of page numbers.)
5. Annie Friedberg to Harold Spivacke, Feb. 21, 1939, WC-MDLC.
6. Harold Spivacke to Annie Friedberg, Feb. 23, 1939, WC-MDLC.
7. Washington *Evening Star*, Dec. 9, 1938.
8. Undated, unspecified newspaper, Papers of Boris Kroyt, in possession of Yanna Kroyt Brandt. (Hereafter referred to as Kroyt Papers.) The reviewer was G. R. Harvey.
9. Undated, unsigned, unspecified newspaper review of Mar. 12, 1939, concert at Cambridge Theatre, London, Kroyt Papers.
10. Dinu Lipatti, *Libertatea*, No. 10 (May 1939), Kroyt Papers.
11. M. Schneider-Interview.
12. Ibbs & Tillett to Mischa Schneider, Sept. 6, 1939, Kroyt Papers. Members of the Quartet alternately shared keeping store of the group's correspondence, recording statements, and other material. Kroyt kept those of the mid-1940s.
13. Annie Friedberg to Harold Spivacke, Sept. 15, 1939, WC-MDLC.
14. Harold Spivacke to Annie Friedberg, Sept. 16, 1939, WC-MDLC.
15. Mischa Schneider to Harold Spivacke, Nov. 20, 1939, WC-MDLC.
16. Agreement, between Gertrude Clarke Whittall Foundation and Budapest Quartet, May 10, 1940, WC-MDLC.
17. Paul Hume-I. Mrs. Whittall was always accompanied by a companion friend, a woman slightly younger than herself, Dolly Adams.
18. Washington *Post*, Oct. 8, 1957, Kroyt Papers.

19. "Resident Quartet."

20. *Potomac* magazine, Washington *Post*, Dec. 17, 1961, Kroyt Papers.

21. Edward N. Waters to Mischa Schneider, Jan. 11, 1942, WC-MDLC.

22. Mischa Schneider to Edward N. Waters, Mar. 11, 1953, Budapest Quartet, Concert Files, MDLC. (Hereafter referred to as BQ-MDLC. These files are also arranged by concert-season year.)

23. Mischa Schneider to Edward N. Waters, Sept. 10, 1948, BQ-MDLC.

24. Davidson Taylor to Harold Spivacke, June 25, 1942, WC-MDLC.

25. Carbon copy, untitled analysis of "correspondence received from listeners," Kroyt Papers.

26. Washington *Sunday Star*, Nov. 4, 1945, Kroyt Papers.

27. Ibid.

28. "My Day" column, Washington *Daily News*, Mar. 25, 1941, Kroyt Papers. Mrs. Roosevelt attended the 2:15 P.M. Saturday concert, which included Beethoven's Trio in C Minor, Opus 9, No. 3; Haydn's Quartet in G, Opus 76, No. 1, and Debussy's Quartet in G Minor.

29. James C. Petrillo to Josef Roismano (*sic*), July 23, 1941, Kroyt Papers.

30. Carbon copy of letter from Alexander and Mischa Schneider to James C. Petrillo, July 17, 1941, Kroyt Papers.

31. M. Schneider-Interview.

32. Alexander Schneider to Harold Spivacke, Jan. 25, 1943, Alexander Schneider, Personal Files, Budapest Quartet Collection, Music Division. (Hereafter designated A. Schneider-Files.) Schneider wrote that "this morning I received a little more disagreeable letter" from his local draft board, which notified him that "after considering your status as an alien, the Navy has found that you are, if otherwise qualified, acceptable for training and service in the Armed Forces of the United States." He wired the board that he was about to leave on an extended tour of the Midwest and West Coast with the Quartet. He told Spivacke, "Of course, I do hope that this may postpone my joining the Navy until the war is over, but, as I remember last time when I saw you in Washington, you mentioned to me some conductor of a Navy Band with whom you might talk about my joining in the Navy orchestra. Would you be so kind and think this matter over as to what steps you or I could take now."

33. Copy of letter, Major Edward G. Huey to Major Howard C. Bronson, May 30, 1942, Whittall Collection, WC-MDLC, Camp Lee.

34. Mischa Schneider to Harold Spivacke, Aug. 7, 1944, BQ-MDLC.

35. Harold Spivacke to Mischa Schneider, Aug. 15, 1944, BQ-MDLC.

36. Copy of letter, undated and unsigned, undoubtedly Mischa Schneider to Glenn Dillard Gunn, Kroyt Papers. The Pan American Union concert was on Apr. 8, 1942.

37. Paul Hume-I.

38. Many years later, Ruth Weddle of Granada Hills, Calif., wrote to the *Saturday Review* that she attended a concert of an ensemble called the

Budapest String Quartet in the Koniggratz City Library in German-occupied Czechoslovakia in late January 1945. The magazine carried her letter in its issue of Sept. 25, 1969.

39. *N.Z. Radio Record*, Aug. 13, 1937, Kroyt Papers.

40. Mischa Schneider to Harold Spivacke, Feb. 27, 1943, BQ-MDLC.

41. M. Schneider-Interview.

42. New York *Herald-Tribune*, Oct. 21, 1940, Kroyt Papers.

43. *New York Times*, Oct. 21, 1940, Kroyt Papers.

44. *Nation*, Jan. 2, 1943.

45. Buffalo *Courier-Express*, Jan. 6, 1941, Kroyt Papers. The reviewer was Isabelle Workman Evans.

46. Dallas *Morning News*, Jan. 2, 1943, Kroyt Papers. The reviewer was John Rosenfield.

47. Chicago *Sun*, Aug. 14, 1942, Kroyt Papers. The reviewer was Claudia Cassidy.

48. San Francisco *Chronicle*, Aug. 5, 1941, Kroyt Papers. The reviewer was Alfred Frankenstein.

49. Chicago *Daily Tribune*, Aug. 18, 1941, Kroyt Papers. The reviewer was Cecil Smith.

50. *Time*, Dec. 20, 1943, Kroyt Papers.

4. Allegro: *Joe*

1. Edgar Ortenberg, interview conducted by Nat Brandt. (Hereafter referred to as Ortenberg-Interview.)

2. Eulogy delivered by Edward N. Waters, Oct. 13, 1974, at memorial service for Joseph Roisman in Gawler's Chapel, Washington, D.C. BQ-MDLC.

3. M. Schneider-Interview.

5. *Budapesti Vónosnégyes*

1. David G. Hughes, *A History of European Music: The Art Music Tradition of Western Culture* (New York: McGraw-Hill, 1974), 337.

2. It was assumed, because of a medal struck in Holland on the tenth anniversary of the Budapest String Quartet's first appearance there, that the Quartet first started in 1918. Emil Hauser continually confused the issue. In a letter to Tibor Bartok, Nov. 18, 1968, he wrote, "In 1917, using my experience in two quartets, I founded the Budapest String Quartet." On the other hand, he also offered a different impression when he said that in 1919 the Quartet "fled Hungarian communism and went to Holland. Our first concert was in the Scheveningen Kurhaus before critics of the international press." At the same time, in the same letter, he said, "Our first concert in Budapest was in 1918 at the Urania Theatre." Annie Friedberg, in a letter to Edgar Ortenberg, Oct. 21, 1947, Kroyt Papers, reported: "Emil Hauser called

me up today. He is back in New York and most anxious to see you. He told me that in December it will be 30 years that the Budapest Quartet is in existence, and he wants to do something special for that, so I advised him to wait until you come back here." (There is no indication that any special celebration was held.) Volume Three of the *New Grove's Dictionary of Music and Musicians,* 1980 edition, also gives 1917 as the debut date and also cites Kolzsvar as the place of the debut.

3. Much of the information dealing with the early lives of the original Budapest String Quartet members comes from a two-part article by Sergio Andreoni—"Il 'Quartetto di Budapest' (prima parte 1918–1932)" and "il 'Quartetto di Budapest' (second parte 1932–1967)"—that appeared in the Italian magazine *Musica* in Mar. and June 1982. Tibor Bartok and Alan M. Kriegsman contacted survivors of the Quartet in the early 1960s and received some brief additional information, but nothing substantive.

4. Felix Galimir-I.

5. Transcription, Classical Performances-Concerts from the Library of Congress, second hour of first radio program released in 1990, BQ-MDLC.

6. Artur Balsam-I.

7. Andreoni, "Il 'Quartetto di Budapest' (prima parte)," 49. The Bartók was performed first in Turin, and then in Cologne.

8. Ibid., 51.

9. Ibid., 49–50.

10. Wechsberg, "Profiles," 77.

11. Andreoni, "Il 'Quartetto di Budapest' (prima parte)," 52.

12. Ibid.

13. Roisman Papers.

14. Istvan Ipolyi to Alexander Schneider, Sept. 17, 1945, Papers of Mischa Schneider, in possession of June Schneider. (Hereafter referred to as M. Schneider Papers.)

15. Roisman Papers.

16. In the divorce papers, dated Mar. 22, 1934 and granted Apr. 16, 1934, in Berlin, Mischa Schneider's name is given as Michael Schnejder and his wife as Lottchen Schnejder. However, in a carbon copy of a letter sent by Annie Friedberg to Bryon H. Uhl, U.S. Department of Justice, May 1, 1941, File Number 99290/845, in which Friedberg requested a six-month extension of the visas of the Schneider brothers, Friedberg gave Mischa's name as Mojzesz Sznejder. Both, Mischa Papers.

6. Thème Russe: Allegro: *Mischa*

1. M. Schneider-Interview.

2. Untitled, unfinished autobiography by Mischa Schneider, in possession of June Schneider, 36. (Hereafter referred to as M. Schneider-Autobio.) Apparent discrepancies in the pagination occur in citing from this auto-

biography because portions of it were rewritten without renumbering earlier pages to conform with the revisions, or sometimes without even numbering the page. For example, in footnote 17 below, one would expect that the page number would be higher than the previous footnote, because the autobiography is written in chronological order, but the number is actually lower. Note also that no page number is available for footnote 21.

3. M. Schneider-Interview.

4. Ibid.

5. M. Schneider-Autobio, 38.

6. Ibid., 39.

7. M. Schneider-Interview.

8. M. Schneider-Autobio, 7.

9. Ibid.

10. Ibid., 5.

11. Ibid., 6.

12. Tamara Ortenberg told me this story on the day that I visited her husband Edgar to interview him.

13. M. Schneider-Autobio, 12.

14. Ibid., 19–20.

15. Ibid., 21.

16. Ibid., 22.

17. Ibid., 15–16.

18. Ibid., 19.

19. Ibid., 23.

20. Ibid., 32.

21. Ibid., unnumbered page.

22. New York *Herald-Tribune*, Jan. 5, 1931, Roisman scrapbook, BQ-MDLC. The reviewer's initials were given as J. D. B.—Jerome B. Bohm.

23. *New York Times*, Jan. 5, 1931, Roisman Scrapbook, BQ-MDLC. The reviewer's name was not given.

24. Uncited, undated Ithaca newspaper, Scrapbooks, Music Department, Cornell University. (Hereafter referred to as Cornell.) The reviewer's initials are given as G. A. L.

25. *New York Times*, Feb. 4, 1931. Roisman Scrapbook, BQ-MDLC. The reviewer's name was not given.

26. New York *Herald-Tribune*, Feb. 4, 1931, Roisman Scrapbook, BQ-MDLC. The reviewer's name was not given.

27. M. Schneider-Interview.

28. Roisman Papers.

29. RCA Victor, Artists and Repertoire files, Bertelsmann Music Group, New York City.

30. Kroyt Papers.

31. A. Schneider-Autobio, 27.

7. Allegretto Vivace e Sempre Scherzando: *Sasha*

1. The brief characterizations quoted are from taped interviews with— in the order of the respective quotes—R. Peter Munves, Mrs. Cameron (Jane) Baird, Samuel Rhodes, Caroline Levine, Natasha Schneider Furst, Walter Trampler, again Caroline Levine, Ruth Laredo, Howard Scott, and again Walter Trampler.

2. A. Schneider-Autobio, 3.

3. Ibid., 7.

4. Ibid., 3–4.

5. Ibid., 7.

6. Ibid., 13.

7. Ibid., 15.

8. Ibid., 14.

9. Ibid., 19.

10. Otto Friedrich, *Before the Deluge: A Portrait of Berlin in the 1920's* (New York: Harper & Row, 1972), 345.

11. Ibid., 406.

12. Ibid., 407.

13. Andreoni, "Il 'Quartetto di Budapest' (prima parte)," 164.

14. Undated, unspecified Ithaca newspaper, Cornell.

15. *New York Times*, Mar. 8, 1933, Kroyt Papers.

16. A. Schneider-Autobio, 31.

17. Ibid., 38.

18. *Wireless Weekly*, May 28, 1937, 3, Kroyt Papers.

19. Ortenberg-Interview.

20. *Wireless Weekly*, May 28, 1937, 3, Kroyt Papers.

21. Istvan Ipolyi to Alexander Schneider, Feb. 24, 1946, M. Schneider Papers.

22. Istvan Ipolyi to Alexander Schneider, Apr. 15, 1946, M. Schneider Papers.

23. Istvan Ipolyi to Alexander Schneider, Nov. 20, 1945, M. Schneider Papers.

24. Ortenberg-Interview.

8. Adagio Molto e Mesto: *Boris*

1. The brief characterizations quoted are from taped interviews with Julius Levine, Howard Scott, and Walter Trampler.

2. Interviews with Artur Balsam and Leslie Parnas.

3. Ortenberg-Interview.

4. The quotation here is a combination derived from Kroyt-Interview and Wechsberg, "Profiles," 98.

5. Kroyt-Interview.

6. Ibid.

7. Friedrich, *Before the Deluge*, 19.

8. Kroyt-Interview.

9. Ibid.

10. Ibid.

11. Ibid. A program announcement for a concert of Das Fiedemann-Quartett at the Music Hall, Hamburg, on Jan. 25, 1919 (Kroyt Papers), listed the members of the quartet as A. Fiedemann, Heinr. Drobatschewski, Kroyt, and J. Sakom. The quartet performed a Schubert cello quintet that night with Hans Kraus of the Charlottenburger Opera Orchestra.

12. Ibid. It is not clear when this concert took place. Kroyt saved some announcements of his concerts and recitals in the 1920s but nowhere near a complete set of his public appearances.

13. Ibid.

14. Artur Balsam-I.

15. Friedrich, *Before the Deluge*, 19.

16. Ibid., 195.

17. Ibid., 23.

18. Ibid., 24.

19. Ibid., 195.

20. Douglas Jarman, *Kurt Weill: An Illustrated Biography* (Bloomington: Indiana Univ. Press, 1982), 31.

21. Friedrich, *Before the Deluge*, 24.

22. Ibid., 50.

23. Ibid., 237.

24. Ibid., 141.

25. Artur Schnabel, *My Life and Music* (New York: St. Martin's Press, 1961), 79.

26. Other members of the Guarneri Quartet were Daniel Karpilovsky, first violin; Maurits Stromfeld, second violin; and Walter Lutz, cello. Karpilovsky, a native of St. Petersburg, was a student of Leopold Auer and had played first violin with the Imperial Russian Quartet. He eventually settled in the Hollywood, Calif., area. Stromfeld was a student of Adolph Rebner. Lutz, who was born in Köln, had played in the Berlin Philharmonic Orchestra.

27. Kroyt played first violin in both the quartets that bore his name. The first Kroyt Quartet included Viktor Manusewitsch, who had studied at the Leningrad Conservatory, second violin; Heinz Weiden, a soloist with the Berlin Philharmonic, viola; and Jascha Bernstein, a student of Julius Klengel and soloist with the Leipzig Symphony Orchestra, cello. The second Kroyt Quartet included Benjamin Bernfield, second violin; Weiden; and Godfried Zeelander, cello.

28. Kroyt-Interview.

29. Ibid.

30. A. Schneider-Autobio, 45.

31. A one-year contract, dated June 11, 1936, and written in German (Kroyt Papers), included in its provisions that Kroyt and the other members of the Quartet were obliged to remain together until the end of the 1937–38 season; that they would all share equally in concert fees and record royalties; that all questions pertaining to programming, bookings, and vacations would be decided by majority vote—and if a tie vote resulted, nothing would be undertaken—and that all members were obliged to appear punctually for all concerts unless ill.

32. A. Schneider-Autobio, 45.

33. Kroyt-Interview.

34. M. Schneider-Interview.

35. Ibid.

36. Samuel and Sada Applebaum, "With the Artists: Famous String Players Discuss Their Art—Joseph Roisman," Part 1, *Violins and Violinists,* Vol. 15, No. 2 (Nov.–Dec. 1954), 262.

37. Kroyt-Interview.

38. M. Schneider-Interview.

39. Applebaum, "With the Artists," 260.

40. Ibid.

41. *New York Times,* Jan. 7, 1962, Kroyt Papers.

42. Kroyt-Interview.

43. Samuel and Sada Applebaum, *The Way They Play,* Book 1 (Neptune City, N.J.: Paganianiana Publications, 1972), 168.

44. Kroyt-Interview.

45. Roisman Papers.

46. New York *American,* Nov. 16, 1936, Kroyt Papers. The reviewer was Winthrop Sargent.

47. Undated, unspecified newspaper, Roisman Scrapbook, BQ-MDLC. The review is of a concert of the New Friends of Music at Town Hall.

48. Tour Schedule, 1936–37, Kroyt Papers.

49. Tally handwritten by Kroyt, Kroyt Papers.

50. Undated, unspecified Buffalo newspaper, Kroyt Papers. The reviewer was Edward Durney.

51. *Cornell Daily Sun,* Nov. 18, 1936, Cornell. The reviewer's initials are given as HEJ.

52. San Francisco *Chronicle,* Jan. 6, 1937, Kroyt Papers. The reviewer was Alfred Frankenstein.

53. Los Angeles *Times,* Jan. 9, 1937, Kroyt Papers. The reviewer was Isabel Morse Jones.

54. *Wireless Weekly,* May 28, 1937, 2, Kroyt Papers. The reviewer's name is not given.

55. Undated, unspecified Australian newspaper, Kroyt Papers.

56. The papers of Mischa Schneider contain four letters, dated between Aug. 17, 1939, and Sept. 15, 1939, relating to Mischa's "desire to emigrate to Australia," to quote the last of the letters, written by Lady Zara Gowrie,

Admiralty House, Sydney. The writers of the other letters, who were forwarding his request from one authority to the next, included the private secretary to Prime Minister R. G. Menzies and the Australian Minister of Interior, H. S. Foll.

9. *Twin Peak Number One*

1. Undated, unspecified newspaper, Fremantle, Australia, 1937, Kroyt Papers.

2. A. Schneider-Autobio, 248.

3. Ibid.

4. M. Schneider-Interview.

5. The quotations are from taped interviews with each of the persons cited.

6. Roisman Papers.

7. Ibid.

8. The quotations are from taped interviews with each of the persons cited.

9. Robert C. Marsh, "Vigor and Eloquence for Beethoven's Last Thoughts," *High Fidelity*, Jan. 1963, 65.

10. The quotations are from taped interviewes with each of the persons cited.

11. Vancouver *Sun*, Jan. 19, 1953, Kroyt Papers.

12. Wechsberg, "Profiles," 94.

13. Helen R. Stout to Dear Former Subscriber, Oct. 11, 1937, Records of Education Department, 1937–38, Archives, Young Men's and Young Women's Hebrew Association, New York. (Hereafter referred to as YMHA.) At the time that the Quartet began concertizing at the 92nd Street Y, the institution was known simply as the Young Men's Hebrew Association.

According to the printed program of a Pittsburgh Chamber Music Society concert of Jan. 18, 1965, the Budapest String Quartet had up to then performed the Beethoven cycle "upwards of sixty times." The earliest reported performances of the seventeen quartets took place in London in Nov. 1930. A second cycle was performed in Copenhagen during the 1931–32 season.

When performing the cycle over five concerts, the order of the quartets always stayed the same. However, when in six parts—as, for example, in 1943 and 1949—the order was dramatically different from the order established under the Slee Bequest. However, after the Slee Bequest cycles began in Buffalo in the mid-1950s, the Quartet followed the Slee order for all further six-part cycles, with one major exception: for the six-part series at the Library of Congress, performed between Mar. 17 and Apr. 22, 1960, the Quartet followed the order played at Mills College in 1943—except that it added an arrangement of Beethoven's Piano Sonata in E, Opus 14, No. 1, that he recomposed and transcribed as the Quartet in F, thus performing eighteen works in all. And, at the third concert, it switched the sequence of Opus 135 and Opus 59, No. 2. It was not unusual that the Budapest followed for the Library an order different from the Slee Bequest. The same six-part cycle was performed at the Library between Mar. 9 and May 25, 1944, with Edgar Ortenberg, and between Mar. 24 and Apr. 29, 1949, with Jac Gorodetzky.

The Slee order of the cycle is

FIRST NIGHT: Quartet No. 12, Opus 127 in E-flat; Quartet No. 1, Opus 18, No. 1 in F; Quartet No. 9, Opus 59.

SECOND NIGHT: Quartet No. 10, Opus 74 ("Harp") in E-flat; Quartet No. 2, Opus 18, No. 2 in G ("Compliments"); Quartet No. 14, Opus 131 in C-sharp Minor (seven movements played without pause.).

THIRD NIGHT: Quartet No. 3, Opus 18, No. 3 in D; Quartet No. 16, Opus 133 (*Grosse Fuge*); Quartet No. 7, Opus 59, No. 1 in F.

FOURTH NIGHT: Quartet No. 11, Opus 95 in F Minor; Quartet No. 6, Opus 18, No. 6 in B-flat; Quartet No. 15, Opus 132 in A Minor.

FIFTH NIGHT: Quartet No. 5, Opus 18, No. 5 in A; Quartet No. 13, Opus 130 in B-flat.

SIXTH NIGHT: Quartet No. 4, Opus 18, No. 4 in C Minor; Quartet No. 17, Opus 135 in F; Quartet No. 8, Opus 59, No. 2 in E Minor.

14. Handwritten tally, Kroyt Papers.

15. Carbon copy of contract between Voorzitter van den Bond van N. I. Kunstkringen and Das Budapester Streichquartett, May 11, 1939, Kroyt Papers.

16. The Kroyt Papers contain four letters dated between Dec. 22, 1938, and July 6, 1939, in which Guillermo Gomez of Mexico City proposes a series of concerts in Mexico City. The letters are addressed to Mischa Schneider, care of Annie Friedberg. Gomez reduced the number of concerts of six, concerned that Mexican music lovers could pay the cost of tickets, and he expected that he himself would lose money on the concerts because of the poor peso-to-dollar ratio that was a result of the Mexican government's expropriation of the oil industry. "This matter makes any kind of business in this country very doubtly [*sic*]."

17. *Wireless Weekly*, May 28, 1937, 3, Kroyt Papers.

18. Undated, unspecified Australian newspaper, Kroyt Papers.

19. A. Schneider-Autobio, 50.

20. James Lincoln Collier, *Benny Goodman and the Swing Era* (New York, Oxford Univ. Press, 1989), 339.

21. A. Schneider-Autobio, 50.

22. Benny Goodman, "Contrasts," *Listen: The Guide to Good Music*, Nov. 1940, 4.

23. Log, Studio 2, Budapest String Quartette with Benny Goodman,

Apr. 25, 1938, RCA Victor, Artists and Repertoire Files, Bertelsmann Music Group, New York City.

24. Goodman, "Contrasts," p. 5, photograph accompanying article.

25. Ibid., 4.

26. *New York Times,* Nov. 4, 1938.

27. Harold Schonberg-I.

28. *New York Times,* Nov. 6, 1938.

29. Chicago *Daily Tribune,* Aug. 18, 1941, Kroyt Papers. The reviewer was Cecil Smith.

30. Chicago *Daily Times,* Aug. 18, 1941, Kroyt Papers. The reviewer was Bob Andrews.

10. For the Record

1. F. W. Gaisberg to Mischa Schneider, Nov. 21, 1938, Kroyt Papers.

2. F. W. Gaisberg to Mischa Schneider, Nov. 25, 1938, Kroyt Papers.

3. F. W. Gaisberg to Mischa Schneider, Dec. 20, 1938, Kroyt Papers.

4. Charles O'Connell to Mischa Schneider, Dec. 19, 1939, Kroyt Papers.

5. Charles O'Connell to Mischa Schneider, Dec. 28, 1939, Kroyt Papers.

6. Charles O'Connell to Mischa Schneider, Jan. 19, 1940, Kroyt Papers.

7. Charles O'Connell to Mischa Schneider, July 9, 1940, Kroyt Papers.

8. Telegram, John Hammond to Josef Roismann, June 20, 1939, Kroyt Papers.

9. Moses Smith to Mischa Schneider, Mar. 12, 1940, Kroyt Papers.

10. Moses Smith to Mischa Schneider, May 15, 1940, Kroyt Papers.

11. Moses Smith to Mischa Schneider, June 27, 1940, Kroyt Papers.

12. Charles O'Connell to Mischa Schneider, July 11, 1940, Kroyt Papers.

13. Edward Wallerstein to "Gentlemen," July 31, 1940, Kroyt Papers.

14. Payment vouchers, Kroyt Papers.

15. Moses Smith to Mischa Schneider, Mar. 31, 1942, Kroyt Papers.

16. Moses Smith to Mischa Schneider, May 5, 1942, Kroyt Papers.

17. Goddard Lieberson to Mischa Schneider, Dec. 5, 1947, Kroyt Papers.

18. Recording statements, RCA Victor, Kroyt Papers. The statements are incomplete.

19. Goddard Lieberson to Mischa Schneider, Dec. 5, 1947, Kroyt Papers.

20. Mrs. Cameron (Jane) Baird-I.

21. Wechsberg, "Profiles," 74.

22. Roisman Papers.

23. M. Schneider-Interview.

24. Wechsberg, "Profiles," 74.

25. Ibid.

26. M. Schneider-Interview.

27. Kroyt, "Beethoven's String Quartets," 3–4.

28. Moses Smith to Mischa Schneider, Sept. 18, 1940, Kroyt Papers.

Schneider, in draft of a letter he wrote to Smith five days earlier (Kroyt Papers), said he had spoken to Harold Spivacke about the idea of recording on the Stradivarius instruments and that Spivacke "is very attracted by this idea and he asks you to communicate with him." But Smith replied that the cost of recording at the Library "would not be feasible on our part and would, in any event, entail a greater expense than is warranted by the advantages."

29. Arthur Judson to Mischa Schneider, Oct. 21, 1941, Kroyt Papers.

30. Contract between Annie Friedberg and Budapest String Quartet, Mar. 19, 1942, Kroyt Papers.

11. Exit Sasha

1. Elizabeth Sprague Coolidge to Josef Roismann, Aug. 7, 1941, Kroyt Papers. This letter, written from the Hotel Oakland in Oakland, Calif., is apparently misdated. Mrs. Coolidge wrote that she had heard the Quartet perform on the West Coast, but the Quartet did not perform there until Aug. 12. Perhaps she meant the date of the letter to be Aug. 17.

2. Elizabeth Sprague Coolidge to Josef Roismann, Sept. 21, 1941, Kroyt Papers.

3. Elizabeth Sprague Coolidge to Alexander Schneider, Dec. 4, 1945, A. Schneider-Files.

4. Alexander Schneider to Elizabeth Sprague Coolidge, Dec. 2, 1945, A. Schneider-Files.

5. Alexander Schneider to Elizabeth Sprague Coolidge, Sept. 16, 1945, A. Schneider-Files.

6. Alexander Schneider to Elizabeth Sprague Coolidge, salutations from letters of Sept. 16, 1945, and Dec. 2, 1945, A. Schneider-Files.

7. Alexander Schneider to Elizabeth Sprague Coolidge, Jan. 4, 1948, A. Schneider-Files.

8. A. Schneider-Autobio, 57–58.

9. Alexander Schneider to Elizabeth Sprague Coolidge, Jan. 4, 1948, A. Schneider-Files.

10. Milton Katims-I.

11. Kroyt-Interview.

12. A. Schneider-Autobio, 33.

13. D. R. Martin, "Alexander Schneider: A Passion for Life and Music," *Ovation*, Jan. 1983, 11.

14. Samuel and Sada Applebaum, *The Way They Play*, Book 1, 171.

15. *New York Times*, Jan. 7, 1962, Kroyt Papers.

16. A. Schneider-Autobio, 32.

17. Felix Galimir-I.

18. Mischa Schneider to Harold Spivacke, Nov. 26, 1943, BQ-MDLC.

19. Alexander Schneider to Harold Spivacke, Jan. 1, 1943, BQ-MDLC.

20. Alexander Schneider to Harold Spivacke, undated but written on a Sunday from Cedar Rapids, Iowa, BQ-MDLC. The letter was probably writ-

ten on Sunday, Nov. 28, 1943, when the Quartet was in Cedar Rapids for a concert.

21. Edward N. Waters to Mischa Schneider, Nov. 29, 1943, BQ-MDLC.
22. Mischa Schneider to Harold Spivacke, Nov. 26, 1943, BQ-MDLC.
23. Mischa Schneider to Harold Spivacke, Jan. 1, 1944, BQ-MDLC.
24. Washington *Sunday Star*, Oct. 10, 1954, Kroyt Papers.

12. Second Fiddle Number One

1. Ortenberg-Interview. Unless otherwise noted, all details and quotations regarding Edgar Ortenberg's life and career are from the interview.
2. Mischa Schneider to Harold Spivacke, Feb. 10, 1944, BQ-MDLC.
3. Alexander Schneider to Harold Spivacke, Jan. 7, 1944, BQ-MDLC.
4. Ortenberg-Interview.
5. Washington *Post*, Mar. 10, 1944, scrapbook of clippings and programmes, 1944–45 season, in possession of Edgar and Tamara Ortenberg. (Hereafter referred to as Ortenberg Papers.) The reviewer was Ray C. B. Brown. It is interesting to note that Ortenberg did not save any clippings or programmes after this first year with the Quartet.
6. Washington *Evening Star*, Mar. 11, 1944, Ortenberg Papers.
7. Washington *Times-Herald*, Mar. 24, 1944, Ortenberg Papers.
8. Ortenberg-Interview.
9. Washington *Times-Herald*, May 25, 1944, Ortenberg Papers.
10. Undated, unspecified newspaper of July 4, 1944, concert at San Francisco Museum of Art, Ortenberg Papers. The reviewer was Margaret Gessler.
11. Oakland *Tribune*, Aug. 1, 1944, Ortenberg Papers. The reviewer was Clifford Gessler.
12. Undated, unspecified newspaper review of August 10, 1944, concert at Ravinia, Ortenberg Papers. The reviewer was Felix Borowski.
13. Chicago *Daily Tribune*, undated review of concerts of Aug. 12 and 13, 1944, at Ravinia, Ortenberg Papers. The reviewer was Claudia Cassidy.
14. Undated, unspecified newspaper, Ortenberg Papers. The reviewer was Alexander Fried.
15. Ortenberg-Interview.
16. Indianapolis *News*, Jan. 25, 1945, Ortenberg Papers. The reviewer was Walter Whitworth.
17. Undated, unspecified newspaper review of Feb. 13, 1945, concert in Kimball Hall, Chicago, Ortenberg Papers. The reviewer was Charles Buckley.
18. Ortenberg-Interview.
19. Natasha Schneider Furst-I.
20. Ortenberg-Interview.
21. Kroyt-Interview.
22. M. Schneider-Interview.

23. New York *Sun*, Nov. 5, 1945, Ortenberg Papers.
24. *Nation*, Jan. 5, 1946.
25. Ortenberg-Interview.
26. Annie Friedberg to Mischa Schneider, June 26, 1946, Kroyt Papers.
27. M. Schneider-Interview.
28. Ortenberg-Interview. Sasha—in A. Schneider-Autobio, 52—recalls playing three concerts on Sunday in the early 1940s: from 11 A.M. to noon at the Library of Congress, at 5:30 P.M. for the New Friends of Music in New York, and in the evening a concert in Connecticut.
29. Mrs. Jac (Honey) Gorodetzky-I.
30. M. Schneider-Interview.
31. Ortenberg-Interview.
32. Joseph Roisman to Harold Spivacke, Jan. 17, 1949, BQ-MDLC.
33. Ibid.

13. Second Fiddle Number Two

1. M. Schneider-Interview.
2. Details about Jac Gorodetzky's early life were provided by his wife, Mrs. Jac (Honey) Gorodetzky, in an interview.
3. Kroyt-Interview.
4. *New York Times*, Apr. 15, 1937. The reviewer's initials are given as G. G.
5. Washington *Post*, Mar. 31, 1949, Kroyt Papers.
6. Mischa Schneider to Harold Spivacke, Nov. 22, 1949, BQ-MDLC.
7. Contract dated May 1, 1950, between Whittall Foundation and Budapest Quartet, BQ-MDLC.
8. Miami *Herald*, Jan. 6, 1950, Kroyt Papers. The reviewer was Doris Reno.
9. Pittsburgh *Post-Gazette*, Jan. 10, 1950, Kroyt Papers. The reviewer was Donald Steinfirst.
10. Buffalo *Evening News*, Jan. 23, 1950, Kroyt Papers. The reviewer was Theodolinda C. Boris.
11. Louisville *Courier-Journal*, Feb. 11, 1950, Kroyt Papers. The reviewer was Dwight Anderson.
12. Louisville *Courier-Journal*, Feb. 4, 1951, Kroyt Papers. The reviewer was William Mootz.
13. Ithaca *Journal*, Jan. 9, 1951, Kroyt Papers. The reviewer was Anita Monsees.
14. *Time*, Aug. 20, 1951.
15. Concerts-Attendance 1950–51, YMHA.
16. Subscription brochure, YMHA.
17. Mischa Schneider to Harold Spivacke, Nov. 21, 1944, BQ-MDLC.
18. A. Schneider-Autobio, 96.
19. Virginia Harpham-I. Harpham, a professional violinist, studied

with Roisman for seven years, between 1948 and 1955, and became a personal friend of both Joseph and Pola Roisman. She was for many years principal second violin in the National Symphony.

20. M. Schneider-Interview.

21. Kroyt-Interview.

22. William Lichtenwanger-I. Except when he was in the Army during World War II, Lichtenwanger was an assistant reference librarian in the Music Division of the Library of Congress from 1940 to 1974.

23. M. Schneider-Interview.

24. Kroyt-Interview.

25. Howard Scott-I.

26. M. Schneider-Interview.

27. David Soyer-I.

28. Mrs. Jac (Honey) Gorodetzky-I.

29. Wechsberg, "Profiles," 80.

30. M. Schneider-Interview.

31. Undated, unsigned note, no salutation, on stationery of Nippon Hoso Kyokai, Tokyo, M. Schneider Papers.

32. Yuriko Fukutomi to Joseph Roisman, Jac Gorodetzky, Boris, Mischa Schneider, and Annie Friedberg, Sept. 3, 1952, M. Schneider Papers.

33. Washington *Evening Star*, undated, Kroyt Papers. Alice Eversman wrote this feature article sometime in Sept., after the Quartet's return to Washington.

34. M. Schneider-Interview.

35. Mischa Schneider to Harold Spivacke, Sept. 17, 1952, BQ-MDLC.

36. Wechsberg, "Profiles," 80.

37. *String Player*, Vol. 4, No. 3 [but otherwise undated]: 3.

38. Washington *Evening Star*, Oct. 25, 1952, Kroyt Papers.

39. Washington *Post*, Oct. 18, 1952, Kroyt Papers.

40. Washington *Evening Star*, Oct. 17, 1952, Kroyt Papers.

41. Wechsberg, "Profiles," 80.

42. Portland *Oregonian*, Jan. 12, 1953, Kroyt Papers. The reviewer was Hilmar Grondahl.

43. Mischa Schneider to Harold Spivacke, Jan. 14, 1953, BQ-MDLC.

44. Mischa Schneider to Harold Spivacke, Feb. 7, 1953, BQ-MDLC.

45. Mischa Schneider to Harold Spivacke, Mar. 11, 1953, BQ-MDLC.

46. M. Schneider-Interview.

47. Pittsburgh *Post-Gazette*, Feb. 6, 1951, Kroyt Papers. The reviewer, Donald Steinfirst, wrote, "I had the impression . . . that the Quartet was not playing at its highest level nor did it seem particularly inspired by the music."

48. Washington *Times-Herald*, Mar. 23, 1951, Kroyt Papers. The reviewer was Glenn Dillard Gunn, who said the performance was "not up to the standard of these famous players."

49. Chicago *Daily Tribune*, Feb. 4, 1952, Kroyt Papers. The reviewer was Claudia Cassidy.

50. *Nippon Times*, undated, Kroyt Papers.

51. The *Mainichi*, Mar. 6, 1954, Kroyt Papers.

52. M. Schneider-Interview.

53. Mrs. Isidor (Rose) Alpher-I. The psychiatrist was a Dr. Katzenellenbogen.

54. Kroyt-Interview.

55. Washington *Sunday Star*, Oct. 10, 1954, Kroyt Papers.

56. Mrs. Isidor (Rose) Alpher-I.

57. Sol Schoenbach, interview conducted by Yanna Kroyt Brandt.

58. Mrs. Jac (Honey) Gorodetzky-I.

59. Jac Gorodetzky to Harold Spivacke, Mar. 2, 1955, BQ-MDLC.

60. Mrs. Isidor (Rose) Alpher-I.

61. M. Schneider-Interview.

62. Ibid.

14. Twin Peak Number Two

1. A. Schneider-Files.

2. A. Schneider-Autobio, 58. Mrs. Coolidge had died on Nov. 4, 1953, at the age of eighty-nine.

3. M. Schneider-Interview.

4. A. Schneider-Autobio, 58.

5. The remarks regarding Sasha's returning to the Quartet are from taped interviews with the individuals cited.

6. Washington *Post*, Mar. 22, 1956, Kroyt Papers. The reviewer was John Haskins.

7. Greensboro *Daily News*, Jan. 21, 1956, Kroyt Papers. The reviewer was Henry S. Wootton, Jr.

8. Washington *Evening Star*, undated review of concert of Apr. 5, 1956, at the Library of Congress, Kroyt Papers.

9. *Newsweek*, Jan. 24, 1955.

10. *Life*, May 6, 1957. The photograph appeared on page 164.

11. *New York Times*, Sept. 1, 1968, Kroyt Papers.

12. Roisman Papers.

13. Hans Hirschmann to Nat Brandt, Jan. 24, 1991. Hirschmann was at one time the president of the Cleveland Chamber Music Society.

14. Roisman Papers.

15. A. Schneider-Autobio, 56–57.

16. Wechsberg, "Profiles," 104–6, 111.

17. Washington *Evening Star*, Oct. 8, 1957, Kroyt Papers. The reviewer was Day Thorpe.

18. *Time*, Aug. 20, 1951.

19. Richard D. Heffner to Boris Kroyt, Nov. 2, 1957, Kroyt Papers. The Quartet, incidentally, appeared in a picture, *Library of Congress,* made by the office of War Information. The members were filmed on Nov. 30, 1944, by the Office of War Information, Kroyt Papers.

20. *New York Times,* Oct. 28, 1957, Kroyt Papers.

21. Ibid., Nov. 3, 1957, Kroyt Papers.

22. Ibid., Apr. 11, 1962, Kroyt Papers.

23. Buenos Aires *El Hogar,* June 15, 1956, Kroyt Papers.

15. What the Public Wants

1. A. Schneider-Autobio, 36.

2. *New York Times,* June 9, 1991. The author of the article was Joseph Horowitz.

3. Annie Friedberg to Edgar Ortenberg, Feb. 5, 1947, Kroyt Papers. For a time, Ortenberg handled the Quartet's correspondence, but it is clear from the letters between Annie Friedberg and him that Mischa Schneider was overseeing all arrangements for the ensemble and had to be checked with regarding all Quartet business.

4. Roisman Papers.

5. Julius Levine-I.

6. M. Schneider-Interview.

7. W. Leslie Barnette, Jr., *An Informal History of the Buffalo Chamber Music Society* (Buffalo: privately printed, 1973). The monograph is unpaginated.

8. "From the Institute of Arts and Sciences, Columbia University," undated form letters mailed to concert subscribers regarding concert of Saturday, Feb. 16, 1946, Kroyt Papers. Kroyt annotated the voting results in red pencil in the margin.

9. Cesar Saerchinger to William Kolodney, Dec. 3, 1957, YMHA. Saerchinger took over managing the Annie Friedberg agency when Annie Friedberg died on Nov. 19, 1952.

10. Memorandum, Betty Fowler to Dr. Kolodney and Sid Lowenberg, Apr. 24, 1958, YMHA.

11. Box Office Cash and Ticket Reconciliation reports, Nov. 11, 1959–Mar. 26, 1960, YMHA.

12. M. Schneider-Interview.

13. Gertrude Weeden to William Kolodney, undated, YMHA. The letter was marked received 11/ /42 (*sic*).

14. Harold Spivacke to Mischa Schneider, Jan. 22, 1942, Kroyt Papers.

15. Harold Spivacke to Mischa Schneider, July 26, 1945, Kroyt Papers.

16. Paul Hindemith to Mischa Schneider, undated, Kroyt Papers. In all, the Kroyt Papers collection contains twelve letters written by Hindemith, all addressed to Mischa Schneider. Only five are dated, and they cover the

period May 5, 1943–Jan. 2, 1946. The letter cited here was obviously written before May 1943.

17. Ernst Křenek to Joseph Roisman, Nov. 19, 1944, Kroyt Papers. The Kroyt Papers collection contains nine letters, dated from Apr. 22, 1944, to Dec. 28, 1945, between Křenek and the Quartet; all but this one are addressed to Mischa Schneider.

18. Ernest Křenek to Mischa Schneider, Mar. 12, 1945, Kroyt Papers.

19. Harold Spivacke to Joseph Roisman, May 29, 1947, BQ-MDLC.

20. Ortenberg-Interview.

21. Kroyt-Interview.

22. Handwritten draft of letter, Boris Kroyt to Artur Schnabel, undated but accompanied by registered-letter receipt (obviously for the score that Kroyt was returning to Schnabel) dated Jan. 20, 1948, Kroyt Papers.

23. Walter Piston to Mischa Schneider, dated only Aug. 14 but written in 1945, Kroyt Papers. A second letter, following up on the first, is dated Aug. 23, 1945, also Kroyt Papers.

24. Henri Temianka, *Facing the Music: An Inside View of the Real Concert World* (Sherman Oaks, Calif.: Alfred Publishing, 1980), 249.

25. Ibid.

26. Wechsberg, "Profiles," 97.

27. Goddard Lieberson to Mischa Schneider, Aug. 5, 1942, Kroyt Papers.

28. Roisman Papers.

29. *New York Times,* Dec. 10, 1942, Kroyt Papers. The reviewer was Howard Taubman.

30. Undated, unspecified newspaper review of Dec. 10, 1944, concert in Jordan Hall, Boston, Kroyt Papers. The reviewer was Winthrop P. Tryon.

31. Ithaca *Journal,* Jan. 9, 1951, Kroyt Papers. The reviewer was Anita Monsees.

32. New York *Herald-Tribune,* Jan. 12, 1951, Kroyt Papers. The reviewer's initials are given as P. G-H—Peggy Glanville-Hicks, who was herself a composer.

33. Cleveland *News,* Feb. 7, 1951, Kroyt Papers. The reviewer was Elmore Bacon.

34. Washington *Times-Herald,* Mar. 23, 1951, Kroyt Papers.

35. Undated, unspecified newspaper review of concert of Jan. 23, 1945 in Kimball Hall, Chicago, Kroyt Papers.

36. Buffalo *Courier-Express,* undated review of concert of Nov. 13, 1944, in Mary Seaton Kleinhaus Music Room, Kleinhaus Music Hall, Buffalo, Kroyt Papers. The reviewer was Isabelle Evans.

37. Seattle *Post Intelligencer,* Jan. 18, 1953, Kroyt Papers. The reviewer was Maxine Cushing Gray.

38. Indianapolis *Times,* Feb. 27, 1958, Kroyt Papers. The reviewer was Henry Butler.

39. Chicago *Sun-Times*, Jan. 24, 1945, Kroyt Papers. The reviewer was Felix Borowski.

40. Washington *Post*, undated review of concert of Mar. 30, 1951, at the Library of Congress, Kroyt Papers.

41. Pittsburgh *Sun-Telegram*, Feb. 5, 1952, Kroyt Papers. The reviewer was J. Fred Lissfelt.

42. Washington *Post*, Nov. 12, 1953, Kroyt Papers.

43. Chicago *Daily Tribune*, Jan. 18, 1954, Kroyt Papers. The reviewer was Seymour Raven.

44. Hartford *Courant*, Dec. 1, 1959, Kroyt Papers. The reviewer was Edward W. Pliska.

45. New York *Herald-Tribune*, undated review of all-Mozart program at concert of Dec. 17, 1944, at Town Hall sponsored by New Friends of Music, Kroyt Papers. The reviewer's initials are given as A. V. B.—Arthur V. Berger.

46. Unspecified newspaper, Jan. 27, 1945, Kroyt Papers. The reviewer was Herbert Elwell.

47. Nashville *Tennessean*, Nov. 21, 1951, Kroyt Papers. The reviewer was Louis Nicholas.

48. Chicago *Daily Tribune*, Jan. 18, 1952, Kroyt Papers. The reviewer was Seymour Raven.

49. Indianapolis *Times*, Feb. 26, 1953, Kroyt Papers. The reviewer was Henry Butler.

50. London *Free Press*, Mar. 28, 1961, Kroyt Papers. The reviewer was Lenore Crawford.

51. Unspecified newspaper, Mar. 31, 1961, Kroyt Papers. The reviewer was Donald Mintz.

52. Washington *Times-Herald*, undated review of concert of Apr. 27, 1944, at the Library of Congress, Kroyt Papers.

53. Buffalo *Evening News*, Sept. 25, 1963, Kroyt Papers. The reviewer was John Dwyer.

54. Roisman Papers.

55. Michael Tree-I.

56. M. Schneider-Interview.

57. Mrs. Cameron (Jane) Baird-I.

58. Kroyt-Interview.

59. Tom Z. Shepard-I.

60. *Time*, July 26, 1968.

61. Applebaum, *The Way They Play*, 168.

62. Mischa Schneider to Harold Spivacke, Feb. 14, 1956, BQ-MDLC.

63. Milton J. Bach to Jack Salter, Apr. 17, 1942, YMHA. Bach was chairman of the Committee on Music; Salter was a concert manager.

64. Copy of telegram, Harold Spivacke to Mitchell Lurie, Sept. 30, 1942, Kroyt Papers. Lurie subsequently performed with the Quartet in Pasadena in Feb. 1943.

65. Julius Levine-I.

66. David Oppenheim-I.

67. Howard Scott-I.

68. M. Schneider-Interview.

69. George Szell to Harold Spivacke, Sept. 21, 1945, BQ-MDLC.

70. Artur Balsam-I.

71. Paul Hume-I.

72. Milton Katims to Nat Brandt, Oct. 4, 1990.

73. Walter Trampler-I.

74. Paul Katz-I.

75. Milton Katims to Nat Brandt, Oct. 4, 1990.

76. Undated, unspecified newspaper, Kroyt Papers. Barnes later worked for the *New York Times* and most recently for the New York *Post.*

77. A. Schneider-Autobio, 30.

16. *Opus Oops!*

1. A. Schneider-Autobio, 46.

2. Ibid., 47, and M. Schneider-Interview.

3. M. Schneider-Interview.

4. Yanna Kroyt Brandt.

5. *Saturday Review,* Nov. 3, 1962, 29, Kroyt Papers.

6. M. Schneider-Interview.

7. Julius Levine-I.

8. Samuel Rhodes-I.

9. A. Schneider-Autobio, 60.

10. M. Schneider-Interview.

11. Kroyt-Interview.

12. Lee Fairley-I. Fairley was a music reference librarian in the Music Division, Library of Congress, who took William Lichtenwanger's place during World War II.

13. M. Schneider-Interview.

14. A. Schneider-Autobio, 30.

15. Ibid., 59–60.

16. Howard Scott-I.

17. Buffalo *Evening News,* Nov. 26, 1973.

18. Undated, unspecified newspaper review of concert at Baird Hall, Univ. of Buffalo, Kroyt Papers.

19. Barnette, *An Informal History.*

20. William Lichtenwanger-I.

21. *New York Times,* undated, Kroyt Papers. The reviewer was Alan Rich.

22. Felix Galimir-I.

23. Roisman Papers.

24. Undated, unspecified Atlanta newspaper, Kroyt Papers. The reviewer was Howell Jones.

25. Miami *Herald,* undated, Kroyt Papers. The reviewer was Doris Reno.

26. Chicago *Daily Tribune,* Aug. 18, 1952, Kroyt Papers. The reviewer was Seymour Raven.

27. Chicago *Sun-Times,* July 9, 1958, Kroyt Papers. The reviewer was Glenna Syse.

28. Mischa Schneider to Harold Spivacke, Aug. 7, 1944, BQ-MDLC.

29. Chicago *Daily Tribune,* Aug. 15, 1952, Kroyt Papers. The reviewer was Seymour Raven.

30. Chicago *American,* July 8, 1958, Kroyt Papers. The reviewer was Roger Dettmer.

31. Chicago *Daily Tribune,* Aug. 15, 1952, Kroyt Papers. The reviewer was Seymour Raven.

32. Chicago *Daily News,* July 6, 1961, Kroyt Papers.

33. Buffalo *Evening News,* undated, review of concert of Oct. 22, 1965, in Baird Hall, Univ. of Buffalo, Kroyt Papers. The reviewer was John Dwyer.

34. Toledo *Times,* Feb. 14, 1951, Kroyt Papers. The reviewer was Frederick J. Kountz.

35. Washington *Star,* May 2, 1948, Kroyt Papers.

36. Howard Scott-I.

37. Mary Rogers-I. Rogers was administrative assistant for concerts in the Music Division, Library of Congress.

38. Howard Scott-I.

39. *New York Times,* Nov. 8, 1948, Kroyt Papers.

40. Chicago *Daily Tribune,* Aug. 13, 1952, Kroyt Papers. The reviewer was Seymour Raven.

41. Mrs. Cameron (Jane) Baird-I.

42. William Lichtenwanger-I.

43. Julius Levine-I.

44. Transcript, Program 1, Classic Performances from Library of Congress, 1990, BQ-MDLC. Rich Kleinfeldt was the host of the program, one of fifteen hour-long broadcasts devoted to the Quartet that were aired around the country on National Public Radio.

45. *New Yorker,* undated, Kroyt Papers.

46. *Saturday Evening Post,* Mar. 9, 1953, 62, Kroyt Papers.

17. *"Mr. Chamber Music"*

1. *New York Times,* June 23, 1957, Kroyt Papers.
2. Ibid.
3. "Viola" to Boris Kroyt, Aug. 2, 1942, Kroyt Papers.
4. *Nation,* Oct. 2, 1943.

5. Mrs. Worth (Cornelia) Ryder to Mischa Schneider, undated, Kroyt Papers.

6. Abe Fortas to Mischa Schneider, Oct. 14, 1965, M. Schneider Papers.

7. Yuriko Fukutomi to Joseph Roisman, Jac Gorodetzky, Boris, Mischa Schneider, and Annie Friedberg, Sept. 3, 1952, M. Schneider Papers.

8. Robert McAfee Brown, "Of Horsehair, Catgut and Sublimity," *Christian Century*, Sept. 26, 1979, 912.

9. Kroyt-Interview.

10. Hans Hirschmann to Nat Brandt, Jan. 24, 1991.

11. New Orleans *States*, Jan. 28, 1956, Kroyt Papers. The reviewer was Charles L. Dufour. He wrote, "The crowd, indeed, was surprising, with very few empty seats being noted. The balcony was filled with Tulane and Newcomb students."

12. Phoenix *Arizona Republic*, Mar. 6, 1965, Kroyt Papers.

13. Portland *Oregonian*, June 26, 1942, Kroyt Papers. The reviewer was Hilmar Grondhal.

14. Undated, unspecified Detroit newspaper review of Jan. 22, 1945, concert in Lecture Hall, Detroit Institute of Arts, Kroyt Papers.

15. San Francisco *Chronicle*, undated, Kroyt Papers. The reviewer was Alfred Frankenstein.

16. Ibid., Aug. 5, 1943, Kroyt Papers. The reviewer was Alfred Frankenstein.

17. Indianapolis *News*, undated, Kroyt Papers. The reviewer was Walter Whitworth.

18. Ithaca *Journal*, Nov. 30, 1955, Kroyt Papers. The reviewer was Rey Morgan Longyear.

19. Undated, unspecified Minneapolis newspaper, Kroyt Papers. The reporter was John H. Harvey.

20. *Newsweek*, Jan. 24, 1955.

21. *Life*, May 6, 1957, 163.

22. *Christian Science Monitor*, Nov. 17, 1958, Kroyt Papers. The reviewer was Jules Wolffers.

23. Undated, unspecified Montgomery newspaper, Kroyt Papers. The reviewer's initials are given as J. F. W.

24. Buffalo *Evening News*, Apr. 20, 1963, Kroyt Papers. The reviewer was Bob Williams.

25. Ibid., undated, Kroyt Papers. The reviewer was John Dwyer.

26. Barnette, *An Informal History*.

27. M. Schneider-Interview.

28. Margaret McClure-I. Mrs. McClure was an early concertgoer at the Ravinia Festival who attended the first chamber-music recitals given there by the Pro Arte Quartet.

29. Francis M. Knight to Annie Friedberg, Aug. 19, 1941, Kroyt Papers. Knight, a banker, was responsible for securing artists for the Ravinia Festival.

30. Contract, Edward Schein for League of Music Lovers and Young Men's Hebrew Association, May 2, 1938, YMHA.

31. Mark Levine to William Kolodney, Nov. 8, 1938, YMHA.

32. Elsie Illingworth to William Kolodney, Mar. 13, 1945, YMHA.

33. Luther Marchant to Mischa Schneider, Jan. 5, 1945, Kroyt Papers.

34. Annie Friedberg to Mischa Schneider, Jan. 13, 1947, Kroyt Papers.

35. George Harvey to Annie Friedberg, Jan. 30, 1947, Kroyt Papers.

36. Annie Friedberg to Mischa Schneider, Dec. 22, 1947, Kroyt Papers.

37. Annie Friedberg to Edgar Ortenberg, Mar. 22, 1947, Kroyt Papers.

38. Annie Friedberg to Edgar Ortenberg, Mar. 27, 1947, Kroyt Papers.

39. Ivan Langstroth to Mischa Schneider, Nov. 24, 1947, Kroyt Papers. The Quartet played two concerts for the Mozart Society, on January 6 and 20, 1948, each for $700, a reduction of $100 from the Quartet's usual fee.

40. Annie Friedberg to Mischa Schneider, Sept. 8, 1947, Kroyt Papers.

41. Untitled fee list, 1964–65, Buffalo Chamber Music Society.

42. David Soyer-I.

43. M. Schneider-Interview.

44. Ibid.

45. M. Schneider-Autobio, 20.

46. M. Schneider-Interview.

47. Ibid.

48. Boris Kroyt to Nat Brandt, Feb. 2, 1964.

18. Silence in the Library

1. M. Schneider-Interview.

2. Ortenberg-Interview.

3. Carbon of letter, Joseph Roisman to Ira Hirschmann, Oct. 24, 1945, Kroyt Papers.

4. Ibid.

5. Ira Hirschmann to Joseph Roisman, Oct. 30, 1945, Kroyt Papers.

6. Ira Hirschmann to Joseph Roisman, Nov. 5, 1945, Kroyt Papers.

7. Washington *Evening Star*, undated review of concert of either Apr. 13 or 14, 1944, at Library of Congress, Kroyt Papers.

8. Chicago *Sun-Times*, undated review of Ravinia concert of Aug. 13, 1944, Kroyt Papers. The reviewer was Felix Borowski.

9. Chicago *Daily Tribune*, undated review of Ravinia concert of Aug. 15, 1944, Kroyt Papers. The reviewer was Claudia Cassidy.

10. Pittsburgh *Post-Gazette*, Jan. 11, 1945, Kroyt Papers. The reviewer was Donald Steinfirst.

11. New York *Sun*, Nov. 5, 1945, Kroyt Papers. The reviewer was Irving Kolodin.

12. *New York Times*, Nov. 26, 1945, Kroyt Papers. The reviewer's initials are given as H. W.

13. Washington *Evening Star*, Oct. 8, 1948, Kroyt Papers.

14. *New York Times*, undated review of Town Hall concert of Nov. 8, 1948, Kroyt Papers. The reviewer was Carter Harman.

15. Los Angeles *Examiner*, Feb. 3, 1959, Kroyt Papers. The reviewer was Herbert Donaldson.

16. San Francisco *Chronicle*, Feb. 7, 1959, Kroyt Papers. The reviewer was Alfred Frankenstein.

17. San Francisco *Call-Bulletin*, Feb. 7, 1959, Kroyt Papers. The reviewer was Arthur Bloomfield.

18. London *Times*, Feb. 15, 1960, Kroyt Papers.

19. *Il Resto del Carlino*, Jan. 21, 1960, Kroyt Papers.

20. New York *Herald-Tribune*, Nov. 14, 1960, Kroyt Papers. The reviewer was Jay S. Harrison.

21. Mischa Schneider to Harold Spivacke, Feb. 15, 1961, BQ-MDLC.

22. M. Schneider-Interview.

23. Jerusalem *Post*, Sept. 17, 1961, Kroyt Papers.

24. Anonymous to Day Thorpe, Mar. 27, 1960, copy, Kroyt Papers.

25. Washington *Post*, Nov. 5, 1960, Kroyt Papers. The writer of the letter was Robert Evett. He was responding to a critical letter sent to the *Post* by Robert Parris.

26. Ibid., Mar. 19, 1960, Kroyt Papers.

27. Ibid., Mar. 26, 1960, Kroyt Papers.

28. Mischa Schneider to Harold Spivacke, Feb. 18, 1955, BQ-MDLC.

29. Contract between Whittall Foundation and Budapest Quartet, Apr. 20, 1961, BQ-MDLC.

30. Kroyt-Interview.

31. Marginal note in response to letter, Nat Brandt to Alexander Schneider, Mar. 24, 1991. In his autobiography, 253, he wrote, "I often played Kreisler's violin at Library of Congress concerts with the Budapest Quartet."

32. William Lichtenwanger-I. Mrs. Edward N. (Lilly) Waters, whose husband was Harold Spivacke's assistant and subsequently succeeded him as head of the Music Division, said she understood that other violinists had also been allowed to use the Kreisler instrument—among them, Robert Mann of the Juillliard Quartet and Nathan Milstein, who borrowed the Kreisler when his own violin was undergoing repairs. Evidently, the loaning of the Kreisler Guarneri was done without publicity.

33. Frances Gewehr-I. Mrs. Gewehr was administrative assistant to Spivacke.

34. M. Schneider-Interview.

35. A. Schneider-Autobio, 61. Mrs. Whittall died three years later, in 1965, at the age of ninety-seven.

36. *New York Times*, Apr. 1, 1962, Kroyt Papers.

37. Washington *Evening Star*, Mar. 30, 1962, Kroyt Papers. The reviewer was Wendell Margrave.

38. Transcript, Patrick Hayes broadcast of Sunday, Jan. 7, 1962, Station WGMS, Kroyt Papers.

39. Washington *Post*, undated, Kroyt Papers.

40. Buffalo *Evening News*, Aug. 8, 1962, Kroyt Papers. The journalist was music critic John Dwyer.

41. Kroyt-Interview.

42. M. Schneider-Interview.

43. Louisville *Courier-Journal*, Mar. 4, 1963, Kroyt Papers. The reviewer was William Mootz.

44. Joseph Roisman to William Kolodney, Jan. 24, 1963, YMHA.

45. Adelaide *Advertiser*, July 9, 1963, Kroyt Papers. The reviewer was John Horner. He was reviewing what he called "the longest programme (though it seemed the shortest)," which was necessitated by the Quartet's adding the Brahms Quartet in B-flat, Opus 67. Three nights earlier, Roisman had had to quit performing after the first movement of the piece.

46. M. Schneider-Interview.

47. Kroyt Papers.

48. Roisman Papers.

49. Melbourne *Age*, July 11, 1963, Kroyt Papers. The reviewer was Dorian Le Gallienne.

50. Joseph Roisman to Boris Kroyt, May 1, 1964, Kroyt Papers. A similar note is in M. Schneider Papers.

51. Joseph Roisman to Mischa Schneider, May 10, 1964, M. Schneider Papers. This second letter from Roisman was written in response to a reply he had received from Schneider. Roisman said, "I am sorry if I shocked you with my letter, but this was not my intention."

52. Ibid.

19. The Marlboro Men

1. Julius Levine-I.

2. A. Schneider-Autobio, 160. The Schneiders' father had died in 1928.

3. Rudolf Serkin to Budapest String Quartet, undated, M. Schneider Papers.

4. Except as otherwise noted, the quotations in this chapter are from interviews with the individuals cited.

5. Ruth Laredo-I.

6. A. Schneider-Autobio, 64.

7. Roisman's quotations are an amalgam from parts 1 and 2 of Samuel and Sada Applebaum, "With the Artists: Famous String Players Discuss Their Art—Joseph Roisman," which appeared in *Violins and Violinists*, Vol. 15, No. 2 (Nov.–Dec. 1954), 260–64, and Vol. 16, No. 2 (Mar.–Apr. 1955), 57–60.

8. Jaime Laredo-I.

9. Arnold Steinhardt-I.

10. Michael Tree-I.

11. Jaime Laredo-I.

12. M. Schneider-Interview.

13. Jaime Laredo-I.

14. Kroyt-Interview.

15. Michael Tree-I.

16. Jaime Laredo-I.

17. Ruth Laredo-I.

18. Paul Katz-I.

19. Kroyt-Interview.

20. Michael Tree-I.

21. M. Schneider-Interview.

22. Michael Tree-I.

23. Ibid.

24. David Soyer-I.

25. Michael Tree-I.

20. Coda

1. Kroyt-Interview.

2. M. Schneider-Interview.

3. Subscriber renewal letter, Mar. 1, 1962, YMHA.

4. Los Angeles *Times*, Apr. 21, 1964, Kroyt Papers. The reviewer was Raymond Kendall.

5. *New York Times*, Dec. 12, 1964, Kroyt Papers. The reviewer was Theodore Strongin.

6. M. Schneider-Interview.

7. *New York Times*, Oct. 11, 1962, Kroyt Papers. The reviewer was Alan Rich.

8. M. Schneider-Interview.

9. Kroyt-Interview.

10. M. Schneider-Interview.

11. Kroyt-Interview.

12. *New York Times*, Jan. 7, 1962, Kroyt Papers. The reporter was Eric Salzman.

13. M. Schneider-Interview.

14. David Soyer-I.

15. Ibid.

16. Kroyt-Interview.

17. A. Schneider-Autobio, 108.

18. Julius Levine-I.

19. Joseph Roisman to Mischa Schneider, May 10, 1964, M. Schneider Papers.

20. Kroyt-Interview.

21. A. Schneider-Autobio, 32.

22. Kroyt-Interview.

23. M. Schneider-Interview.

24. Wechsberg, "Profiles," 69.

25. Edward Waters to Mischa Schneider, Oct. 11, 1973, M. Schneider Papers. Mischa, in a letter to Waters, Oct. 2, 1973, requested a tape of the Rachmaninoff sonata "in order to hear how nervous and badly I played it."

26. Washington *Evening Star*, Nov. 20, 1965, Kroyt Papers. The reviewer was Donald McCorkle.

27. Walter Trampler-I.

28. Arnold Steinhardt-I.

29. Yanna Kroyt Brandt.

30. M. Schneider-Autobio, 26. He added, "Before sleeping, Hauser gave me a massage but the pain kept me up much of the night. I was afraid it was pneumonia."

31. June Schneider-I.

32. Apparently the last Budapest Quartet concert in which Mischa Schneider participated was that of Oct. 22, 1965, in Baird Hall, Univ. of Buffalo. There was no indication that he was having any trouble. The reviewer for the Buffalo *Evening News*, John Dwyer, said, "The balances and blends were exceptional." Undated, Kroyt Papers.

33. Cornell Univ. *Spectrum*, Feb. 24, 1967, Cornell. The reviewer was Stephen Kamholtz.

34. Buffalo *Evening News*, Feb. 18, 1967, Kroyt Papers. The reviewer was C. Wesley Steiner.

35. Buffalo *Courier-Express*, Feb. 21, 1967, Kroyt Papers. The reviewer was Thomas Putnam.

36. Cornell Univ. *Spectrum*, Feb. 24, 1967, Cornell.

37. *New York Times*, Dec. 19, 1968, Kroyt Papers.

38. M. Schneider Papers.

39. A. Schneider-Autobio, 169.

40. Julius Levine-I.

41. A. Schneider-Autobio, 96.

42. Washington *Evening Star*, Mar. 5, 1966, Kroyt Papers. The reviewer was Donald McCorkle.

43. Yanna Kroyt Brandt.

44. M. Schneider-Interview.

45. Julius Levine-I.

46. A. Schneider-Autobio, Preface.

47. Alexander Schneider to Elizabeth Sprague Coolidge, Jan. 4, 1948, A. Schneider-Files.

21. The Legacy

1. *New York Times*, Jan. 6, 1991.

2. Washington *Post*, Jan. 6, 1962, Kroyt Papers.

3. *New Grove Dictionary of American Music,* Vol. 1 (New York: Macmillan, 1986), 401.

4. *National Endowment for the Arts Five-Year Planning Document, 1986–1990* (Washington, D.C.: Government Printing Office, 1984), 63.

5. Irene Busch Serkin, editor, *Adolf Busch: Letters—Pictures— Memories,* Vol. 2 (Walpole, N.H.: Arts & Letters Press, 1991), 427. From a letter from Adolf Busch to Volkmar Andreae, Aug. 23, 1941.

6. Serkin, *Adolf Busch,* Vol. 2, 437. From a letter from Adolf Busch to May Fahrlander, Aug. 11, 1942.

7. *New York Times,* Sept. 3, 1966, Kroyt Papers.

8. Except as otherwise noted, all quotations are from interviews with the individuals cited.

9. *Music for Mischa* (California Institute of the Arts, 1988), 10.

10. Transcript, Classic Performances–Library of Congress, 4, BQ-MDLC.

11. Washington *Post,* undated 1970 article, Kroyt Papers.

12. Ibid., Dec. 15, 1968, Kroyt Papers.

13. Ibid., Mar. 31, 1962, Kroyt Papers.

14. Pittsburgh *Sun-Telegraph,* May 15, 1951, Kroyt Papers.

15. Washington *Post,* Oct. 13, 1985.

16. Roisman Papers.

17. *New York,* Aug. 11, 1975.

18. Wechsberg, "Profiles," 78.

19. Undated, unspecified magazine review of 1975 reissue of four recordings made in the Library of Congress in 1952, Kroyt Papers.

20. *Audio and Record Review,* Vol. 3, No. 3 (Nov. 1963), 18.

21. Kroyt-Interview.

22. M. Schneider-Interview.

23. Transcript, "Critic's Choice: Farewell to Strings," Jan. 21, 1969, 5, Roisman Papers.

24. A. Schneider-Autobio, 65.

Bibliography

Archives and Manuscript Sources

American Heritage Center, University of Wyoming, Laramie, Wyo.
    Papers of Tibor Bartok (regarding Joseph Roisman)
Bertelsmann Music Group, New York City
    RCA Victor, Artists and Repertoire files
Yanna Kroyt Brandt, New York City
    Correspondence, Budapest String Quartet, 1935–1948
    Papers of Boris Kroyt
    Kinescope, "Budapest String Quartet," Dec. 1, 1957, televised broadcast
Buffalo Chamber Music Society
    Concert Files
Music Department, Cornell University, Ithaca, N.Y.
    Scrapbooks
Alan B. Kriegsman, Chevy Chase, Md.
    Papers of Tibor Bartok and Alan M. Kriegsman (regarding Joseph Roisman)
Music Division, Library of Congress, Washington, D.C.
    Budapest Concert Files
    Busch–Serkin Concert Files
    General Concert Files
    Miscellaneous Correspondence, Alexander Schneider Files
    Gertrude Clarke Whittall Collection
Mills College, Oakland, Calif.

Rare Books and Archives Department
Library, Museum of Broadcasting, New York City
  "Festival of the Performing Arts: Budapest String Quartet with Rudolf
  Serkin," Apr. 12, 1962, televised broadcast (T88:0189)
Edgar and Tamara Ortenberg, Philadelphia
  Scrapbook of clippings and programs, 1944–45 concert season
Ravinia Festival Association, Highland Park, Ill.
  Administrative Offices Files
June Schneider, Washington, D.C.
  Papers of Mischa Schneider
University Musical Society, University of Michigan, Ann Arbor, Mich.
  Concert Records
Archives, Young Men's and Young Women's Hebrew Associations, New
  York City
  Records of Education Department

Printed Documents

Catalogs, 1925–1948. Victor Records.
Concert Night: The Library of Congress. Washington, D.C.: Library of Con-
  gress, n.d.
Coolidge Auditorium and the Whittall Pavilion in the Library of Congress.
  Washington, D.C.: Library of Congress, n.d.
Music for Mischa. California Institute of the Arts, 1988.
National Endowment for the Arts Five-Year Planning Document, 1986–
  1990. Washington, D.C.: U.S. Government Printing Office, 1984.
Programs, Budapest String Quartet, Library of Congress. Three bound vol-
  umes covering years 1938–49, 1949–55, and 1954–62.
Programs, *Marlboro Music,* Marlboro Music School and Festival. Two
  bound volumes covering years 1954–75 and 1954–84.
Three Masters: The Stringed Instrument Collection in the Library of Con-
  gress. Washington, D.C.: Library of Congress, 1983.
Tribute to Sasha Schneider. Special Edition, Catalogue no. 222. Israel Museum, Jerusalem, Oct.–Dec. 1981.

Taped interviews

Mrs. Isidor (Rose) Alpher: Oct. 24, 1990
Mrs. Cameron (Jane) Baird: Mar. 28, 1991
Artur Balsam: Oct. 5, 1990
Natasha Schneider Furst: Jan. 12, 1991
Felix Galimir: March 12, 1991
Mrs. Jac ("Honey") Gorodetzky: Jan. 11, 1991
Paul Hume: Oct. 25, 1990
Anna Lou Kapell-Dehavenon: Dec. 4, 1990

Paul Katz: Apr. 9, 1991
Alan M. Kriegsman: Oct. 24, 1990
Boris Kroyt: June 10–11, July 11, Aug. 10–21, 27, Dec. 3, 1964; June 13, 16, 1966
Jaime Laredo: Jan. 30, 1991
Ruth Laredo: Oct. 16, 1990
Caroline Levine: Oct. 5, 1990
Julius Levine: Oct. 11, 1990
Joseph Machlis: Oct. 16, 1990
Irving Moskovitz: Dec. 5, 1990
R. Peter Munves: Dec. 19, 1990
David Oppenheim: Oct. 1, 1990
Edgar Ortenberg: Sept. 20, 1990
Leslie Parnas: Dec. 27, 1990
Samuel Rhodes: Nov. 30, 1990
June Schneider: Oct. 22–23, 1990
Mischa Schneider: Dec. 3, 1964 (not available on tape); Jan. 14, 1965; Mar. 11, 1983
Sol Schoenbach: Nov. 2, 1990 (conducted by Yanna Kroyt Brandt)
Harold Schonberg: Nov. 14, 1990
Howard Scott: Nov. 16, 1990
Thomas Z. Shepard: Dec. 3, 1990
David Soyer: Nov. 28, 1990
Arnold Steinhardt: May 21, 1991
Walter Trampler: Nov. 21, 1990
Michael Tree: Feb. 1, 1991

Telephone Interviews

Howard R. Brubeck: Jan. 7, 1991
Lee Fairley: Apr. 16, 1991
Frances Gewehr: Oct. 26, 1990
Virginia Harpham: Oct. 26, 1990
Milton Katims: Oct. 13, 1990
Mrs. Ernst Křenek: Jan. 2, 1991
William Lichtenwanger: Oct. 27, 29, 1990
Margaret McClure: Dec. 4, 1990
Gale Rector: Feb. 20, 1991
Mary Rogers: Oct. 27, 1990
Mrs. Edward N. (Lilly) Waters: Oct. 26, 1990

In-person Interview

Madeleine Milhaud: July 13, 1991

Books

Applebaum, Samuel and Sada. *The Way They Play*. Book 1. Neptune City, N.J.: Paganianiana, 1972.

Barnette, W. Leslie, Jr. *An Informal History of the Buffalo Chamber Music Society*. Buffalo: Buffalo Chamber Music Society, 1973.

Baumol, William J., and William G. Bowen. *Performing Arts: The Economic Dilemma*. New York: 20th-Century Fund, 1966.

Bithel, Jethro, ed. *Germany: A Companion to German Studies*. London: Methuen, 1955.

Brinkle, Lydle. *Hippocrene Companion Guide to Romania*. New York: Hippocrene Books, 1990.

Coleman Chamber Concerts, 1904–1964. Pasadena, Calif.: Coleman Chamber Music Association, 1963.

Collier, James Lincoln. *Benny Goodman and the Swing Era*. New York: Oxford Univ. Press, 1989.

Connor, D. Russell and Warren W. Hicks. *BG On the Record: A Bio-Discography of Benny Goodman*. New Rochelle, N.Y.: Arlington House, 1969.

Dent, Bob. *Hungary*. New York: W W Norton, 1990.

Friedrich, Otto. *Before the Deluge: A Portrait of Berlin in the 1920's*. New York: Harper & Row, 1972.

Grove's Dictionary of Music and Musicians. 10 vols. New York: St. Martin's, 1954–1961.

Haggin, B. H. *Music in the Nation*. New York: William Sloane Associates, 1949.

Harvith, John and Susan Edwards, eds. *Edison, Musicians and the Phonograph*. New York: Greenwood Press, 1987.

Hirschmann, Ira. *Caution to the Winds*. New York: David McKay Company, 1962.

Hughes, David G. *A History of European Music: The Art Music Tradition of Western Culture*. New York: McGraw-Hill, 1974.

International Who Is Who in Music. 5th Edition. Chicago: Who Is Who in Music, Inc., Ltd., 1951.

Jarman, Douglas. *Kurt Weill: An Illustrated Biography*. Bloomington: Indiana Univ. Press, 1982.

Kilburn, Nicholas. *Chamber Music and Its Masters in the Past and in the Present*. London: William Reeves, 1932.

———. *The Story of Chamber Music*. New York: Charles Scribner's Sons, 1904.

Machlis, Joseph. *The Enjoyment of Music*. 4th Edition. New York: W W Norton, 1977.

———. *Introduction to Contemporary Music*. New York: W W Norton, 1979.

Marteens, Frederick H. *String Mastery: Talks With Master Violinists, Viola Players and Violoncellists.* New York: Frederick A. Stokes, 1923.

Milaud, Darius. *Notes Without Music.* New York: Knopf, 1953.

New Grove Dictionary of American Music. 4 vols. New York: Macmillan, 1986.

New Grove Dictionary of Music and Musicians. 20 vols. London: Macmillan, 1980.

Norton, M. D. Herter. *The Art of String Quartet Playing.* New York: Simon & Schuster, 1966.

O'Connell, Charles. *The Other Side of the Record.* New York: Knopf, 1947.

Piatigorsky, Gregor. *Cellist.* Garden City, N.Y.: Doubleday, 1965.

Rubinstein, Arthur. *My Young Years.* New York: Knopf, 1973.

Ruttencutter, Helen Drees. *Quartet: A Profile of the Guarneri Quartet.* New York: Lippincott & Crowell, 1980.

Schnabel, Artur. *My Life and Music.* London: Longmans, 1961.

Schneider, Alexander. *Sasha: A Musician's Life.* New York: privately published, 1988.

Serkin, Irene Busch, ed., Russell Stockman, trans. *Adolf Busch: Letters—Pictures—Memories.* 2 vols. Walpole, N.H.: Arts & Letters Press, 1991.

Temianka, Henri. *Facing the Music: An Inside View of the Real Concert World.* Sherman Oaks, Calif.: Alfred Publishing, 1980.

Thomson, Virgil. *The Musical Scene.* New York: Knopf, 1945.

Ulrich, Homer. *Chamber Music: The Growth & Practice of an Intimate Art.* New York: Columbia Univ. Press, 1965.

Vizetelly, Henry. *Berlin under the New Empire.* 2 vols. Tinslex Bros., 1879; reprint, New York: Greenwood Press, 1968.

Weingartner, Fannia. *Ravinia: The Festival at Its Half Century.* New York: Ravinia Festival Association in conjunction with Rand McNally, 1985.

Articles

Andreoni, Sergio. "Il 'Quartetto di Budapest' (prima parte 1918–1932)." *Musica,* Mar., 1982, 46–54.

———. "Il 'Quartetto di Budapest' (seconda parte 1932–1967)." *Musica,* June, 1982, 164–72.

Applebaum, Samuel and Sada. "With the Artists: Famous String Players Discuss Their Art—Joseph Roisman." Part 1. *Violins and Violinists,* Vol. 15, No. 2 (Nov.–Dec. 1954): 260–64.

———. "With the Artists: Famous String Players Discuss Their Art—Joseph Roisman." Part 2. *Violins and Violinists,* Vol. 16, No. 2 (Mar.–Apr. 1955): 57–60.

Barter, Christie. "25 Years in Recordings." *Cue,* Mar. 26, 1960.

"Big Four." *Time,* Dec. 20, 1943, 79.

Breuer, Janos. "A Survey of the Contemporary Music Scene in Hungary."
    Hungarian Music News, Vol. 3, No. 1 (1986): 3–9.
Brown, Robert McAfee. "Of Horsehair, Catgut and Sublimity." *Christian
    Century*, Sept. 26, 1979, 911–12.
"Budapest Quartet: Four Russians Make Up the Finest Chamber Music
    Group Playing Today." *Life*, Apr. 2, 1945, 75–76, 78.
Clough and Cuming. "Discography." *Audio and Record Review*, Vol. 3, No.
    3 (Nov. 1963): 16–19.
Coeuroy, Andre. "Further Aspects of Contemporary Music—The Musical
    Thought, and Its Forms: Contemporary Themes." *The Musical Quar-
    terly*, Vol. 15, No. 4 (Oct. 1929): 547–73.
"Cuarteto de Cuerdas Budapest: Un reportaje a curatro voces." *El Hogar*,
    June 15, 1956.
"Farewell to the Budapest." *Time*, Jan. 10, 1969.
Frank, Mortimer H. "The Budapest Quartet's Stunning Legacy." *Books &
    Arts*, Feb. 22, 1980, 28–29.
Goldsmith, Harris. "The Budapest's Missing Links." *High Fidelity*, May
    1978, 85–88.
Goodman, Benny. "Contrasts." *Listen: The Guide to Good Music*, Nov.
    1940, 4–5.
Goossens, Eugene. "The String Quartet Since Brahms." *Music and Letters*,
    Vol. 3, No. 4 (Oct. 1922): 335–48.
Hart, Philip. "Four Russians Called Budapest." *High Fidelity*, May 1961, 30–
    34, 91–93.
Haskins, John. "Best Buy in Chamber Music: Washingtonians Line Up for
    Library of Congress Concerts." *Americas*, Aug. 1955, 31–34.
Hayes, Patrick. "My Monday Morning Country Store." *Quarterly Journal of
    the Library of Congress*, Fall 1982, 213–23.
Hume, Paul. "The Budapest." *Potomac*, Dec. 17, 1961, unpaginated.
"It's Chamber Music Time Across the Land: The Budapest Quartet Is a Big
    Hit Even Out West." *Life*, May 6, 1957, 161–64, 166.
Kolkebech, David. "The 'Magic Chamber.'" *Washington Post*, Apr. 9, 1982.
Kerner, Estelle. "The Fading Sad Sound of an Era." *Today* (distributed by the
    Philadelphia Inquirer), July 24, 1977.
Kolodin, Irving. "The Big World of Don Pablo." *Saturday Review*, Dec. 31,
    1966, 43–47, 59.
Kriegsman, Alan M. "Budapest String Quartet Honored on Reaching Golden
    Anniversary." *Washington Post*, Dec. 15, 1968.
———. "Farewell to the Budapest Quartet." *Saturday Review*, Nov. 30,
    1968, 69–70, 84–85.
Kroyt, Boris. "Beethoven's String Quartets: Their Performance." *Listen: The
    Guide to Good Music*, May 1945, 3–8.
"Longhair for All." *Time*, Aug. 20. 1951, 66.
Marsh, Robert C. "A Posthumous Farewell from the Budapest." *High Fidel-
    ity*, July 1974, 92.

————. "Vigor and Eloquence for Beethoven's Last Thoughts." *High Fidelity*, Jan. 1963, 65–66.

Martin, D. R. "Alexander Schneider: A Passion for Life and Music." *Ovation*, Jan. 1983, 8–11, 36.

Mayer, Martin. "The Budapest String Quartet." *Harper's*, Vol. 216, No. 1294 (Mar. 1958): 78–84.

"Meet Your Colleague." *Colleague* (publication of State University of New York at Buffalo), Vol. 4, No. 5 (Jan. 1968): 10–11.

Munves, R. Peter. "How the Legendary Budapest 78s Got onto LP." *High Fidelity*, May 1978, 86–87.

Pelleg, Frank. "Music in Israel." *The Atlantic*, Nov. 1961, 146–49.

Piatigorsky, Gregor. "My Life, My Cello." *The Atlantic*, May 1957, 42–46.

Rich, Alan. "Budapest Revisited." *New York*, Aug. 11, 1975, 61.

————. "The Ghost of Budapest Bygone." *New York*, Oct. 22, 1979, 122.

————. "Past Presence." *New York*, Feb. 6, 1979, 91.

Salzman, Eric. "Reminiscing About the Budapest." *New York Times*, Jan. 7, 1962.

"Second Fiddle, *con Brio.*" *Time*, July 26, 1968, 4–49.

Smith, H. Allen. "The Unsound and the Fury." *Saturday Evening Post*, Mar. 9, 1963.

Smolian, Steven. "Four Decades of the Budapest Quartet: A Discography, 1926–1966." *American Record Guide*, Vol. 37, No. 4 (Dec. 1970): 220–27.

"Spell of the Strings." *Newsweek*, Jan. 24, 1955.

Stoddard, Hope. "Chamber Music." *Etude*, Vol. 49 (June 1931): 444–45.

Storer, H. J. "Chamber Music—Something About Its Present State and Developement [*sic*]." *Musician*, Vol. 9, No. 5 (May 1904): 184.

Tallian, Tibor. "Hungarian Opera and the Outside World." *Hungarian Music News*, Vol. 2, No. 1 (Winter 1985): 3–6.

Taber, Bernard. "Casals at Ninety-two." *New Yorker*, Apr. 19, 1969, 123–24, 126, 129–30, 132, 134.

"Think You Own a Strad?" *Saturday Evening Post*, Dec. 19, 1959, 26–27, 78–80.

Weschsberg, Joseph. "Profiles: The Budapest." *New Yorker*, Nov. 14, 1959, 59–60, 62, 64, 67, 69–70, 72, 74, 76–78, 80–82, 87, 89–90, 92, 94, 97–98, 100, 102–6, 111–12.

"Where Are the Customers?" *American Musical Digest*, prepublication issue, spring 1969, 12–13.

Wirthmann, Julianna. "An Interview with Mr. Miklos Borsa, engineer-in-charge of the Budapest Opera House." *Hungarian Music News*, Vol. 2, No. 1 (Winter 1985): 7–9.

"WQXR: Radio's Gift to Musical Culture." *Musical Digest*, Feb. 1947, 14–15, 38.

Yaple, Carol and Kara Larson. "The Chamber Music Boom." *The Instrumentalist*, Vol. 42, No. 5 (Dec. 1987): 25–26, 28, 31.

Index